D0884465

Spies of the First World War

James Morton

SPIES OF THE

FIRST WORLD WAR

Under Cover for King and Kaiser

The National Archives

First published in 2010 by
The National Archives
Kew, Richmond
Surrey, TW9 4DU, UK

www.nationalarchives.gov.uk

The National Archives brings together
the Public Record Office,
Historical Manuscripts Commission,
Office of Public Sector Information
and Her Majesty's Stationery Office.

A catalogue card for this book
is available from the British Library.
ISBN   978 1 905615 46 9

Jacket illustrations:
Front, top Edith Cavell (1865–1915), the British nurse
executed by the Germans after helping hundreds
of Allied soldiers escape from occupied Belgium.
(Print Collector/HIP/TopFoto TopFoto.co.uk)
Front, bottom Vernon Kell (1873–1942), the first head
of what was to become MI5, *c.*1920. (Getty Images)
Back Mata Hari (1876–1917), shot by the French
as a German spy. (The National Archives KV 2/2)

Designed and typeset by Ken Wilson | point 918
Printed in the UK by Cromwell Press Group,
Trowbridge, Wilts

CONTENTS

ACKNOWLEDGEMENTS

To a certain extent any book on espionage in the First World War must now be a posy of other men's flowers, or at the very least a series of wayleaves, and particular tribute is due to Nicholas P. Hiley for his seminal articles in the *Historical Journal* and the *English Historical Review* in the 1980s as well as to Christopher Andrew for his *Secret Service*. I hope that by the end of this book—in which I have adopted a more anecdotal than historical approach—the reader will think I have added a few more wayleaves, and perhaps a few flowers of my own.

Although the name MI5 was not officially adopted until 1915, for the sake of convenience I have often used the name from its effective founding under Kell in 1909.

My thanks are due first of all to Dock Bateson without whose constant encouragement and help this would never have seen light of day. My particular thanks go to Joyce Holland, Fred Judge and Alan Edwards of the Intelligence Corps Archives, Chicksands, and then, in strictly alphabetical order, to J. P. Bean, Catherine Bradley, Edward Hampshire, Peter Higginson, Sheila Knight, Barbara Levy, Tim Newark, Sheila Thompson and Tom Wharton, as well as to the staff at the British Library; the National Archives, Kew; the British Newspaper Library, Colindale; the Liddell Hart Centre for Military Archives, King's College, London; the Imperial War Museum; New York Public Library and, in France, the Bibliothèque Marguerite Duras; Bibliothèque des Littératures Policières; Bibliothèque Historique de Ville de Paris; the Archives Nationales de France; and the Musée de Police, 5eme, Paris.

JAMES MORTON, *February 2010*

Germany has realised that special men ought to be employed for this special, necessary but, at the same time, despicable business. Your perfect spy is a man of criminal impulse, a moral pervert of sorts.

The German Spy System from Within Ex-Intelligence Officer [1]

INTRODUCTION

Before James Bond, spies generally did not have a good press.

In the opening decades of the twentieth century, public opinion, influenced by the popular press, divided spies into good and bad categories. The good were 'our' spies, such as nurse Edith Cavell and Lawrence of Arabia (although, in retrospect, he may not be quite such a good example), who were motivated by patriotism and displayed the utmost heroism. The bad were 'theirs': Mata Hari and Dr Armgaard Karl Graves, underhand and motivated by greed. Occasionally, as in the case of the German officer Carl Lody, 'their' spies could generate grudging or even real admiration. The general perception was that, riddled with disease and dependent on drugs, the First World War women spies such as Fräulein Doktor and Despina Storch lounged in silk underwear, smoked Turkish cigarettes in long holders and seduced our gallant boys with their wiles. Their male counterparts, who like the women smoked Turkish cigarettes in long holders, also carried whips and wore silk dressing-gowns.

These were the spies romanticized by *Thomson's Weekly News* and *Le Petit Journal*. For the majority in the profession, life was very different. For example, ex-Scotland Yard officer Herbert Fitch thought that: 'Often it is deputed to criminals, who, having formerly shown considerable cunning are released from a long prison sentence on promising to act as secret service agents abroad.'[2]

The espionage services generally were not much more highly regarded. At the time of the Dreyfus affair, when the French Secret Service was admittedly thoroughly in disgrace, the Paris correspondent of *The Times* wrote:

> The espionage department is only a small section of the General Staff and indeed is not in great favour with it but stands a little apart as a police bureau consisting of officers of a particular turn of mind. Friendships between them and other officers are extremely rare and to judge from all that has happened it is evident that those officers have abnormal manners.[3]

In November 1894 the long-serving French agent Marie Bastian, known as *l'agent Auguste*, found a piece of paper in the wastepaper basket of Maximilian von Schwartzkoppen, the German military attaché in Paris—an event which led to the Dreyfus scandal and the subsequent fall from grace of the French Secret Service.

Bastian's cover was to work for the Service de Renseignements as a cleaning lady. She supplied all the foreign embassies in Paris with maids, as a result of which all their wastepaper baskets were searched on a daily basis. She had previously been involved in stealing a document from the safe of another German military attaché, which led to the arrest of Schnabele and a diplomatic incident in the spring of 1887. She was also involved when Boutonnet was found to have given training documents to the military attaché Huene. Boutonnet, who had been receiving 250 French francs a month for his troubles, got five years, and Huene was declared *persona non grata*.

Now, Alfred Dreyfus, a young artillery officer from Alsace, was charged with communicating French military secrets to the German embassy, including details of a new Howitzer gun. The writer of the note Bastian found had signed off saying he was about to go on manoeuvres. There was no evidence against Dreyfus, except the doubtful evidence of Alphonse Bertillon, then claiming to be a handwriting expert. There was, however, some exculpatory evidence: as a young officer of the Troisième Bureau, Dreyfus would not be sent on manoeuvres. What was against him was that he was austere, personally wealthy and, worst of all, Jewish.

Whole swathes of France were at the time, and would remain for decades, very anti-semitic. When, at the turn of the 20th century, the swindler Madame Humbert defrauded the Jewish bankers of vast sums of money, there was a sly feeling that they had deserved all they got.

In November 1894 Dreyfus was convicted, stripped of his insignia and sent to Devil's Island. Two years later Lieutenant Colonel Georges Picquart was sent a second note by Marie Bastian which showed that Dreyfus was *not* the traitor. The culprit was an army major, Ferdinand Walsin Esterhazy, who was improperly using the title of count—a gambler with an expensive mistress. This was not a scenario which pleased the high command and, in a cover-up, French counter-intelligence under Colonel Hubert-Joseph Henry faked documents so that the evidence again pointed to Dreyfus. On the second day of a trial behind closed doors that started on 10 January 1898, Esterhazy was acquitted.

This was not a situation that would go unchallenged. Led by the writer Emile Zola and the future President of France Georges Clemenceau, a campaign began to overturn the conviction.[4] Following lengthy public support for Dreyfus, counter-campaigning by the anti-Dreyfusards, anti-Jewish rioting, and before a series of trials in which Zola was convicted and left France and Piquard was charged with forging the second note, Dreyfus' first conviction was quashed. At a retrial he was again found guilty and sentenced to 10 years. After the German embassy agreed to release documents showing that Dreyfus was not the originator of the notes (in a deal which anticipated that of Abdel Basset al-Megrahi and the Lockerbie bombing by a century), he was pardoned when he withdrew his appeal. Dreyfus was not officially cleared until 1906, when the Cours de Cassation quashed the conviction.[5] One result of the fiasco was that serious counter-espionage in France largely ground to a halt.

Generally, in the early 20th century it was thought better not to admit there was any such thing as espionage. 'It must be understood that I speak of the methods of foreign countries—if Great Britain employs spies, I know nothing of them,' lied Herbert Fitch.

That spying was dirty business was an attitude held by the top brass. As far back as the Crimean War an English officer called Kingslake wrote: 'The gathering of knowledge by clandestine means was repulsive to the feelings of an English gentleman', while General Sir Douglas Haig pontificated: 'I would not authorise my men being used as spies. Officers must act straightforwardly and as Englishmen. "Espionage" among our men was hateful to us Army men.'[6]

These attitudes were mirrored in the general populace. When Marthe McKenna, a nurse who spied for the British in Belgium, was first approached by a female friend, she thought:

> I knew what she must mean, a spy, and for a moment I was filled with horror. I knew that spies existed in Belgium and that they were serving their country, yet somehow I had regarded them as inhuman and far removed from my own sphere.[7]

Members of the heroic First World War Belgium-based network *La Dame Blanche* refused to be called spies. So far as they were concerned they were agents or soldiers.

It may have been a case of special pleading, but when Hans Tauscher, the arms dealer and husband of New York opera singer Joanna Gadski, was on remand for conspiracy to blow up the Welland canal, she told the *New York Herald* that her husband was not the kind of man who could spy, but that *she* would have no such scruples.[8]

Nor did spies necessarily hold themselves in very high esteem. Franz von Papen, the German military attaché in America, busy organizing blowing up munitions factories, is said to have remarked at one dinner: 'My God, I would give everything to be in the trenches where I could do the work of a gentleman.'[9]

Some spies at least stuck up for themselves: Max Schultz, who spied pre-war for England, said:

> I was a spy in Germany and I am not only not ashamed of the fact but proud of the risks I ran in getting information which I may fairly claim has helped us win the war.[10]

The life of a spy was certainly difficult financially. Herbert Fitch felt really rather sorry for spies (other people's, of course), writing that, 'The life of the spy is difficult. He is reliant on his master sending him money and this is often only paid by results'. Indeed, the German spies' letters almost invariably begged for money and if spy and master fell out it was the master who could twitch the thread and threaten to denounce him.

In the early 1900s, the British spy Henry Dale Long was on and off half pay for the better part of five years while, on 19 March 1906,

Belgian-born Hely Claeys wrote a piteous letter to his master Colonel Charles Repington begging to be given an allowance so that he and his family could exist in Belgium. Claeys had been employed since 1898, when he was used to provide information in the Anglo-French spat over the Nile port of Fashoda, seized by Major Marchand and retrieved by Lord Kitchener. In March the next year Claeys and his wife were arrested in Cherbourg, and he was jailed for two years for making drawings of forts. On his release he went to Africa for three years for the Intelligence Office and then in February 1906 he was, to use a modern term, made redundant. Repington applied for funds to Sir Charles Hardinge, who in turn asked Sir Thomas Sanderson, his predecessor, what he should do. Money was found for Claeys by the Foreign Office, but probably not the £120 annual retainer he was seeking. Perhaps Sanderson thought along the same lines as the German spymaster Gustav Steinhauer: 'A discarded spy—like a discarded mistress—is dangerous for any man', but he advised Hardinge to take care to distance himself from Claeys: 'It would be prudent to tell him [Repington] that you never have any dealings with agents of this kind. Perhaps you might add that that was also my rule.'[11]

In times of war, however, an agent's pay improved commensurately with the risk attached to the job. The usual pay for a German spy working in Britain in the early days of the First World War was between £10 and £25 a month with a bonus of 10 shillings a page for copies of secret documents. By June 1916 it was £100 a month and in 1918 it had risen to £180. According to Sir Vernon Kell, the first head of MI5, by the last months of the war a good spy could name his own price. The supply of volunteers had dried up completely.[12]

> There can be no doubt that Germany, through lack of choice, employed agents who very largely lived on their wits in normal times. It seems to have been a settled principle with their secret service to get hold of semi-destitute people with a penchant for extravagant living and induce them to spy on the promise of liberal remuneration according to results.[13]

There have, of course, been exceptions, one of whom was Baron August Schluga von Rastenfeld, designated by the German Secret Service IIIb as Agent 17, whose career ran for over 50 years. Born in Zsolna, Hungary, Schluga first came to prominence when in June

1866 he brought Berlin the battle order of the Austrian army along with profiles of some of its more important commanders.

Charming, well-educated and aristocratic, Schluga was rarely used, living in Paris from where he informed Bismarck of the plans of General MacMahon during the Franco-Prussian War of 1870–1871. He seems to have been both independent and autocratic, arguing that it was the value of his reports to IIIb that mattered, rather than that his masters should know exactly where he was at any given time. He does seem to have been sufficiently immodest to have allowed a portrait of himself to be painted and exhibited in London in 1908 by the then fashionable artist Maurice Romberg.

In recent years there has been a tendency to downgrade Schluga's 20th-century reports as open secrets garnered from the cocktail party circuit, but on the eve of the First World War he delivered an account of how the French would deploy their troops on the fifth day of their mobilization, which provided a key to how the Germans would defeat a counter attack. Unfortunately for the Germans, the information was not used properly.

In ill-health and possibly losing his nerve, Schluga moved to Geneva during the war without informing IIIb but, on a visit to Wiesbaden, he was interned by Colonel Nicolai, the head of the service, first there and later in Brussels. He died before the war ended.[14]

In the 1930s when Kell gave a lecture on spies of the First World War, he said that at its outbreak there were six recognizable classes of foreign agent: the travelling agent working under the cover of a commercial traveller, amateur yachtsman or journalist; the stationary agent such as the German Gustav Ernst who collected news and was used as a post-box—these would include waiters, photographers, language teachers, hairdressers and pub landlords; paymasters, who financed the agents; inspecting or head agents such as Steinhauer; commercial enquiry agents such as Schimmelfengs Agency;[15] and British traitors.

The first five could in varying degrees fall under the heading of patriot, and the shining example of this was the German officer Carl Lody, the first spy to be shot in the Tower of London during the war, of whom nothing but praise for his courage and bearing has been written, although he was abysmally incompetent. Lady Kell thought of him: 'Here indeed was a man who had undertaken a job which must have been very foreign to his nature, from purely patriotic motives.'[16]

Patriotic spies garnered admiration whatever they may have done and there was respect also for Franz von Rintelen who came to live in England in the 1930s. When questions were asked in the House of Lords about his wartime activities, which included placing bombs on merchant ships, the Earl of Lucan told their lordships: 'I should think he was working all he knew for his country during the war, and I do not think I should blame him for that.'[17]

Edwin Woodhall, the Scotland Yard detective who was in Intelligence during the war, included in an 'adventurers' category both Sir John Norton-Griffiths, known as 'Hell-Fire Jack' and another Scotland Yard detective, Inspector Hubert (Huibert Cornelius) Ginhoven. He thought that Ginhoven, a man of Dutch origin who spoke several languages and was a master of disguise, went behind enemy lines in Germany, Turkey and Austria.[18]

Norton-Griffiths, also known as 'Empire Jack', was certainly an adventurer, but whether he qualifies as a spy rather than a saboteur is more doubtful. When the war broke out he joined the 2nd King Edward's Horse and, developing a technique of pouring cement down wells, almost single-handedly destroyed 70 refineries. He also devised a system of tunnelling known as 'clay-kicking' which facilitated the eavesdropping on and interception of German communications in 1915. Later in the war General Ludendorff attributed German shortages to him.

Some men, such as Charles Ullmo, became traitors over women. In the 1900s, Toulon was a hotbed of opium smoking: to have a few pipes after dinner was the thing for polite society in general and young naval officers in particular. During a visit to Indochina Charles Benjamin Ullmo, a French naval ensign, born to a wealthy family in Lyon in February 1882, took to the habit. On his return to Toulon he became infatuated with the music hall singer Marie Louise Welsch, 'La belle Lison', who ran one of the 70 opium dens in the city. Whether she was actually a German spy placed to entrap him or other likely lieutenants is open to question. Certainly Paul Lanoir thought so, describing her as: 'One of those foul creatures with nothing womanly about them but their bodily form.'[19]

In his confessions, which may or not have been up St Augustine's and which were published 30 years after his conviction, Ullmo says that one of Welsch's previous relationships had been broken up because of suggestions that she might have been a spy.

Once he had run through his inheritance—spending, it was said, £3,000 to finance his relationship with Welsch and his opium habit of 20 pipes a day, and to stop her leaving him for another officer—in October 1907 Ullmo stole secret codes and details of French mobilization plans from a torpedo boat of which he was temporarily in command while his superior officer was on leave. Lanoir says quite specifically that La belle Lison told Ullmo how to do it.

Whether that is correct, Ullmo certainly tried to sell the plans through Brussels, which in 1909 was a headquarters of German intelligence. After he failed to sell them through the International Spy Bureau—its agent Talbot, also known as Theissen, both doubted their authenticity and baulked at the price—Ullmo then tried to blackmail the Minister of Marine, Gaston Thomson, writing to him on 10 September 1907 and naively offering the documents for 150,000 French francs. 'If the price seems too high then suggest your last price.' An advertisement was to be put in *Le Journal*, 'Paul à Pierre accepte prix demandé ou tel prix.'

Several meeting places were suggested which fell through. Finally the Gorges des Ollioules near Olliers was agreed upon. It was, naturally, a trap and Ullmo, met by detective Sulsbach backed up by an ex-prizefighter, was arrested. The trial, watched by La belle Lison sitting between Captain Jaures and the chief of staff of the Maritime Prefect, was a foregone conclusion. A number of others were swept up in the inquiry including the German naval attaché, Admiral Siegel, but he was soon released. There were also raids on opium dens in the city, some of which moved down the coast to Hyères.

To the delight of thousands brought in on excursion trains, and watched by naval recruits, on 12 June 1908 Ullmo's chevrons were stripped and his sword broken. He was marched around the parade ground in an impressive ceremony in St Roch Square, then was sent to serve his 25-year sentence on Devil's Island where he was given the cell formerly occupied by Dreyfus.

In January 1937 Ullmo published his story in the magazine *Confessions*, claiming that he had met the German purchaser, a man over two metres in height, in a hotel in Brussels. The man had told him that the information he was peddling was worthless because he already knew it. What he *would* be interested in, however, was details of submarines. Ullmo justified his actions, saying that if there had been a war the plans would have been changed immediately.[20]

On this occasion Ullmo had exonerated La belle Lison, but over the years her name cropped up again and again until, on 1 April 1915, she was arrested in Paris and accused of selling intelligence secrets and consorting with another spy.[21]

Others turned to spying because they were being blackmailed. On 25 May 1913 the Austro-Hungarian spymaster Colonel Alfred Redl shot himself in his room at the Hotel Klomser in Vienna. Redl, the ninth child of a railway clerk, was born in Lemberg, Galicia, now the Ukraine. A man of exceptional ability and intelligence, he joined the army in 1881 and was sent to the Imperial War College. In 1898 he went to Kazan in Russia to improve his command of the language. He joined Austrian counter-intelligence and, over the years, introduced serious reforms including recording conversations on wax cylinders, pioneering the use of fingerprints (a science then in its infancy), the use of secret cameras, and exchanging military intelligence with Germany. In 1907 he was made Chief of Intelligence and on 1 May 1912 he was promoted to colonel, then the highest rank in the Austrian army.

That was the plus side. On the debit side was an overwhelming minus. For some years he had been blackmailed by the Russians, who had discovered he was homosexual, a fact which, if revealed, would have ended his military career as well as exposing him to prosecution. Apart from dalliances with young men Redl had for a time carried on an affair with Stefan Hromodka, a young cavalry officer, passing him off as his nephew.

Perhaps the strangest thing is that he was not exposed earlier. The Russians had known about Redl's homosexuality from 1901; indeed a 'married' woman with whom he had conducted a tentative affair when he was at Kazan had actually been spying on him. The Russian spymaster Colonel Nikolai Batyushin had not only been blackmailing Redl but also financing his lifestyle; there was no way in which Redl, the son of a mere clerk, could keep himself in the required style in the army.

In 1903 the Austrians had discovered the Russians had full details of their battle plan, and Redl was given the task of finding the traitors. He first unmasked Lieutenant Colonel Sigmund Hekailo and then Major von Wieckowski after persuading his six-year-old daughter to show him where her father kept his secret papers. The third in the trio, all of whom received hard labour despite Redl about-facing and pleading for them, was Captain Alexander Acht.

In July 1904 Simon Lanrow and Bronislaus Drycz were prosecuted in Austria as Russian spies; they had been fed to Redl by Batyushin. In turn Redl sent Austrian spies to be caught in Russia.

Not everyone, however, was happy with Redl; a report from 1907 described him as 'more sly and false than intelligent and talented'. Despite this, his rise continued. When he was promoted to colonel in 1912 his successor at counter-intelligence was Major Maximilian Ronge, whom he had trained—and it was Ronge who brought him down, quite by mischance.

In the spring of 1913 an unclaimed package addressed to 'Nikon Nizetas' in Vienna was returned to Berlin, where it was opened by the security services. It contained 600 Austrian crowns and known espionage addresses. A duplicate letter was sent and when Redl went to collect it he was traced to his hotel. By an amazing coincidence the detectives took the same cab as Redl had taken earlier and in which he had dropped a sheath knife. The hotel management was instructed to ask which guest had lost the knife and when Redl claimed it he was questioned. A Browning revolver was placed in his room and several hours later he committed suicide leaving a note: 'Passion and levity have destroyed me. I pay with my life for my sins. Pray for me.'

Redl's greatest betrayal of his country was when he informed the Russians of Austria's Plan III for the invasion of Serbia along with its battle order at a time when mobilization was crucial. The Russians duly passed this to the Serbs so that when Serbia was invaded it was well prepared. As a result Redl is credited with the deaths of half a million Austrians.[22]

It is difficult to determine into which category of spy l'abbé Heurtebout could be fitted. After a trip to Austria and Germany, Heurtebout, the *curé* of a small village in Normandy, was caught in July 1914 trying to photograph mobilization plans for northern France which he had bought from the local stationmaster for £20. A detective punctured the tyres of his bicycle while he was at work, and when the abbé put down his camera to repair the puncture the detective seized it and the plates. Apparently the good *abbé* had led a double life, frequenting the night spots in Paris in disguise and, to finance this habit, he had answered an advertisement for a correspondent for a German military review. His parishioners were reported to have known of and accepted his Paris visits but to have been horrified that he was a spy.[23]

In truth, a spy's work was often dull and repetitive. The playwright Edward Knoblock, who in the First World War worked for Sir Mansfield Cumming, the first head of MI6, later wrote:

> If people think that being attached to 'Secret Service' means a life of continual 'hair-breadth scapes' let me tell them at once they are sadly mistaken. It means hours of infinite drudgery in which, only very rarely, there occur moments approaching the dramatic. Information can only be pieced together like the parts of a jigsaw puzzle, very occasionally producing results after endless labour and patience.[24]

Another of Mansfield Cumming's agents, Hector Bywater, pointed out that the trouble with recruiting agents was to find people with sufficient technical knowledge so that they were able to sort the wheat from the chaff when it came to gathering information.

Espionage was certainly more dangerous on the ground in a foreign country than sitting at home directing operations. The Hague Rules applied in wartime, so a convicted spy could be executed but, conversely and perversely, belligerent states could obtain information about the enemy in peace time under the same rules and so no protest could be made. Fortunately for him, Franz von Rintelen spied in America before the country entered the war; as such he was tried for espionage but not as a war spy.[25]

How should a spy behave? William Melville, often cited as MI5's master spy, thought that:

> Above all, the mysterious manner should be avoided. It only engenders distrust. A frank and apparently open style generally gains confidence… people as a rule are not averse to seeing you again. One can joke and humbug much in a jovial manner; one can talk a great deal and say nothing.[26]

The Nachrichten Bureau had a *vade mecum* for the behaviour of spies and, while much of the advice is out of date, some of the principles apply today:

Tell nobody of your missions.
Never take notes.
If you are compelled to carry a message, write it on the thinnest paper

and roll it in a cigarette. In case of danger, light it.
Do not join any other agent, even one belonging to the same service.
Abstain from alcoholic drinks.
When you travel, get a friend to take your ticket.
Never take a ticket as far as your destination; pay the supplement
   on arrival.
Try to change compartments while travelling.[27]

Other advice said to come from the same bureau included:

Not speaking at restaurants and on railway platforms; destroying all
paper including blotting paper and not putting it in wastepaper
baskets; to get a corner table in a public room; sit with one's back to the
wall. It was permissible to have a South German accent if the speaker
made it clear he was a Roman Catholic.[28]

Spies come in all shapes and sizes; full-time or part-time. It has been
suggested that one of the latter may have been the escapologist and
magician Eric Weiss, better known as Harry Houdini. The story is
based on thin evidence. It goes that on 14 June 1900 when the relatively unknown Houdini came to London, he met William Melville,
then still in the police force at Scotland Yard. Houdini demonstrated
just how quickly he could escape from a pair of the best British hand-
cuffs with which Melville had locked him to a pillar. Melville had
locked him up, intending to go out to lunch with the theatrical manager C. Dundas Slater. Before they had even left the room, Houdini
joined them. Slater immediately signed him for a two-week engagement at the Alhambra music hall off Leicester Square. In their biography of Houdini, William Kalush and Larry Sloman suggest that he
was not really auditioning for the Alhambra but for Melville. Certainly, he had some credentials: a good cover story for a spy is essential, and music hall artists, circus people and dancers have instant
cover. As a touring magician Houdini would certainly have had good
reason to be in Germany, and could have moved about without creating suspicion. He spoke the language and he would have been in a
position to mix with high and low society alike.

At the end of September that year—if HH was indeed Melville's
code for Houdini—the magician may have sent his first known report
from Berlin. But apart from one further journal entry in which Melville
says 'Waiting to hear from HH', there are no further references.

It may well be just a good story.[29]

There have been many good stories. The writer John Maclaren wrote that:

> The 1920s and 30s saw the publication of a number of personal 'memories' of alleged British agents. It was all too easy for someone to claim this dubious honour. No authority would normally deny or confirm their claims. Some of the stories they told have entered the folklore of the history of the war.[30]

It was the same in France where Louis Rivière wrote that 'Most spies' stories are an agreeable blend of fact and fiction intended to amuse the reader'.[31]

One problem with any memoir is that the author will play down his or her failures and correspondingly play up any successes. There is also the problem of writing for a commercial publisher: memoirs have to be spiced with tales of derring-do. There is little of interest in an opening sentence which reads, 'There were 27 letters in my in-tray that May morning…' Instead, 'Waiting for me that night in that dangerous drinking den filled with apaches who would cut my throat without a thought, in the depths of Soho/Montmartre/Berlin, was the Master Spy who would give me information which would save England…' makes for much better reading and sales, but is likely to be a simple piece of fiction. It is, for example, impossible to know how much truth there is in Marthe McKenna's account of retaining her virtue when she was sent to spend several days in Brussels with a German officer or when for a time she was trapped in a house with two other soldiers. Certainly for the purposes of sales, her resistance made for a good story and, although there is no evidence she did so in life, she was certainly not allowed to succumb in the text.

Another problem is that full names will not always be known, or cannot be revealed; conversations will certainly be fictionalized; memories will have dimmed after a few years; and books will have been used to settle old scores.

PART ONE

THE FOUNDING OF MI5 AND MI6

Chapter One

The evidence which was produced left no doubt in the minds of the sub-committee than an extensive system of German espionage exists in this country and that we have no organisation for keeping in touch with that espionage and for accurately determining its existence or objectives. Foreign Espionage in the United Kingdom: Report and Proceedings 1909[1]

SPY PANIC

As the years have gone by, people have forgotten, if indeed some now ever knew, just who was allied with whom when war was declared in August 1914, and why. Children have been taught that the First World War began with the assassination of Archduke Franz Ferdinand of Austria as if he were killed at six in the evening and the war began an hour later. People now also have a tendency to mix the players of the Great War with those of the Second World War.

Of course, war did not happen overnight. There had been tensions brewing in Europe for the last half century as old alliances were broken and new ones formed, upsetting the balance of power. Perhaps the German Chancellor Otto von Bismarck was responsible for the first turn of the screw when, in the 1860s, he set out to unify the loose collection of German states. Ten years later the Franco-Prussian war left resentment in France over its occupation and its loss of Alsace-Lorraine. In 1888 Kaiser Wilhelm II came to the German throne and Bismarck was dismissed. As Wilhelm was regarded as mentally unstable and Germany was to some extent ruled by an autonomy—rather than benefiting from some checks, along the lines of the British Parliament—stability went out with Bismarck. Russia's new alliance with France meant that Germany was in a pincer, and pressure increased as a result of Britain's 1904 *entente cordiale* with its traditional enemy, France, and its agreement with Russia three years later.

The British *entente* with France was over earlier colonial problems. In the summer of 1898 the two nations nearly came to blows over an expedition to Fashoda by Major Jean-Baptiste Marchand to set up an uninterrupted route from the Niger to the Nile, a development which the British feared might lead to water supply problems throughout Egypt. France, in return, took issue with the British occupation of Egypt. On 18 July Sir Herbert Kitchener, later Field Marshal Lord Kitchener (and British hero of the Boer War), arrived at Fashoda with a flotilla of gunboats, and for a time it seemed as though there might be a small war. By November, however, with the case of Captain Dreyfus—the French army officer controversially accused of selling military secrets to the Germans—once more on the front pages, the French ordered their soldiers to withdraw.[2]

The Balkans—generally under Austrian control but claimed by both Russia and Austria—was another area of contention, as was Africa, which Europe was in the process of colonizing, leading to a series of diplomatic incidents, particularly in Morocco, and to minor wars.

Tension also came from competition between Germany and England at the turn of the 20th century over the development of their navies. Each sought to be the best in the world, resulting in an arms race to build bigger and better battleships. The first of these, which put all others in the shade, was the British *Dreadnought*, launched in 1906, the fastest battleship then in the fleet, with 12-inch guns capable of firing up to a distance of eight miles. After that, it was a question of catch-up—and Germany caught up fast. By 1908 a British election slogan, referring to the number of ships needed, ran: 'We want eight and we won't wait.'

These tensions were acknowledged in October 1908 when Kaiser Wilhelm II gave an interview to the *Daily Telegraph*:

> You English are mad, mad, mad as March hares. What has come over you that you are so completely suspicious, quite unworthy of a great nation? What more can I do than I have done? I declared with all the emphasis at my command that my heart is set upon peace. I am a friend of England ...[3]

It was today's equivalent of saying a football manager has the full support of the board and 'has a job with Rovers for life'—a statement which precedes his sacking within the week. Certainly Foreign Secretary Sir Edward Grey was aware of this irony, writing in the *Daily Telegraph* in November that: 'I don't think there will be a war at present, but it will be difficult to keep the peace of Europe for another five years.'[4]

That year, with Russia still in military tatters after its defeat by the Japanese three years earlier, Austria took the opportunity to annexe Bosnia and Herzegovina. Russia would not let such a thing happen a second time without reprisal.

The modern spying trade had already begun. In the early 1890s Europe was, in theory, at peace; the Franco-Prussian war of 1870 was long over, if not forgotten. But over the next two decades there was a series of cases of espionage in which naval secrets, defence plans and munitions information were stolen and sold with increasing regularity. There were a number of countries' agents roving abroad, including from England. The English spied on the French and later the Germans; the Italians on the French; the French on the Italians and the Germans; the Russians on the Germans and anyone else they thought necessary. The Germans spied on everyone. Whatever their fine thoughts and words, statesmen all over Europe were aware of the developing political situation, and were quite prepared to use spies when it suited them. Espionage may have been on an ad hoc basis, but there was money to be made out of it and good use could be made of the information when it arrived. Some of its players may have been amateurish in the extreme, but those possessed of natural cunning would have been surprisingly effective.

From then until the war spies were arrested throughout Europe on a monthly basis. From time to time those who appeared in court said they had been trying to sell information to England, and from time to time Englishmen themselves were arrested. For example, on 26 December 1891 John Samuel Cooper and Walter Bedwell went on trial in France, charged with attempting to obtain a specimen of a Russian rifle made at a factory in St Étienne. The prosecution's case was that Cooper, who had already tried to obtain the prototype rifle in Tulle and Châtelleraut before going to St Étienne, had made the acquaintance, over a game of billiards, of an employee from the factory and offered him 10,000 French francs for the rifle. The worker reported the approach and a trap was set. He brought a worthless rifle to Cooper, who had by now been joined by Bedwell. Before the police could swoop, Cooper went back to Birmingham. When he returned to St Étienne, a supper party was arranged with the factory worker and 'some ladies'. Instead of the ladies, the police arrived.

Cooper claimed he had been asked to obtain the rifle by a man named Harrison in the Tower Bridge area of London, but was unable, or more likely unwilling, to give any further description of his employer. He maintained that as he had been trying to buy the gun from a commercial as opposed to a state factory he could not be convicted of espionage. He was wrong. He and Bedwell were sentenced to 15 months' imprisonment, which was increased in Cooper's case to two years on appeal. It was then disclosed that witnesses in the proceedings, which had been held *in camera*, had claimed that Cooper had also tried to obtain a Lebel cartridge.[5]

Around the same time another Englishman, Purdie, was arrested in Paris on suspicion of espionage, but was released.

In late May 1904 a retired English colonel, Edward Smith-Gordon (ex-Royal Artillery), was arrested for spying at Belle Isle, in northwest France. *The Times* for one thought this another bit of hysterical behaviour by the French: 'Many charges are brought but soon dismissed after a little investigation.' How could this elderly gentleman sketching a 'picturesque antiquated fortress' be a spy? The French took it all much more seriously, and Smith-Gordon's arrest was the cover story of *Le Petit Journal*. The paper believed the Englishman had been a spy for some time, and had already been officially warned about his behaviour. He was eventually released without a trial some weeks later.[6]

The growth of international suspicion and underground activity was mirrored—even stimulated by—an emerging trend in literary culture; sometimes fiction can help to create fact. The French had traditionally been the enemy of the British in military fiction, but in 1893, in Louis Tracey's *The Final War*, they went a step further, joining Germany to invade Britain. Fortunately, at the last minute the Germans changed sides, and Paris was taken by the British commander Lord Roberts. Then prolific pulpwriter William Le Queux, who would do so much to bring about a British Secret Service fifteen years later, imagined the Russians and French invading England in *The Poisoned Bullet*, published the same year.[7] In his later *England's Peril: A Story of the Secret Service*, the moustache-twirling Gaston La Touche was the villainous head of the French Secret Service. *The Campaign of Douai, London's Peril, The Great Trench War of 1901*, George Chesney's *The Battle of Dorking*[8] and *The Coming Waterloo* were all Francophobe novels, one of which included a French invasion via a Channel tunnel.

But then allegiances began to shift, and a new enemy marshalled its army. In 1899 Headon Hill wrote *The Spies of Wight*, which postulated German spies in the English countryside. It was followed in 1901 by Max Pemberton's *Pro Patria* in which the French invaded, again through a Channel tunnel. In the same year Louis Tracey's French were joined by the Germans in *The Invader*. The next year A. C. Curtis' *A New Trafalgar* described another combined German-French invasion with a German naval attack, fortunately defeated by Britain's fine new battleship.[9]

One of the most remarkable novels of the genre was *The Great War of 189–*, by Philip Colomb, published in 1891 as a serial in *Black and White* magazine. In its pages war broke out in the Balkans, with an assassination attempt on Prince Ferdinand of Bulgaria, after which Serbia declared war on Austria, Russia sent troops to Bulgaria, Germany mobilized against Russia in support of Austria-Hungary, and the French declared war on the Germans, who disregarded Belgian neutrality. Britain remained neutral but then joined forces with Turkey, which caused France and Russia to declare war on her. With a few changes here and there it was all remarkably prophetic.

In 1903 came the best and most enduring of the pre-war German invasion novels, Erskine Childers' *The Riddle of the Sands*, in which the heroes, on a sailing holiday on the North Sea, uncovered a plot to invade England. It was an extremely clever piece of writing purporting to be a document the author had discovered. The novelist John Buchan considered *The Riddle of the Sands* to be the best adventure story in the last 25 years. It had an immediate impact, leading eventually to the establishment of the Committee of Imperial Defence designed to advise the Prime Minister on the military services—a small body but more proactive than the Defence Committee, which tended only to meet in times of crisis. And in Southampton a senior naval figure, the apparently retired old sea dog Mansfield Cumming, set up a reserve of motor-boat owners to help combat any invasion.

In 1905 the immensely popular novelist E. Phillips Oppenheim, whose spies invariably wore silk and smoked Turkish cigarettes, described in *A Maker of History* a Captain X, head of German Intelligence, and a waiter who claimed there were thousands of German intelligence gatherers in London. Two years later in *The Message*, A. J. Dawson dealt with the hitherto unmentionable prospect of occupation, describing a scenario where the Germans had been gathering intelligence for years and knew 'almost to a bale of hay what provender lay between London and the coast'.

British readers were not alone in having their fears fuelled. Both the French and the Germans had their own fantasy war novels, including *La Guerre avec Angleterre* (1900), Karl Eisenhart's 1900 epic *The Reckoning with England* and August Niemann's *World War— German Dreams,* published in 1904, which has Germany, France and Russia combining to attack England and landing in the Firth of Forth.

But was all this pure fantasy? By now reports were filtering through to the Home Office suggesting that Germans were indeed wandering around English farms noting the number of working draught horses. There is no doubt that German agents were operating in England, and probably had been since the 1890s. They were active in France and Russia—while Britain had men in locations including Europe, Samara and Mozambique—so it would have been naive to suppose that they were not having a quiet look at defences in England. The questions that preoccupied officials always concerned the degree, nature and efficacy of foreign spying: were there more than a handful of spies, and what exactly were they looking into? And to what degree did their activities profit Germany?

There had already been murmurings, if not stirrings, in the forest of counter-espionage. In 1903 William Melville, who had been head of the Special Branch of Scotland Yard, was invited by Colonel James Trotter of the War Office, to open an 'agency' as part of MO3, later MO5, a section covering secret service left over from the Boer War (having been formed in 1899 as Section H).

There was no more suitable person for the job of spy-finder than Kerry-born Melville. He had joined the Metropolitan Police in September 1872 and his career, like many another in the police, was a chequered one. By 1879 he had been promoted to detective sergeant in the Criminal Investigation Department. In March 1883 he was recruited into a new section, known as the Special Irish Branch, and the next year was posted to Le Havre as part of a port surveillance effort to control the movements of Fenians. He remained in France for the next four years. His superior, Sir Francis Davies, later remarked snobbishly: 'He has a really good working knowledge of French which is most uncommon in men of his class... His accent would certainly appal you.'[10]

The Special Irish Branch was reorganized and Melville was promoted to inspector and moved to a new, very small and secret section, called simply the Special Branch. This had a brief to watch not only Fenians, but also social revolutionaries and anarchists. In 1893 Melville became superintendent of the branch when his predecessor John Littlechild retired to become a private investigator.

In this period, Britain was the only European country that did not restrict immigration, and it had become a refuge for many foreign anarchists. While anarchist violence, as opposed to Fenian violence, was not yet a problem, Britain was becoming very unpopular with her neighbours because of what they saw as its policy of sheltering anarchist refugees.

At this point, and very conveniently, Melville uncovered an anarchist bomb plot in Walsall. Six anarchists were arrested in early 1892, and charged with the manufacture of bombs to be used against the Russian regime. Three of them were each given ten years' imprisonment, and a fourth received five years.

This was the case that made Melville's reputation. His reward was promotion to head of the Special Branch. There is now little doubt that the plot was a sting engineered by Melville through an *agent provocateur*, Auguste Coulon, who encouraged the anarchists to make some rudimentary bombs and then informed on them. But when in 1895 a disgruntled ex-Special Branch officer, Sergeant Patrick McIntyre, alleged in *Reynolds News* that the bomb plot was a Scotland Yard operation—as had been a number of other so-called Fenian and anarchist plots—fortunately for Melville, no one believed him. Apart from anything else McIntyre had already compromised himself—he had been demoted for fiddling his expenses and for getting too close to the good-looking daughter of a known anarchist—and was forced to resign in 1894.[11]

In the next ten years, Melville embarked on a series of well-publicized raids against anarchists. In one of these he went to Victoria station personally to arrest bomber Théodule Meunier. In 1896

Melville recruited Shlomo Rosenblum—later and far better known as Sidney Reilly—as an informer in an organization he suspected to be involved with Russian anarchists. In 1901 he worked with Gustav Steinhauer, then head of the German Secret Service, to thwart a plot against the Kaiser during the state funeral of Queen Victoria.

And then suddenly, and apparently inexplicably, in early November 1903 Melville retired to look after his garden in Lydon Road, Clapham, in south London. Tributes flowed and embassies fell over each other to join a subscription list for a presentation to him the following May at City Hall, Westminster.

In fact, there was no retirement; Melville was just going undercover and changing jobs. At a salary of £400 a year in addition to his police pension, on 1 December Melville opened his two-roomed offices at 25 Victoria Street just across Parliament Square from Scotland Yard, under the name W. Morgan, General Agent, working for the War Office and under the immediate supervision of Sir Francis Davies.[12] The rooms had been chosen because there were two entrances to the building; Melville could use the second, tucked around the corner, to avoid people. He found to his great surprise that although, as he modestly put it, 'few men at the time were better known in London', in five years he never ran into anyone who knew him while going in or out.

Melville's new 'agency' began to watch for suspicious 'Germans, French and foreigners generally'. There had been some earlier rudimentary intelligence gathering by and about the Germans, concentrating on naval strengths and defences (for the moment the army did not really count in such matters). For example in 1902, while still in the police, Melville had trailed a United States citizen and potential German spy named Allain, purportedly a dealer in wine, who had been questioning soldiers about the manning of forts in Portsmouth. Although nothing was proved, it was thought that Allain had paid money to at least three soldiers. Somehow, during his crossing to France on the Dover–Calais ferry, Allain was cleverly separated from a packet of documents containing his researches, which made its way back to London. The year Melville opened his agency Allain was to be found teaching English in Cherbourg. He was asking the same sort of questions as before, and was deported.[13]

Working under Melville was Henry Dale Long, a former sergeant in the Army Service Corps, subsequently employed by the Foreign

Office, who would become a long-serving agent. He was a man to be sent here and there. In 1900 he had been in Madagascar and in April 1903 he had sent a report to Colonel Sir Francis Davies, 'considered fairly good and accurate', on the defence of beaches at Dover.[14] After this, he was despatched by Melville to Hamburg to 'get in' with employees in German manufacturing companies. Whether the experienced Long was pleased to have Melville give him 'Full instructions. Everything is to be done in a commercial way. To this end [you] will present attached card which explains itself' is a moot point. In February 1905 Long was sent off again, this time to Diego Suarez in Madagascar.

The third semi-permanent member of staff was the Austrian-born Byzewski, a professional spy based in Berlin, who was certainly in place by 1906. And there were other payments to agents in Overburg, Baku, Petrovsk and Samara as well as Malta and Montevideo.[15]

There was, however, discontent in the ranks when Melville discovered that Long, off on mission, was earning £100 a year more than he was. Melville immediately applied for an increase. After all, he said, Inspector Littlechild was now earning £1,500 as a private investigator, while of two other former Scotland Yard men, the former Inspector Sweeney, now also acting in a private capacity, was getting £850 and a man called Thorpe, who had been a mere sergeant, was on a salary of £450 a year from the Russian government to report on an-archists.

It was pointed out to Melville that Long 'can at anytime be called on to undertake duty which may lead him into a foreign prison and that considering the risks he has often run and will shortly run again, his salary is not as high as it seems'. At the time Long was on his way to Zanzibar, where imprisonment would no doubt have been extremely unpleasant. Davies wrote to Sir Thomas Sanderson adding, 'The last [the money] is an unfortunate circumstance and one which I always hoped he might not discover, to which end I have always paid Long direct.'

Melville would not have been much of a detective if he had not found out. He was given an immediate pay increase of £50 and a further £50 after a year. There was also a new proviso that if his employment were ended through no fault of his own he would be given a year's salary. Poor Long, back after two years in and around East Africa, was put on half pay.[16]

Melville was also engaged in proactive espionage. Shortly before Christmas 1904 his agent Hely Claeys, then in Brussels, tried to obtain the new cartridges for the Lebel gun, which were apparently being sold there by a French soldier from the supplies division of the French War Office. It was this weapon which had brought grief down on the heads of John Cooper and Walter Bedwell back in 1891. The deal went sour and, to his annoyance, Melville had to travel to Belgium over Christmas to retrieve the situation. In the end, the sale came to nothing because the soldier was selling out-of-date cartridges, but soon Melville obtained an example of the new cartridge in London.

In 1906, the *Daily Express* reported that Melville had gone to work for the Russian secret police. He denied the allegation, saying he was quietly enjoying his well-earned retirement, and claiming in *Police Review* to be extremely hurt by the suggestion he would work for a foreign power.[17]

That year Melville investigated a suspected spy ring in Epping where a rotating group of Germans was living at the Forest Gate Inn, taking photographs of a disused fort and going on long drives to the east coast. When Melville mentioned to the local superintendent of police that they might be spies, the man replied, 'Spies — what could they spy here?'[18] After that Melville went to Hamburg shadowing another possible spy, C. Werner, continuing to indulge his appetite for travel, disguise and a touch of danger.

Melville emphasized the need to introduce a surveillance system for foreigners in Britain with co-operation between the police, post office and coastguard. The next summer three Germans were found photographing the beaches at West Hartlepool and there were others doing the same at Holyhead. Melville's investigations continued, hampered rather than helped by the local constabulary; its senior officers would not believe there was any such thing as espionage.

Around 1906 spy fever really started to grip the public — which might explain the accusations levelled against Melville. It began with a serialization in the *Daily Mail* of William Le Queux's *The Invasion of 1910*, in which a 40,000-strong German army invaded Britain; he followed this with *The Battle of Royston*. The year after Le Queux's books, the German forces had grown by a third in Patrick Vaux's *When the Eagle Flies Seaward*, but happily they were still defeated. In 1909

London was occupied overnight in Henry Curties' *When England Slept*; no one had noticed the build-up of a German army on UK territory in the previous weeks.

Few people in authority seem to have believed in Le Queux's scares. Edward Henry, who was chief commissioner of the Metropolitan Police from March 1903 to 1918 thought that 'In his own eyes he is a person of importance and dangerous to the enemy', adding that Le Queux was, 'Not to be taken seriously'.[19] Le Queux thought no better of Henry, writing of him in a non-fiction book about German spies in England that the commissioner was 'utterly incapable' and his Metropolitan Police department 'hopeless'.[20]

But Le Queux was a winner both ways. When no spies were discovered, he simply pointed out that this showed just how cunning they were. In February 1909 the magazine *Weekly News* ran a column:

FOREIGN SPIES IN BRITAIN / £10 given for information
Have you seen a spy?... you may have had adventures with them, you may have seen the photographs, charts and plans they are preparing.

And, not surprisingly, many had.

One of the more curious men who believed Britain was to be invaded by German spies was Roger Pocock, the adventurer and writer whose book *On the Frontier* was highly regarded by Baden-Powell and who, unsurprisingly, was a friend of Le Queux. In 1898 Pocock organized an expedition to the Klondyke to prospect for gold. On 10 June the expedition cook Sir Arthur Curtis disappeared, and it was popularly believed that Pocock had killed him for his share of the profits. (Another view is that Curtis, who had matrimonial troubles, may have staged his disappearance, got lost and died.) In December 1904 Pocock formed the Legion of Frontiersmen, a patriotic imperialist auxiliary force, part-time, but uniformed and armed (a child could own a revolver at the time). Greatly influenced by Le Queux, the Legion trained for war and gathered information on potential German spies.[21]

It was not just the popular papers that feared German invasion. In June 1907 the military correspondent of *The Times*, Charles À Court Repington, a former army officer who the previous year had been working in the Foreign Office and was now running agent Claeys, took a delegation to the urbane and generally unrufflable (except when playing tennis) former Prime Minister Arthur Balfour, leader of the Conservative opposition, and gave him *Notes on an Invasion*, which argued that a German invasion could be mounted with both stealth and speed.

According to *The Times* this would not be difficult. Circumstances had changed since a report on the possible threat of an invasion by the French four years earlier. The assembly of an invading force could be explained away as manoeuvres or annual training, and whereas once a concentration of a fleet near Heligoland had been regarded with suspicion, it was no longer out of the ordinary.[22] Initially, *Notes* was poohpoohed both by Sir George Clarke, the secretary of the Committee of Imperial Defence, and First Sea Lord 'Jackie' Fisher, who nevertheless commissioned Edmond Slade, then head of the naval war college, to write a paper on the possible invasion. Slade concluded that, while the German strength was impressive, there could not be less than two days' notice of even a small attack. Even so, the question was referred to the Committee of Imperial Defence and an inquiry was held in November 1909.[23]

This inquiry concentrated the minds of the War Office and the Admiralty on how, if an invasion were planned, they would hear about it. The problem was two-fold—home and away. First, intelligence on German invasionary tactics had to be obtained, and secondly, little was known of German intelligence in England. There was no real system of obtaining information in advance. British espionage, *pace* Melville, was not proactive at the time. Agents, such as there were, were generally paid on results.

The Foreign Office had no overall policy on espionage. 'Extracurricular activities' were frowned upon, and it would not permit the ungentlemanly conduct of its consulate employees acting as spies. Indeed under-secretary Sir Charles Hardinge warned that such activities would be regarded as a disciplinary offence. On 5 March 1908 Captain Edmond Slade, then director of Naval Intelligence, noted in his diary that the British consul in Cherbourg had refused to pay 1,000 French francs for the plans of French submarines on the grounds that this would be ungentlemanly.[24] Nevertheless, provided its own hands were clean, the Foreign Office was happy there should be some informal spying on an *ad hoc* basis: 'An occasional artist or commercial traveller might prove useful'.[25] In October 1906 Norman Haag had been appointed vice-consul at Bremerhaven with the idea of procuring 'as much information about naval matters as can properly be obtained by a Consular Officer'.

The War Office's Directorate of Military Operations did, at least, have MO5 as a source of information, but it was shamefully run down.[26] By the time Major-General John Spencer Ewart was appointed director in 1906 he found there was no proper funding, and that the section was being run 'in a very light-hearted way'. The next year things took a turn for the better with the appointment of Le Queux's friend Lieutenant-Colonel James Edmonds—known in the department as Archimedes because of his enthusiasm for engineering —who was transferred from the Far Eastern section.

Edmonds, an outstanding intellect and experienced army official, was later to become an official historian of the Great War. His background was relevant to MO5: for example, in 1891 he had visited Germany, where he made contact with Major Dame, head of the German Secret Service, the Nachrichten Bureau, which had two branches conducting operations in France and Germany. Edmonds and Dame maintained a close friendship until Dame, considered excessively pro-English by his superiors, was replaced in 1900 by Major Brose, known for his anti-British views. Shortly after, Edmonds learned that a third branch—to deal specifically with England, working mainly out of Brussels but also from New York—had been added to the Nachrichten Bureau.

Back in 1899, Edmonds, on joining the intelligence division, had begun to recruit agents. Subsequently he had monitored events for the Far Eastern section of the Committee of Imperial Defence, and then it was off to South Africa to watch British interests there. He returned to England on 22 March 1904 and reported next morning to the Director of Military Operations and Intelligence.

When in October 1907 Edmonds was transferred to MO5, the refreshed intelligence service which had taken over most of Section H's records and remit, he found Major A. A. Adam in charge, a Conservative parliamentary candidate more interested in nursing his potential constituency than minding the office in Victoria Street, which was left in the day-to-day charge of Melville. As for the service's files, Edmonds claimed in his memoirs that there was some material about Russia and France and nothing at all about Germany.

In a giant step in February 1907, MO5 Special Duties Section (Interior Economy) was permitted to 'assume duties of an executive nature'; that is, breaking and entering, eavesdropping and shadowing.

In the same year Herbert Henry Asquith, then Prime Minister, insisted that the Committee of Imperial Defence should inquire about preparations in the event of a German invasion. Progress was being made, albeit slowly.

Edmonds had a tendency to see spies under the bed, and his memoirs recount how he approached German friends to ask them 'to look for and report on certain matters, notably the movement of warships, work in dockyards and arsenals and air progress and the erection of munition factories'.

Occasionally, there were small nuggets of evidence of German spies. A barber in Dover and a photographer in Sheerness had each been offered the munificent sum of £1 a month 'for information services'. The agents were paid by a former German officer named Gordon who got into trouble for bouncing cheques. In fact the information about the photographer was several years out of date. In another case that fizzled out, Franz Heinrich Losel appeared in court after being charged with spying in 1905. Losel had been seen by workmen apparently photographing the Ravelin battery in Sheerness—but it was found that the only photograph in his camera was of the High Street, and Losel claimed he was intending to sell it to a tradesman to make picture postcards. The Director of Public Prosecutions offered no evidence.[27]

Much of Edmonds' theorizing was based on the former French agent Emil Lajoux's memoirs, *Mes souvenirs d'espionage,* which took the view that any German living abroad was a spy. Some of Edmonds' logic left much to be desired—for example, he reasoned that as many of the waiters at the Queen's Hotel near Aldershot were Germans, and many English officers patronized the hotel, the waiters were therefore spies.

In December 1908 Edmonds presented a report at a Home Office conference urging co-operation between the Home Office and Post Office 'with a view to obtaining their assistance in marking down and tracing the German agents in England'. Quoting a territorial officer, he said that German officers were being given districts to investigate thoroughly, and that this had been going on since 1900. He went on to say:

We are in the position of the French in 1870; our enemy is 'in training' for the conflict, we are not. The French had no Secret Service, and on the 16th July, 1870 General Frossard was ordered to improvise one. As he says, it was then 'too late'; such a Service requires careful preparation in peacetime.[28]

Edmonds' superior, Major-General Ewart, had some sympathy with this view, and wanted the Secretary of State to allow him to try to arrange a meeting of interested agencies. The next year, Henry Dale Long was sent to East Anglia to try to bolster Edmonds' case with some up-to-date reports. On 5 March 1909 he delivered a report about alleged 'spies' in Lynn, writing that one local German, Sommerfeld, was a man of 'solid and honourable reputation'—and so dismissed thoughts of his being a spy. Melville thought that 'reputation' did not prevent a man from being a 'TR' or 'Tariff Reformer', the agency's name for a German agent; 'I think it may be the contrary', he said. In fact Melville was much more willing to see Tariff Reformers than many others and was no respecter of 'respectability'.

Long was initially based in Norwich; his next objective was to find out what was happening in Yarmouth. There were allegedly three Tariff Reformers staying on a farm near Dereham and another two at Fakenham. On 10 March Edmonds wrote to Long wanting to know the source of this claim, and asking for more exact information. On 23 March 1909, after reporting that the party's emissaries had 'worked the district', Long was called off.[29]

Partly based on this very thin evidence, Edmonds told the Committee that the Germans had undertaken espionage at 50 places, from the Wash on the Lincolnshire–East Anglia borders to the south coast. The previous year they had taken great interest in the new railway junction at Hither Green. Later, there were claims that in 1908, 68 German officers—far too many for comfort—had been hunting with local packs of hounds in England.[30]

What became clear, from an earlier (November 1906) report by the naval attaché in Berlin to Edmonds, was that while a German invasion remained unlikely, it was not impossible. It could be done, provided it did not embark from Hamburg where there was an English consul and a large English community, as well as a local population which was generally sympathetic to England. The bankers Rothschilds felt that, in the event of impending invasion, there would be sufficient movement in the financial markets for them to be able to detect mobilization. Sir John Pender of the Eastern Telegraph Company claimed that a change in telegraphs would soon be detected: 'Our customers are as regular as a butcher's'. But, reasoned MO2c, the German section of the War Office, if the Germans could stop cipher telegrams and newspaper reports as well as controlling passenger railway traffic into France, Belgium and Holland, then: 'We might not have our suspicions aroused until some friendly person who had escaped over the Dutch border wired us from Holland.'[31]

What the War Office wanted was to be warned within hours, not days, of mobilization. So Edmonds began recruiting more agents. But espionage was still a pretty amateur affair. Friends of Edmonds travelling to Germany were asked to go into police stations and enquire which English were living in the area, on the pretext that they required a document witnessed by an Englishman. The next step was for the people identified to be asked to report on military and naval preparations. The amazing thing was that German intelligence in Britain was using the same blundering method of recruitment.[32]

Egged on by Le Queux, Edmonds became obsessed with Germany's intentions, and the invasion of German spies. He began pressing the Secretary of State for War, Lord Haldane, to take the question of German espionage on the home front seriously. In many ways, Le Queux's next book, the factional *Spies of the Kaiser,* which described a German secret service network operating in Britain, was the clincher. Serialisation began in early March 1909, and on the last day of that month a sub-committee of the Committee of Imperial Defence was convened under Lord Haldane. Members, including the Home Secretary; the First Lord of the Admiralty; the Post Master General; Admiral Alexander Edward Bethell, Director of Naval Intelligence; Major-General John Ewart, Director of Military Operations; and Le Queux's *bête noire,* the Metropolitan Police Commissioner, Sir Edward Henry, began to consider the 'question of Foreign espionage in the United Kingdom'. Now Edmonds had his chance to outline his evidence. But with only Le Queux's book, some unconfirmed stories in newspapers, and Melville's experiences, it was thin. But, however easy it is to mock Edmonds, there was still something in his belief that England needed an operating secret service.

Edmonds presented his case on the basis of German intelligence in peacetime, and cited the consular official Count Victor Eulenburg, who in 1904 had been found in a dinghy apparently watching the landing of troops at Clacton manoeuvres. Edmonds claimed that Brussels, Geneva and New York were German espionage centres and in this, at least, he was correct.

Much of the 'evidence' Edmonds was able to produce was anecdotal. For example, he told the story of how when the German military attaché Major Ronald Ostertag (known as Easter Egg), complained at Wyndham's Theatre in January 1909 that the actors playing German officers in Guy du Maurier's play *An Englishman's Home* (about England being invaded) used 'raucous voices', Lieutenant-General William Thwaites raised his eyeglass and said, 'Bad conscience, Ostertag, bad conscience'.[33] A great deal of weight was also given to reports based on tales from Le Queux; from Edmonds' friend Fred Jane, who had published *Jane's All the World's Fighting Ships*; to letters received, some of which offered only copies of stories from *Spies of the Kaiser*, and to reports in the newspapers.[34] He had, he said, been hampered by the apathy of the general public: for example, one boarding house proprietress in Wells had refused to help him, saying that German money was as good as any other.[35]

Some dubious statistics helped to bolster Edmonds' case. He told the committee that in 1907 there had been five incidents; 1908 had seen a huge leap to a total of 48; while in the first three months of 1909 there had been 24. Edmonds also produced a map on which the 77 cases of espionage were marked with red dots. They were mainly in the southeast, from which it could be deduced that any invasion would land there.

Apart from the reports of people who had written to Le Queux or to Fred Jane, there was some support for Edmonds from Captain R.C. Temple in naval intelligence, who spoke of a series of advertisements placed by a man called Trianoud in the *Daily Mail* the previous year, asking for British naval men to write for American newspapers and magazines published in Brussels. It had been assumed that this was a German intelligence operation, but no direct evidence was forthcoming. Temple's department had absolutely no effective counter-intelligence, and any information it received was passed to Edmonds.

Neither Haldane nor Lord Esher, Commander of the London Territorial Force, was impressed with the case presented. Esher thought Edmonds was: 'A silly witness from the War Office. Spy catchers get espionage on the brain. Rats are everywhere—behind every arras.'[36]

Haldane wanted more evidence before he would act, and took himself off on holiday to Germany where, unsurprisingly, his friends told him there was nothing at all in the spy question. At a second meeting of the sub-committee on 20 April, Haldane reported that the Prussian General Staff had collected some intelligence—nothing to do with any projected invasion, but rather to help with sabotage before or at the beginning of any war. This was undoubtedly correct and, following Melville's line of thought on controlling the correspondence of aliens, the sub-committee spent much of its time redrafting the Official Secrets Act 1889.

However, when the sub-committee met for the third and last time on 12 July that year, 1909, Haldane had changed his mind. It was a moment for back-covering. He had come under considerable pressure from rising political stars such as Winston Churchill, and had been asked in Parliament if he knew that there were 66,000 trained German soldiers in England, with weapons and ammunitions stored near Charing Cross. He had also been told of a Frenchman who had come across an official German invasion plan, which he had copied to the British authorities. Although the plan was almost certainly a fake, General Ewart and General Murray, Head of Military Training, had convinced Haldane to take it seriously.

It was a question of better safe than sorry. The sub-committee now resolved that there was an extensive German system operating in the country and they were without the means to monitor or prevent it. As a sop to Cerberus, a department would be formed—initially to run for a two year period—to do so. After which, when it had found nothing —as was confidently expected—it could be scrapped, but at least the Opposition could not claim that nothing was being done.

Years later in his autobiography, Edmonds would say:

> I doubt whether the Germans in 1906–14 seriously contemplated invasion. The intention was intimidation. [The German General] Molthe who had shied off crossing a quarter mile arm of the sea in the Danish war said to a Kriegsakadamie audience, 'I can always land a pair of army corps in England but I cannot hope to supply them or get them out again.'[37]

Edmonds believed that the 'invasion threat' was to frighten the War Office from sending any troops from England to the Continent should a war break out between France and Germany. It was certainly a tactic later employed by Germany in an effort to keep America out of the war.

And so another set of rooms was taken in Victoria Street, and MI5 and MI6 were conceived.

Chapter Two

It was in August 1909 that an opportunity arose for Vernon Kell to do something vitally necessary for the safety of his country. There was the risk that should he fail to carry it through it would leave him with his career wrecked and bring about the dismal prospect of having to provide for his family with no adequate means of doing it. But he was young and an optimist—why should he fail? Lady Kell[1]

KELL AND COUNTER-ESPIONAGE

By the end of August 1909 plans were in place for the establishment of a bureau overseeing intelligence in the United Kingdom, at 64 Victoria Street, London S.W. Its cover was that of a detective agency owned and run by the former Scotland Yard officer Edward Drew, known in his days at the Yard as 'Tricky Dicky' and 'Sketchley'. Drew was one of the best thief-takers of the time.

The offices were principally for the use of Vernon Kell, Mansfield Cumming and William Melville. There was also a clerk whom Drew could use if the others did not need him.

It was to be a small operation, with everyone known by initials—not that this was much help in concealing identities: Drew was 'D', Melville was 'M' and Cumming 'C'. Henry Dale Long, 'L', was the bureau's foreign agent, based in Brussels but working as far afield as East Africa. As time went by, the fashion spread and initials became *de rigueur*. Compton Mackenzie, the author and agent working in Greece, became 'Z'; the head of Athens intelligence, Colonel Rhys Sampson, was 'R'; 'V' was Major Max, who ran the 'V' bureau, to whom Mackenzie reported.[2]

As for the spymasters, the privately educated, asthmatic Captain Vernon Kell, 'K', was to be in charge, leading a small team of home counter-espionage agents—later to become MI5—working with the

Special Branch of Scotland Yard. A fine linguist who could speak six languages (and whose grandmother had married a Polish Count, Aleksander Konaraki), Kell had been backed for the post by Sir Francis Davies, now General, known as Frankie or Joe. The tall, austere Kell had been at Sandhurst a year ahead of Winston Churchill, and had spent time in China, and in Russia where he learned the language while in a Moscow hospital recovering from scarlet fever. He had also served in India but, because of his ill-health, he had returned to England to work as a staff captain in the German section at the War Office. On 19 September 1909 he retired from the army and signed on at the new bureau for £500 a year in addition to his pension. Afraid that he was sacrificing a career for what might simply be a short-term appointment, he insisted that his contract was for a minimum of two years.[3] Given his circumstances, it was in his personal as well as professional interest to ensure that the bureau was a success.

On 10 August 1909, Rear Admiral A.E. Bethell, then Director of Naval Intelligence, wrote to Mansfield Cumming suggesting that he had a job for him that he thought would prove more interesting than the project on which Cumming had been working for the previous decade, Boom Defence—a series of underwater nets and wires designed to keep out enemy shipping, in particular submarines, in the event of war.

The short, stocky, balding Cumming, who looked a little like Punch, was described by the author Valentine Williams as having 'eyes as grey as the North Sea, a jutting imperious nose and a massive chin'.[4] Born on 1 April 1859, Mansfield George Smith took the name Cumming on his second marriage. At the age of 12 he went to the Royal Navy's officer training college at Dartmouth, which was regarded as the cheapest way of educating a pre-teen boy. The course lasted up to 18 months, and Cumming's disciplinary record was not good: diverse offences were recorded, including bullying and throwing a bottle at a train.

Once commissioned, Cumming saw service in China, around the Malay peninsula and Malta as well as Canada, but he was signed off on health grounds on 21 December 1885. (The precise nature of the health grounds was never satisfactorily explained.) On his retirement he worked in Ireland as a land agent for the Earl of Meath, until he was placed on the active retired list on 30 April 1898. From then on he worked on Boom Defence in Southampton. He spoke adequate French and had a taste for photography and electricity. An early pioneer of motor racing, he had taken part in the Paris–Madrid race in 1903 in which, as in today's Tour de France, crowds gathered on the roads, leaping out of the way at the last minute. Cumming, whose car had earlier been timed at over 110 kilometres an hour, crashed near Chartres—or rather his co-driver did: Cumming had provided the Wolseley, but it was driven by the company's test driver Sidney Girling.[5]

Sir Paul Dukes, who worked for Cumming in Russia, wrote of him, 'He was a British Officer and an English gentleman of the finest stamp, absolutely fearless and with limitless resources of subtle ingenuity.'[6]

There have been suggestions that Cumming was a womanizer, and he certainly kept a portfolio of 'artistic' studies, *Le Nu au Salon*, which he showed to favoured colleagues. The playwright Edward Knoblock thought that this was merely evidence of a childish naughtiness. According to Knoblock, Cumming was adored by his staff, and particularly his secretary, a Miss LeB.[7]

Like Kell, Cumming was happy to accept a salary of £500 and his military pension.

By the beginning of October 1909 the bureau was up and running. Staggering is probably a better word; it was hopelessly underfunded and under-manned. On 4 October there was a meeting attended by Kell, Cumming and their immediate superiors Sir James Edmonds and Colonel, later General, George Macdonogh, at which the rules under which Kell and Cumming were to operate were clearly spelled out. For a start they were not permitted to interview potential agents without Melville's presence.

On 7 October, three days before he was expected, Cumming arrived at the Victoria Street offices—and, unsurprisingly, found that there was nothing to do. Neither he nor Kell were to receive visitors there; nor were they to send or receive letters. To keep himself occupied, Cumming began to learn German. At the beginning of December, however, the workload grew and he had 'as much as I can tackle'.[8] He now employed a principal agent, the Austrian-born Byzewski, known as 'B', who had three men working under him.

At the start, there was friction between Kell and Cumming.

Although in theory they were joint heads and equal in status, in War Office eyes Kell was the more equal. Unless Kell—who was to have control of all naval and military espionage and counter-espionage in the United Kingdom—was on leave, Macdonogh would communicate with him rather than with Cumming. Cumming, fifteen years his senior, resented this, but the Foreign Office, which was paying for the enterprise, wanted no part in any squabble. Cumming began to lobby for his own quarters away from Victoria Street, and by November he had his way and had taken rooms in Whitehall Court.

In the meantime Kell, committedly anti-German and a firm believer in Edmonds' stories of spies under every bush, had thrown himself into his work enthusiastically, if adopting a rather scattergun approach.

Over the years Kell put in place a secret register of possible suspects on whom reports should be made every three months. But he failed to investigate the Edmonds/Le Queux list of spies that was used to lobby the 1909 committee: once it had served its purpose, no one in authority took it seriously. Ironically, and almost by chance, Edmonds had had one genuine German agent on his list. This was Paul Brodtmann, a director of the Continental Tyre Company in London, who had been recruited as early as 1903 by the Admiralstab (the German Admiralty Staff) to report on British battleships. At the time of the bureau's formation he was reporting to Major Ronald Ostertag, the German military attaché, on a Guards' motor trip to Hastings.[9] But the new bureau failed to investigate him, and Brodtmann went about his business unhindered for another five years.[10] Indeed, at the outbreak of the war, a list of 34 army officers to be used by the Admiralstab included Brodtmann.

The War Office, as well as a number of the Legion of Frontiersmen, had come to believe that the Legion's founder, Roger Pocock, was himself a German spy. In 1908 he was replaced as secretary and the following year expelled from the Legion. Even this did not allay suspicions, and on 6 June 1910 Kell ordered Henry Dale Long to join the Frontiersmen to investigate, possibly also with a view to recruiting a few unpaid agents. Legionnaires had to purchase their own uniform of stetson, neckerchief, breeches and boots as well as equipment—an outlay which kept out the working classes—and by 5 July Long had been warned to keep his expenses down, which suggests that the infiltration did not occur.[11]

Although there were reports of German activity, for the best part of the first year of the embryonic MI5 there was no positive proof. This was in spite of the fact that some of the so-called German spying seems to have been conducted quite openly with, for example, rudimentary questioning of estate workers by visiting and returning Germans. One farmer's letter reported a German in East Anglia asking about the number of draught horses 'more than four years ago' and referring to the area as his 'district'.[12]

Kell suspected that a German who gave his name as De Corvina, and who was running a poultry farm at Bartley Hill near Frant in Sussex, was a spy. The farm was secluded and it was thought that De Corvina could not be making a living from it. It was believed, but never proved, that the farm served as a rendezvous for Germans who, in properly sinister fashion, spent most of their time cycling around the country.

There was a similar case in nearby Rusper. Two Germans, apparently unknown to each other, took lodgings at the same address. They quickly became friends, but when Melville was sent to investigate they purported to quarrel, and were keen to know if he spoke a foreign language. Suspicious—but no proof of espionage was found.

In June 1910 Melville reported that a German named Stiewe visited waiters in Dover and Folkestone, who seemed afraid of him. Nothing further came of this inquiry either. Similarly, investigations were made of the many Germans who learned to ride at a London equestrian centre, and an officer was sent to walk the Essex and Sussex coastline to look for potential beachheads. No spies were uncovered.

That nothing much emerged from the bureau for some time was not wholly Kell's fault. Spencer Ewart wrote to Churchill asking for a general letter of introduction to chief constables. 'He is in every way most discreet and reliable.'[13] Now Kell stomped the country, trying to convince recalcitrant chief constables that there could be spies in their areas, until on 1 January 1911 he was given the services of Captain F.L. Stanley Clarke of the Suffolk Regiment, and his part of the bureau was divided into two branches — Passive (Preventive) and Active (Detective).

Clarke soon made a substantial contribution to the bureau when he overheard a conversation on a train between two Germans, one of whom said that he had received a curious letter from a Mrs Tony Reimers in Potsdam asking for information about Britain's preparations for war. Mrs Reimers was, in fact, a senior member of Gustav Steinhauer's staff and, once permission was given to Kell to intercept similar letters, it became clear that there was a ring of agents using a series of post-boxes.

In the summer of 1910 the bureau at last proved its worth with the arrest of the first of the pre-war German spies, Lieutenant Siegfried Helm of the 21st Nassau Battalion, who was found making sketches at Portsmouth docks.

The previous summer, a young woman called Hannah Wodehouse travelled to Germany and had an affair with Hans Wohlfahrt of the 8th Rhenish Pioneer Battalion. The next year she returned to see him in Berlin. He told her of a colleague coming to England, and asked her to show him around, and to speak English to him. The comrade was Helm, who wrote to Hannah saying he would be visiting Portsmouth. She obtained lodgings for him, but when he described his visits to the dockyard she became suspicious and alerted the authorities.

Although Helm had been making sketches of a number of installations and fortresses, the local magistrates, perhaps charitably, declined to commit him for trial on espionage. In November at Winchester Assizes he pleaded guilty to a breach of the Official Secrets Act and was released on his own recognizance by the equally kindly Mr Justice Eldon Bankes, who told him:

> We may be vigilant and perhaps from your point of view, too vigilant, in the detection of offenders against our laws yet, in the administration of those laws we are just and merciful, not only to those who are subjects of this realm but also to those who, like yourself, seek the hospitality of our shores.

In fact, Helm's sketches were made of an out-of-date fort which would have been of no possible use to German intelligence.[14]

In 1911 Phil Max Schultz of the 13th Hussars (the 'Phil' came from his doctorate of philosophy; he signed himself Phil Max Schultz) was charged with procuring a Plymouth solicitor, Samuel Duff, and businessman Edward Tarran, to commit offences against the Official Secrets Act. Schultz had a houseboat on the River Yealm, and offered the men an initial £50 and then £60 a month for information on how quickly vessels in the Mediterranean could return to base. The solicitor drew up a formal contract and, under the guidance of Special Branch, began supplying what might be called Duff information.

Sentencing Schultz to 21 months' imprisonment at Exeter Assizes on 4 November 1911, Baron Alverstone commented, also perhaps naively, 'No one would repudiate and condemn the practices of which you have been guilty more strongly than all the leading men in Germany'.[15] Schultz had sent letters to Pierre Thissen at 22 rue d'Ouest, Ostend, Belgium, which the police knew to be the address of Max Tobler, head of a German spy school at Rotterdam.[16] Tobler dropped out after the Schultz affair, and R.H. Peterssen, who ran the International Spy Bureau in Brussels and who would be a long standing thorn in British flesh, took over.[17] Schultz was released on 12 April 1913.

In the same year, 1911, Heinrich Grosse was unmasked. William Salter, a former naval rating who had opened a private detective agency, advertised for work, and a reply came from Captain Hugh Grant, who named 'a German magnate', the same Mr Peterssen, who would pay for information about British warships. Salter went to the admiral superintendent at Portsmouth, who handed the case over to the Special Branch. Salter was assigned the role of double agent, and a later search of Grant's rooms produced a number of incriminating letters. Captain Grant was arrested and turned out to be Grosse, a merchant navy officer who had served a 10-year sentence for forgery in Singapore. Questioned, he claimed that he had also spied for England—and was sentenced to three years. After his release in April 1914 he was arrested again in August, and died in an internment camp. Grosse was one of the few genuine spies observed by Le Queux, who had seen him with Steinhauer, the Kaiser's self-proclaimed master-spy, in the naval dockyards at Portsmouth in 1902.

Suddenly there seemed to be spies everywhere. In 1911, Dr Armgaard Karl Graves was denounced by his Edinburgh landlady, but it was not until April 1912 that a search of his hotel room revealed letters relating to a new 14-inch naval gun. An eclectic collection of equipment, including a number of phials containing poison, a hypodermic syringe and rifle cartridge cases, was also found.

Graves was a splendid confidence trickster. His name may have been Max Meincke; he was probably born in Berlin on 7 May 1882. In his none-too-reliable memoirs he claimed to have been recruited into the German Secret Service shortly after the Boer War, and to have been imprisoned twice in Serbia and South Africa. This may have been correct, but he chose to exclude his imprisonment on fraud charges in New South Wales in 1910. On his return he was sentenced to six months in Wiesbaden, and after that he may have persuaded the German Admiralty or Peterssen's International Spy Bureau in Brussels to send him to the United Kingdom to investigate the Rosyth naval base and the arms manufacturers Beardmore & Sons based in Glasgow. (If the former, it seems the Admiralty bypassed Steinhauer when employing Graves because, admittedly with the gift of hindsight, Steinhauer thought Graves to be a 'double-dyed' rascal.)

Offering faked Australian medical qualifications, Graves applied for a *locum* position in Scotland with a Dr James Mackay who, fortunately for his patients, thought Graves' strong German accent would 'not go' in Leith. Graves then became a friend of the assistant manager at the Central Hotel in Glasgow, who actually introduced him to members of the Art Club as 'my friend the German spy'.

Arrested at his rooms, Graves was charged with spying and 'making or obtaining a telegraphic code for the purposes of communicating information relating to the British Navy and land fortifications'.

At first Graves represented himself, but changed his mind and asked Crabb Watt QC to appear for him. In his biography, generally regarded as thoroughly mendacious, he claims that actually the trial judge forced him to use Watt, and also that during the trial the judge sent him half his own dinners. The charge of espionage failed, and in July 1912 Graves received 18 months on the telegraphic code charge. As with all good conmen he received his sentence well, saying, 'Exit Armgaard Karl Graves. Well, it was a fair trial'. He was sent to Barlinnie prison.

Graves was released in December 1912. According to his memoirs —and there seems to be at least some truth in this story—he was summoned to the prison governor's office, where Kell was present and asked him to work for the British. Graves claims to have immediately recognized Kell as a cavalry officer, and agreed to work for MI5—but only after he had been convinced that the German Secret Service had betrayed him. He was brought down to London and put up in the Russell Square Hotel. He lunched the next day with Melville at the Imperial, after which he was taken to Downing Street, where he signed the visitors' book as Trenton Snell, and met Sir Edward Grey, the Foreign Secretary.

Graves' landlady seems to have had sharper antennae than Vernon Kell. He thoroughly conned the spymaster, who had had the idea to employ Graves at £2 a week under the name of Schnell or Snell. Graves told him of German plots to blow up the Forth Bridge and to employ other undesirable persons to commit terrorist acts. He claimed to know all the German spies in Britain and, with a Detective Fitzgerald, it seems he was employed to hunt them down. Unsurprisingly he failed to find a single one. Kell was continually duped by him.[18]

If Graves ever did any real work for Kell, which is unlikely—although he claims that he went to Berlin to report on the bureau's behalf—it must have been for a very short period because, six months after his release from prison, the good doctor could be found in New York boasting of how he had deceived the British.[19] And indeed he had. Kell had sent him money in Germany and Austria on a number of occasions before he realized it was being wasted.

By June 1913 questions were being asked in Parliament about the reasons for Graves' early release. McKinnon Wood, on behalf of the Foreign Office, told the House of Commons:

> It would not be in accordance with precedent to state reasons for the exercise of the prerogative [of mercy]. I have no knowledge of his nationality. The sentence did not include any recommendation for deportation.

He did add, however, that Graves had been in ill-health, then as now a ground for early release.

On the outbreak of war Graves published the vastly entertaining and almost wholly specious *Secrets of the German War Office*. It quickly sold over 100,000 copies.

In spite of such embarrassments, Kell's early years were not without successes. The surveillance of Karl Gustav Ernst, the main resident German agent in Britain, who was operating from a barber's shop at 402A Caledonian Road, north London, provided MI5 with its biggest pre-war coup. Born in Britain and therefore entitled to citizenship, Ernst first came to notice in 1910. At the funeral of King Edward in May, apart from providing security, the bureau kept round-the-clock surveillance on Captain von Reuber-Paschwitz, a senior member of the Kaiser's staff who was thought to be an intelligence officer. After dining at the Café Royal one night, the captain returned to his hotel, left by a back door, and went to Ernst's shop where he stayed the rest of the night—singular behaviour for a German officer. The next day a warrant was obtained to intercept Ernst's mail, and for the next three years it was faithfully opened, copied, translated, re-sealed and re-posted.

Colonel James Edmonds later wrote: 'I was opposed to the arrest of even undoubted espionage agents: it was better to let Germany live in a fool's paradise that we had no counter-espionage system.'[20]

Steinhauer claimed to have discovered that after Ernst was under suspicion, secure in the knowledge that his correspondence would be opened, he continued to write to him, now sending misleading information. One particularly puzzling message was a telegram which read 'Father deceased await instructions'. A second read, 'Father deceased, what action' and a reply 'Father dead or deceased, please explain'.[21]

In 1911 the Official Secrets Act was tightened to allow the confiscation of mail for examination and copying. The Germans took exception to this, somewhat ironically complaining of the British practice of controlling German agents without arresting them.

In June 1912 Ernst's monitored correspondence turned up the name of George Parrott, a warrant officer in charge of the navy's rifle range at Sheerness barracks, who had been chief gunner of HMS *Agamemnon*. When Parrott applied for leave he omitted to mention that this was in order to visit Richard Dinger, a friend in Berlin. He was followed to Ostend and on his return dismissed from the service. He then went to live in Battersea, south London, where more correspondence was sent to him by Ernst. A German language teacher, Karl Hentschel, also came forward to say that since 1909 he and his wife had been in Parrott's pay. Hentschel betrayed him because their wages had been cut. Parrott received four years at the Old Bailey in January 1913; Hentschel was merely cautioned.

On 15 October 1912, Levi Rosenthal, a hairdresser in Portsmouth, reported to the authorities that a William Klare had asked him to obtain details of submarines in the dockyard. Klare, a hunchback whose real name was Klauer, had arrived in London 10 years earlier. He had married a prostitute and, for a time, set up a dentist's practice patronized by a handful of sailors. It was arranged that Rosenthal should introduce Charles Bishop, a senior officer in the paymaster's office, to Klare. The two met, and agreed a fee for smuggling the annual Torpedo Report from Bishop's employers. Bishop duly delivered the report, and Klare was arrested as he left Rosenthal's shop. On 26 June 1913 he received five years' imprisonment at Hampshire Assizes.

Frederick Gould, or Schroeder, was sentenced in April 1914 and received six years. He and his wife, Maud, had run the Queen Charlotte public house in Rochester. A new landlord found two Admiralty maps there, as well as a copy letter dated 8 October 1903 which was an application to join the German Secret Service. A watch was kept on the Schroeders, and Maud was arrested at Charing Cross after buying a ticket to Ostend. On the way to Bow Street police station she tore up some envelopes and tried to throw them out of the cab window. They contained the Admiralty's chart for Spithead and Bergen. At the Schroeders' new home in Merton Road, Wandsworth, south London, a six-page questionnaire relating to Royal Navy warships was discovered. Rather generously no evidence was offered against Maud, on the grounds that she did not know what was in the envelopes. Her husband had done his best for her, claiming she was completely innocent.

In May 1914 Ordinary Signalman Herbert Ernest Hutton was arrested in Sheerness and was court-martialled, charged with obtaining confidential documents from the battleship *Queen* on which he was serving. On 18 February the key to the signal-box was lost and the flotilla signal-book went missing; he was suspected of sending it to Flushing on 23 February. He received four years' penal servitude and his name was added to the list of German spies.

The final pre-war arrest was in June when an electrician called Samuel Maddicks boasted at Portsmouth dockyard that he was a spy. He had offered his services to Germany in April 1914, and an agent calling himself A. Ransom in Potsdam took him up. Maddicks had been sent £4 travelling expenses for a visit, but had not made the journey.

However, when he appeared at the magistrates' court Maddicks was found to be of unsound mind. He had, said his solicitor, 'the great intention to hoodwink foreign nations' but had realized the task was too great for him alone and had sought help. Perhaps charitably, he was sent to a mental asylum, from which he escaped. On his recapture he was interned and not released until 27 January 1919.[22]

Not all espionage cases ended in prosecution. As war approached the attention of German intelligence shifted from personnel on ships to those on shore. In February 1914 there were reports that Edwin Gregory was sending information from Portsmouth to A. Kutusow, who had recruited him by pretending he was an editor writing about the navies of the world. In fact, it was a retired dock worker, Peter Gregory, who had been in correspondence with Kutusow, who was really the hard-working Peterssen, now operating out of Pacheco Street, Brussels. At first, the articles concerned were of a general nature, but then they became more and more specific, with the editor wishing to know details of the fittings of tubes on the Iron Duke class ships. Melville was sent to interview Gregory, but the Director of Public Prosecutions took the case no further. What saved Gregory was the fact he had written that he wasn't a spy, and certainly not for the £2 offered him.[23]

The next month 21-year-old Clare Fouguet (who was also known as Lina Mary Heine) and Max Power Heinert were investigated. The good-looking Fouguet arrived in Portsmouth in March 1914 and began giving German lessons to British officers, as well as to Heinert. In fact Heinert was Fouguet's husband, and could speak German perfectly well. Between them they sent a sketch of searchlights at Portsmouth back to Germany. She claimed she had been recruited through an advertisement in *Berliner Tägeblatt* around Christmas the previous year. She had been receiving £15 a month and had travelled to Germany to meet her contact, Fels.

Fouguet and her husband were not prosecuted, but simply interned. She was sent to the harsh women's prison in Aylesbury, and he died in prison on 1 December 1914. It was thought that her conduct was worth a minimum of three years; when she petitioned for release in 1916 it was refused on the grounds that she would only start spying again. She was eventually deported, sailing for Rotterdam on 1 April 1919. A note on her file said that the case showed that the non-prosecution of such cases simply led to endless petitions and false claims that there had been no proof on which to prosecute.[24]

It was never quite clear who Albert Celso Rodriguez, *aka* Garcia, who came to teach at the Berlitz school in Portsmouth, really was — or indeed if he was even a Spaniard. He was another working under the guise of collecting information for a Russian newspaper, offering 5 shillings an answer and £70 for the Annual Torpedo Report, with the replies to go to Harry Ford at a poste restante in Brussels. He was interned.

According to Steinhauer's none-too-reliable memoirs, with war a matter of weeks away he made a lightning visit to Britain and, posing as a Dutchman doing a bit of fishing, he toured his agents in Scotland and England advising them to cease activity and cut and run. A number greeted him with scepticism but, of those who listened, Georg Kiener, a music hall pianist in Edinburgh; Kronauer, a barber in Walthamstow; Walter Reimann in Hull; and Schappman in Exeter, were among the few who escaped the round-up of suspected German spies on the eve of war.

Another who got away, and who had been in Kell's sights, was Francis Charles Bubenheim.[25] Born Karl Franz Josef in Alsace in 1886 and known as Charles Wilson, he trained as a mechanical engineer and in October 1913 worked in Lincoln's Inn at a patent agent's, where he saw plans of aeroplanes. He then wrote to an officer in Strasbourg offering his services to Germany. He met a Colonel Kolbe in Brussels and, offered an appointment at 420 German marks a month for one year, arranged to organize an espionage service for the whole of the south of England with special reference to dockyards and aeroplane stations.

It proved impossible to track down his correspondence so Melville was put on observation duty. Bubenheim applied for a job in Vienna in May and then on 4 July offered his services to the British in Rotterdam— but Inspector Frost, who was stationed there, was told to have nothing to do with him. Melville was sent over to interview Bubenheim, who claimed that he was defecting because of the way the Germans treated him and paid him so badly; they had wanted names of impecunious English officers. Melville gave him £5 but said the British would not be employing him.

Bubenheim managed to avoid arrest after being placed on the Special War List of Germans to be detained, and when his lodgings were searched in December 1915 his landlady had gone and no one knew of him.

On 3 August 1914, just hours before war was declared, 21 of the suspected 22 German agents in Britain were arrested (the 22nd, Reimann, was in Germany at the time). One of them was the biggest fish that landed in Kell's net, or at least the one who received the longest sentence (though Steinhauer thought he was incompetent): the Caledonian Road 'postman', Gustav Ernst.

Ernst was first charged under the Official Secrets Act, a charge which was dismissed by the magistrate at Bow Street. He was then taken to Brixton under the Aliens Registration Act. He contested this, claiming that he was a British subject, which indeed he was. He was released, only to be arrested at the prison gates and charged with communicating information to Steinhauer in Berlin.

It was a question of third time lucky for the authorities. On 13 November Mr Justice Coleridge, sentencing Ernst to seven years' penal servitude, told him:

> You are a mean, mercenary spy, ready to betray your country to the enemy for money, equally ready, I dare say, to betray Germany to us for an increased reward. With such a man I can have no sympathy.[26]

Ernst had sold himself and betrayed his country for £1 a week. This was typical of the sums involved in spying: 'I had forty agents in London but the sum total of their remuneration was hardly worth worrying about,' wrote Steinhauer.[27]

Chapter Three

Clever and effective spies seldom get caught, but the best are not even suspected. George Hill [1]

BRITISH SPIES UNDER CUMMING

For most of the pre-war years Mansfield Cumming had dealt with a few professional spies and a goodly number of rank amateurs, some of whom caused him considerable problems. But by the end of November 1909 he had met his first professional agent, the long-serving Byzewski, who had apparently initially been recommended to the British by the Austrian Director of Military Intelligence, Colonel Hordoiczke, and was said to have the ability to go into a fort, come out and make a completely accurate sketch from memory. On the negative side, he was also regarded as lazy. [2]

The meeting with Byzewski was to take place with Kell, and there was friction between them as to what was to happen. Byzewski had previously been run through Melville by Kell's patron, Sir James Edmonds, but, as he was to be a foreign-based agent, Cumming thought he should be under Admiralty, not War Office, control. Both Kell and Cumming spent the afternoon before the meeting seeking help from their superiors as to who was now to run Byzewski, and Cumming, supported by Rear Admiral Bethell, won. When the meeting finally took place, Byzewski was introduced to Cumming by Edmonds, who then left. (Presumably, as Byzewski was already employed as an agent, Melville did not have to be present.) During the interview Byzewski spoke only German and everything he said had to be translated for Cumming, who was still in the early stages of his

Berlitz lessons. Although he claimed he could follow the conversation, 'but not to understand his ideas and opinions', for both agent and controller this must have been a considerable handicap.

The aim was for Byzewski to recruit a permanent sub-agent in Wilhelmshaven on the western side of Jadebusen, a bay of the North Sea, and a second who would travel around the German dockyards. Cumming was still keen on approaching English people in Germany, but Byzewski seems to have been against this. When it was put to him that Cumming wanted information about the dreadnoughts being built in the Austrian Empire, Byzewski jibbed, saying he would do nothing that would hurt his homeland.

It seems to have been only toward the end of the meeting that they discovered they both spoke French. Cumming noted in his diary that Byzewski 'speaks French as well as or better than he speaks German'. Given Cumming's limited German, how he could have known this is not recorded.[3]

In time, Byzewski would find more sub-agents — but Cumming did not find the wage structure for this employment at all satisfactory. In a *Report on the Workings of the Secret Service Bureau 1910,* Cumming wrote:

> The principal agent — whom I will call 'B' — is employed on peculiar terms. He has three men working under him for whom he is allowed £360, £500 and £642 respectively.
>
> He is not paid anything at all for himself, but is supposed to retain some part of his men's salaries. There is no check whatsoever on the proportion he deducts and I think that this in itself is a mistake, as it invites him to employ the cheapest men he can get. I have no control over these men. I have never seen them or heard their names, and I am not by any means certain that they exist at all. The reports sent in are very meagre and do not up to the present justify the large salaries paid — more than is paid to all other agents put together.

Nor did he find two of the agents, 'B' (not Byzewski) and 'U', satisfactory either. They were to send urgent reports of an imminent war, but at first Cumming thought them, 'so timid that I doubt their finding sufficient courage when the time comes'.[4] Later he thought 'U' had potential. 'U' had reported on what seemed to be experiments in germ warfare near Kiel. Not for the last time, Cumming made a faulty character assessment: shortly before the outbreak of war, 'U' was lured into purchasing a completely sham German code by the talented Mr Peterssen in Brussels.

Kell also seems to have handed Henry Dale Long over to Cumming, who found him, 'a smart looking fellow, very likely, alert and I think careful'. It would be Long's task to recruit men, not facts, so his ignorance of shipping and the navy would not matter that much.[5]

Slowly, Cumming began to assemble a small team of spies. In late 1909 he acquired Captain Cyrus Regnart of the Royal Marines, the Russian-speaking son of an upholsterer, a man with whom he undertook a number of overseas field trips over the coming years. It was at Regnart's flat that Cumming met another agent, WK. And in the fortnight before Christmas he was due to meet with Von de T, another man who had worked for Kell. More agents followed. Not all of them were satisfactory; nor was the method of payment.

Over the next two years, Cumming often disguised himself, sometimes as a German—using the theatrical costumier, arsonist and blackmailer Willie Clarkson[6]—and interviewed many potential spies, some of whom had at least something to commend them. Others were out-and-out bounders; they included a former gunner in the Royal Horse Artillery who engagingly suggested there was no point in Cumming taking up his references. (And he seems to have been one of the better ones.) At the other end of the spectrum was a former major whom Cumming thought to be a blackguard and who claimed to be able to identify a German agent because the man had four rows of teeth. This potential agent claimed he carried a ring containing Peruvian poison which would kill in three seconds—eat your heart out, Phillips Oppenheim. Nevertheless, Cumming took him on for a trial run to Essen.[7] Another potential agent's contribution was to name as spies the Jewish moneylender Braywich Power, and William Guy Delaforce, a disgraced Scotland Yard officer. The information was probably correct.

This was not the only time that Delaforce would be mentioned as a possible spy. One of the most bizarre cases of a woman possibly involved in espionage was that of Australian Eva Mortlock Black, who was married to Braywich Power and sued him for divorce in 1916. She claimed that Delaforce worked for the Secret Service and paid her £20 a month to bring documents to and from France. Those she brought to England she handed over to people in the street or at

railway stations. This came to light when the King's Proctor intervened in the divorce case to argue that because of Black's adultery
with Delaforce she should not be given a divorce. It was never clear
for whom Delaforce was working, if anyone, but he and Eva Black
had, with her husband's agreement, gone to Algeciras, a hotbed of
espionage at the time. Mr Justice Horridge said he thought she believed
she was working for a secret service even if neither he nor she knew
whether it was German or English and, although all parties had
behaved thoroughly irresponsibly, he was not certain she had committed adultery with Delaforce, who by the time of the case had very
sensibly disappeared.[8]

One problem for Britain was that, with France and Spain as its traditional naval foes, by the time Imperial Germany decided to build a
North Sea and Baltic fleet no one knew very much about its strength
as a potential enemy. What the navy required was information on ship-
building capacity, naval bases and coastal defences. To get it, Cumming
continued with the tradition of using military as well as naval officers
to spy out German ship-building while seemingly on walking or sailing
tours; it was the military officers who got into the most trouble.

Back in 1901 an agent identified as 'Z' had reported that, while
there was no naval station or defences at Emden, the area was of
strategic importance to the German navy. This would be particularly
so if the Ems-Jade canal was made navigable for gun and torpedo
boats.[9] This was useful stuff, but there had not been much in the way
of information since and, in pursuit of it, some of the pre-war British
spies operating in Germany seem to have been asking to be caught.
According to Admiralty files, between 1909 and August 1912 11
Britons were arrested for espionage in Germany.[10]

In August 1910 naval officers Lieutenant Vivian Brandon of the
Admiralty Hydrographic Department and Royal Marine Captain
Bernard Trench were sent 'on a walking tour' to reconnoitre the North
Sea coast defences.[11] The pair had already done a little recognizance
work together when, in 1908, they went to look at German naval
resources at Kiel. It is hardly surprising that in 1910 they were caught:
Trench had told a German barber called Schneider in Portsmouth
that he was off to Denmark to learn the language, but would go to
Borkum and other islands to see what he could discover.

They had planned to deposit any incriminating papers in the Netherlands but, hearing of the naval manoeuvres, they went straight to Borkum. Within days Brandon was arrested there, and Trench in Emden two days later. At Borkum they had taken photographs and written notes on postcards which, it was alleged, had been sent to England. They had also taken measurements of landing stages and of the depth of the water at Sylt and Amrum.

The arrest of Brandon was through his own sheer folly. There were military exercises taking place in the area and Trench went through the wire one night into a restricted zone. The next night Brandon did the same, this time holding a camera with a flash attachment. The flashes were seen by a sentry and Brandon was arrested. The affair was managed, as was often the case, in a gentlemanly fashion: Trench should have stayed well away from his co-conspirator but, as Brandon was being taken by train to Emden, Trench was allowed to join the party. At Emden, Trench went back to his hotel to try to hide the incriminating photographs and sketches, and for the moment he succeeded. He was, nevertheless, arrested before he could escape to Holland. Quite properly the British government denied any knowledge of the pair; the official line was that if Brandon and Trench were doing anything suspicious it was on their own account. (Coincidentally, a matter of days later the German officer Lieutenant Siegfried Helm was arrested for espionage in Portsmouth.)

Over the months, evidence against Brandon and Trench was gradually accumulated. Brandon's story, that he was working for the *Daily Sketch*, fell apart when towards the end of September a hotel proprietor in Emden found some of the papers Brandon had hidden in the bolster. It was only a matter of time before the police found more papers under the mattress (the fact they had remained undisturbed for some weeks speaks little for the cleaning arrangements). Brandon's rather careless conduct was in sharp contrast to that of the German spy Horst von der Goltz, who claimed to have eaten 2lbs of incriminating papers in one evening.

Brandon and Trench both gave evidence at their trial in Leipzig, as a result of which the Germans learned a little more about British intelligence. Trench admitted that he had been in the Borkum fortifications, which the Germans did not know, and he also admitted that the 'Reggie' to whom he had written was Captain Cyrus Regnart who 'is connected with the Intelligence Bureau of the Admiralty'. For his part Brandon agreed that he had read *The Riddle of the Sands* three times.

An ingenious, if unsuccessful, argument was advanced that the notes they compiled were to be used for a sort of naval *Baedecker* and that, as British warships had not visited the area, there could be no objection to the men taking down information. It was not an argument which appealed to the judges, but they took into account the fact that Brandon and Trench were officers and gentlemen, not traitors, and had not tried to bribe German functionaries. In no way as lucky as Helm, they each received 46 months' fortress detention. Trench went to Glatz, now Klodzko, in southwestern Poland, and Brandon to Konigstein, southeast of Dresden.

Fortress detention was by no means as bad as imprisonment. The inmates were generally not common criminals and often included a number of officers sentenced for duelling. They would:

> Be allowed to provide their own comforts and to enjoy the society of the other officers, students and others, all men of education and good social position who share the Governor's hospitality in the fortress.....There are no irksome restrictions and it will not be difficult for them to obtain leave to make excursions in the town.

Before they were whisked off to their fortresses, Brandon and Trench spent some time chatting in the well of the court with counsel and the *juge d'instruction*. 'They were very gay and perfectly satisfied with the trial', said *The Times*.[12]

In the following year, on 29 July 1911, with tension between Germany and Britain increasing over the German gunboat sent to Agadir,[13] the clubbable Old Etonian Bertrand Stewart, a 38-year-old London city solicitor and part-time officer in the Queen's Own West Kent Yeomanry, was sent to see Henry Dale Long in Belgium and then on to Germany. He had apparently first approached Cumming two years earlier, volunteering to 'do something for Britain'. It was not simply the Agadir crisis that prompted his journey: the German High Seas fleet had left port and apparently disappeared into the mists of the North Sea. Could this be the beginning of the long-feared attack on England?

The ever-useful Macdonogh, who seems to have been the only person in the War Office who had his head screwed on tightly enough, was contacted to assist with finding the vanished fleet, and it was he who sent Stewart abroad to search. According to another version, Macdonogh sent Stewart on his hopeless mission but as a double agent; apparently Cumming was overruled when he protested.

Meanwhile, British intelligence had found the German fleet, and story has it that Stewart decided to pose as a British traitor to 'worm his way into the confidence of the German Intelligence and so glean information of the utmost value'.[14]

Once in Germany, Stewart contacted Byzewski's sub-agent 'U', the Belgian criminal Frederick Rué whose real name was Arsène Marie Verrue. Born in Courtrai on 14 February 1861, Rué had convictions for fraud and robbery, and had run a soap factory before going bankrupt in 1894. He had then gone to work for Courage's brewery in Hamburg, and had apparently been recruited by the managing director, G.N. Hardinge, on behalf of British intelligence in 1907.

There is a letter in German Intelligence files which, if genuine, shows that Hardinge's approach to Rué was hardly subtle:

> The Intelligence Department of the War Office have a list of individuals in their employ abroad, who give them various information when required… I am therefore writing to ask you whether you would care to have your name entered on the intelligence list in the employ of the War Office, and to give the best information you could when required to.[15]

Rué seems also to have worked for the French and it is likely he was working for the International Spy Bureau in Brussels as well. Hector Bywater, the naval journalist and pre-war spy for Cumming, has it that in 1905 Rué had been convicted in his absence for appropriating cheques and was sentenced to two years' imprisonment, which makes the story of his recruitment doubtful.[16]

Claiming that he was poorly paid by the British, Rué had become a double agent. According to Rué, Stewart went under the name of Martin when he visited him in Holland near the German border on 30 July, offering him money to find out when the German fleet could mobilize in the North Sea. Shortly after a second meeting, Stewart was betrayed by Rué and arrested in Bremen.

If Stewart really was posing as a traitor, then Cumming and others must have known Rué was working for Germany, otherwise why would Stewart be given his name? If they did not, then something was seriously wrong with Byzewski's network—or perhaps he also had doubled. Cumming discussed Rué with French Intelligence on a visit to Paris in March 1912. He claims they did not know he was a double agent—in which case there was a complete lack of liaison between England and France, and the French did not read English news-papers.[17]

On 21 August, Rear Admiral A.E. Bethell wrote phlegmatically to Cumming:

> I am afraid S (Stewart) has made an awful ass of himself and it is very questionable whether U has not been a decoy all through. Anyway our organisation must be pretty well through over there by now and your connection with it as well.

Bethell did not think

> … they can have anything against Brandon and Trench as you never had any dealings with them. It is annoying but we must expect drawbacks such as these in this kind of business.[18]

The Times thought that Stewart's arrest was a mistake which would soon be cleared up—but it was not so. Put on trial on a charge of attempting to obtain knowledge of military matters in Bremen, Heligoland and Wilhelmshaven, Stewart seems to have put up a spir-ited defence at his trial in Leipzig. Told by the president of the court that every German child knew that merchant ships could be con-verted for war purposes, Stewart replied, 'Then children must be bet-ter educated in Germany than in England.'[19]

The repartee did him little good. To show that he had friends in high places, much was made of Stewart's membership of the Carlton, the Athenaeum and five other London clubs. He also admitted that he had scouted during the Boer War. On 31 December 1911 Stewart was sentenced to three years and two months in the same fortress as Trench. His friends were outraged, and on 5 February 1912 barrister Reginald Arkwright wrote indignantly to *The Times*:

> All who knew Stewart at Eton, or who have known him in later years
> as a professional practitioner of the highest reputation, can state
> without fear of contradiction that he is absolutely incapable of a mean
> or dishonourable act, and would never stoop to play the miserable role
> of a spy.

Stewart's father took a rather more measured view along the lines that 'Young men will be young men'. He, for one, did not want to see an international incident come of his son's misfortunes but, even after Stewart's death in 1914, his friends still complained that he had wrongly been labelled a spy.

Spying was legal in Belgium so, quite apart from spies from Germany, France and the home country, there were independent commercial concerns there, such as the International Spy Bureau run by R.H. Peterssen—a.k.a. Müller, Schmidt, Kutusow and Talbot and no doubt a few other names—who advertised freely in the Belgian papers.[20] Peterssen's agency was also used by German intelligence for the purposes of counter-espionage. Peterssen had a £50 monthly salary and £4 and 5 shillings for every spy detected in Germany through his organization. No doubt the trap for Stewart had been laid by Peterssen, who was later mentioned in the Grosse spy trial in England.

At first Brandon, Trench and Stewart were treated well in the fortresses, but then conditions were tightened, principally because of the escape of a French officer, Captain Charles Lux, sentenced to six years' imprisonment for espionage. Lux had been arrested at Friedrichshaven on 4 December 1910 when he was found too close to some Zeppelins. On 27 December 1911 he managed to escape from the fortress by filing the bars of his cell, breaking down a door and letting himself down to the ground with a rope made of handkerchiefs and bed sheets. Disguised as a hunchback, he took a train to Dittersbach, from where he sent his commanding officer a telegram: 'Good journey, best wishes, Charles Noël'. He went on to Italy, from where he took the Paris train from Milan, arriving to great acclaim on New Year's Day 1912. For a time a French professor in Germany was held over the escape, but Lux maintained he had been helped only by his brother and an old school friend.[21]

In February 1912 Brandon also made an escape attempt, but he only reached the courtyard before he was stopped by a sentry. Later, he successfully sued a German newspaper for alleging that he had attempted to bribe a guard, which would have been seriously bad form. He donated his £4 damages to a German charity. Curiously, the Germans regarded his escape and that of Lux as unsporting behaviour akin to breaking parole. Now prisoners convicted of espionage were no longer allowed personal effects or money, were subject to both regular and spot searches and had bars put on their cell windows. It was not until the spring of 1913 that Brandon, Trench and Stewart were released, following pardons from the Emperor Wilhelm marking a visit by King George V to the wedding of his daughter Victoria Louise to Prince Ernest Augustus, Duke of Cumberland.[22]

Trench had written down what he could remember of the trip and managed to smuggle out two letters with a visiting priest. But by the time they arrived, the Admiralty had already received the necessary information — the vice-consul and his wife at Emden reported every time they returned to England. Trench was not pleased.

However, he and Brandon seem to have taken their imprisonment in good part, and on their release their claims for expenses were soon settled. Stewart was not as happy. He began to lobby the Admiralty, trying unsuccessfully to obtain compensation and blaming Cumming for his troubles. He wanted £10,000 and rejected an offer of £1,200.[23]

Cumming may have wanted to place agents abroad, but attitudes were different when spies tried to sell documents to the British government. In April 1913, a man called Maimon, said to be a Mohammedan and a naturalized Englishman, was arrested in Paris. He had tried to sell papers which could have been used to convince Russia that the French and English were co-operating against that country's interests. They had been stolen from the archives of the French Foreign Office, copied and returned. They were offered both to Sir Edward Grey and to a newspaper, both of whom informed the French government.[24]

In September 1911 two Englishmen, Attwood and Steplord, said to be infantry officers, were arrested at Emden when they were found taking photographs at the dockyards. Their cameras were confiscated and the plates exposed. They had been on a yacht flying a Norwegian flag. They were released without charge two days later. *The Times* reported that other newspapers had given their names as Wace and Hagg. In fact, Wace and Hagg were schoolmasters who had been arrested at Kiel on 30 August. They had also been released.[25]

In August 1912, five 'sportsmen of high social standing' were arrested at Eckernförde and their yacht, *Silver Crescent*, impounded. Somehow, they had managed to avoid customs at Kiel, and compounded their mistake by taking photographs of a new torpedo stand. The German newspapers variously claimed the men to be two doctors:

two barristers; one businessman, one engineer; one photographer and one naval painter. The next day they were released, paying tribute to their captors who had sent meals over from the local hotel, and freely admitting they had behaved irresponsibly.[26]

Quite apart from the sometimes clumsy methods employed at the time, much of the intelligence obtained on all sides was of poor quality, either rehashed from technical journals or, worse, completely fabricated. Even so, the agencies could deceive the great and the good at least some of the time. In 1908 Robert Baden-Powell purchased a document detailing plans for a German invasion on the August Bank Holiday. Spies already in England would cut telephone and cable wires and blow up bridges and tunnels. Some 90,000 Germans would then land in Yorkshire, effectively cutting England in half. For a time Baden-Powell seems to have believed this, and lectured on the possibility of such a plot being successful. Later he would claim that, judging by the abuse he received from Germany, he had 'gone even nearer the truth than I had suspected'.[27]

Rather more professional than the unfortunate Stewart, but much more unlucky, was Max Schultz (no relation of the German Phil Max Schultz). Born in Hull in 1884, the son of an immigrant shoemaker, in many ways Schultz was an ideal man for spying. He had been apprenticed to a shipbuilder and had then become a yacht broker, which provided an ideal cover. He married into money in the form of Sarah Hilton, the daughter of a local fish merchant. It is not clear how he came to be recruited by Cumming. Possibly they had met while sailing on the Solent, but there have been suggestions that Cumming held compromising information on him and effectively offered him the choice of arrest or a career as a spy. The best cover for a spy was a business, and Schultz had both that background and the required knowledge.

The first person with whom Schultz made meaningful contact in Germany was the 60-year-old Ernest von Maack, from whom he wanted information about proposals to convert into warships merchant vessels from the Nord-Deutsche Lloyd and Hamburg-Amerika lines. While Schultz was in Germany, von Maack's landlady, Ida Eckermann, introduced Schultz to the 34-year-old naval engineer, Karl Hipsich (she may or may not have been his mistress) and to Bernhardt Wulff. Hipsich, an Austrian by birth, had changed his nationality following a regulation that only Germans could work in German shipyards. During his employment he had made a collection of plans and drawings and in January 1911 he was persuaded by Schultz to bring them to England.

On arrival, Hipsich was treated royally and taken to see the Royal Aero Club at Hendon. He was enchanted, kissing Schultz and trying to kiss the decidedly unenthusiastic Cumming. He was persuaded by Cumming to sign up and was paid £2 a week, with a bonus for information. Schultz went back to Germany at the beginning of March 1911 to discover what he could about the Dreadnought *Thuringen* as well as the first submarine, the *Ersatz Odin*, referring to them in his reports as 'little fishes'. His cover was again that of yacht broker.

He had already been under suspicion on his last visit; now Hipsich was arrested five days after he had produced naval documents quite openly in a café. Schultz had also sent a telegram which indicated that something had been sold. The telegram was duly found.[28]

On 13 December 1911, at the Supreme Court of the Empire, Schultz received a sentence of seven years for spying in Leipzig dockyards, and was kept throughout the war in German prisons. As a former officer, Hipsich received 12 years, and the others lesser sentences. Released in 1919, Schultz returned to Hull where he died in 1924 at the age of 49.

Melville, Kell and Cumming were now recruiting a more talented collection of spies who were, in turn, setting up networks in Europe. Long was still at work and so was Byzewski.

One of the European recruits was Richard Tinsley, who spied on Dutch forts from his offices in Rotterdam. Tinsley, recruited in 1912, and who had been given an RNVR commission as commander, was short and broad-shouldered with piercing eyes and ruddy complexion. The South African, Henry Landau, who worked with him, thought he looked like a 'mix of prize fighter and sea dog'.[29]

Born in Bootle on 12 November 1875, Tinsley was regarded by some, notably Ivone Kirkpatrick (who became Permanent Under Secretary at the Foreign Office), as a liar and first-class intriguer with few scruples, who from time to time dabbled in blackmail. In 1910 Tinsley had set up the Uranium Steamship Company on the Rotterdam waterfront and in February the next year he tried to land two boatloads of rcmigrants, something he had been expressly forbidden to do by the Dutch authorities. He was given a fortnight in which to leave Holland. After appeals to the Dutch royal household this was extended to a month, and he left for Antwerp on 27 March. It was only after lengthy negotiations and fulsome apologies that he was allowed to return.[30]

Cumming's protégé, the journalist Hector Bywater, came from an espionage background. His father had spied for the Union in the American Civil War and his brother Ulysses had posed as an American to get the job as deputy consul general for the United States in Dresden. When Hector joined him there he went along with the fiction. A big man who was a good raconteur, and a fluent German speaker with a genuine liking for German culture (and who sang Schubert *lieder*), Bywater worked on the *Daily Record*, an English-language weekly and also as naval correspondent for the New York *Herald* and the *Navy League Journal*. Soon after he began to write he was invited to meet Cumming in London. Unusually for Cumming's British spies, Bywater demanded money. Given his knowledge of naval matters, he was offered an appointment as a lieutenant commander in the Royal Navy, and undertook a highly successful tour of German dockyards and coastal towns, going as far as Trieste. He returned to England in 1910.[31]

The great spy Sidney Reilly claimed to be doing exactly the same thing for the next three years, writing:

> For three vital years before the outbreak of the First World War the British Admiralty were kept up to date with every new design or modification in the German fleet — tonnage, speeds, armament, crew and every detail even down to cooking equipment.[32]

Cumming, however, maintained he did not meet Reilly until March 1918.[33]

John Herbert-Spottiswoode was another recruit. Fluent in German and financially independent, like Cumming he was a member of the Royal Aero Club. He was persuaded to adopt the cover of an Irish-American to investigate the construction of Zeppelins. He claimed later to have worked in the Zeppelin factory, and to have sent back blueprints of their engines. He remained in Germany after the outbreak of war, when he was arrested. Fortunately, his Irish-American cover held and he was merely interned at the Ruhleben racecourse camp until in March 1915, following representations by James W. Gerard of the American Embassy, he and Joseph Weston were exchanged for German detainees. (Spottiswoode was said to be lame and to have had an operation for appendicitis while in the camp.)[34]

In 1914 an unnamed retired British naval officer and his son were given £1,500 to sail the North Sea looking at the German fleet. To Cumming's great annoyance they considerably overspent their budget. Little more is known about the episode, but it shows the amateur nature of espionage efforts at the time.

As war approached Cumming's men had clearly been busy. In early July 1912 Ewald, an engineer employed by Siemens near Frankfurt to instal telegraphic apparatus in warships, was arrested at Kiel trying to obtain a signal-book for both the French and British. On 30 January the next year he received seven years' penal servitude for giving information to British Intelligence in London, Kiel and Wilhelmshaven. He had visited London after receiving no reply from French Intelligence, to whom he had first offered his services, and had been put on a monthly salary by the British.[35] On 11 October 1912 the German Edmund Kagelmann received six years' penal servitude for selling to British Intelligence naval defence plans relating to the Elbe.[36] On 21 November Petty Officer Zorp, who served on the gunboat Panther, received three years for stealing material at Karlstadt to sell to the British.

One of the last pre-war spying episodes returns us to the realms of cheerful amateurism. The elderly Lord Brassey—founder and editor of Brassey's Naval Annual—caused consternation during Kiel Week at the end of June 1914. He had gone to the regatta in his yacht *Sunbeam*, and one morning before the race went for a little row when, as *The Times* put it, 'he approached too near the mysteries of the Imperial dockyard'. 'Greatly to his amusement' he was arrested and held for an hour and a quarter before his release, having been identified by a German officer. Whether this was a particularly amateurish piece of would-be espionage or a genuine mistake, his Lordship should have known better.[37]

Amateur or not, the spying trade had gained momentum. According to the German spymaster Walter Nicolai, from 1903 until the outbreak of war there were 135 convictions for espionage in Germany. Of those convicted, 107 were German, 11 Russian, 5 French, and 4 English—Trench, Brandon, Stewart and Schultz. In 74 of the cases the spying was for France, 35 for Russia, 15 for England, 1 for each of Italy and Belgium, while in 9 cases the spies were acting for multiple employers. In the first half of 1914 there had been 346 arrests and 21 convictions.

War was now little over a month away.

PART TWO
WAR BEGINS

'It will all be over by Christmas.' Popular belief on both sides

The causes of the First World War, and the alliances that dictated sides, are widely known but are often misremembered or misunderstood. Put at its most simplistic, the catalyst occurred at 6 p.m. on 28 June 1914: Gavrilo Princip, a student from a Serbian nationalist group, shot and killed Archduke Franz Ferdinand of Austria and the Grand Duchess on a state visit to Sarajevo in Bosnia. It was not the first attempt on the life of the Archduke that day; earlier, Nedjelko Cabrinovic had thrown a bomb which had missed. Had Princip not succeeded there doubtless would have been other attempts.[1]

In the first week of July Germany offered the Austro-Hungarian empire total support, and on 28 July 1914 the Central Powers went to war with Serbia. Russia, which had mobilized four days before, then went to the aid of Serbia and, in turn, France to the aid of Russia. (This was unexpected because Britain and France had never before sided with Russia.)

Germany then struck against France by invading Belgium. Britain, which had a moral obligation to defend France and also Belgium—the latter under a 75-year-old treaty—entered the war on 4 August. Britain then negotiated with Italy and Japan, agreeing to transfer to them certain German and Austro-Hungarian land holdings if they joined the Allies. Japan did so on 23 August.

In November, Turkey, then in serious decline but still controlling much of the Middle East, joined the Central Powers. It had no love for England, which in 1906 had compelled it, under threat of war, to cede to Egypt a large area of desert land north of Suez and between the Mediterranean and the Gulf of Akaba.

Italy dithered. Despite holding a treaty with both Germany and Austria-Hungary, she claimed it related to a defensive as opposed to an offensive war. It was not until May 1915 that Italy joined the Allies.

It will be argued for centuries whether the war was always intended to be a short one—aren't they all?—and whether it was primarily defensive (an attempt to unite the German nation and to deal with Russia before it had rebuilt its navy) or deliberately aggressive.[2] Each theory has its supporters. Writing in 2008, Professor Gary Sheffield succinctly summed up the outcome of the posturing and manoeuvring:

At best, Germany and Austria-Hungary launched a reckless gamble that went badly wrong. At worst, 1914 saw a premeditated war of aggression and conquest, a conflict that proved to be far removed from the swift and decisive venture that some had envisaged.[3]

Whichever interpretation you believe, there is no disputing the fact that in the first few weeks of war spies real and imaginary were everywhere on both sides of the Channel. One story was that the aviator Hellmuth Hirth was arrested and shot as a spy in Berlin on 29 August. Allegedly he had been too close to the French aviator Roland Garros, to whom he had written after the outbreak of war. Post, another German aviator, and his passenger were shot by Germans as spies when they went to join up in Denmark. In Hamburg a Danish subject and an English clergyman who was lodging with him were shot as spies; it was alleged that they had a wireless station on the roof of their house and had intercepted messages from the German fleet at Kiel.

Everyone was potentially suspect: on 1 September *The Times* reported that a German of 'high social standing' had been arrested in Britain as a spy. But he was never identified. At the other end of the social scale a lance-corporal in the Territorials was shot near Slough as a spy by a guard from his own regiment when he failed to answer a challenge. It was thought he had failed to hear the man because of a passing train.[4] And the Mayor of Deal, Mr Hussey, was arrested and held as a spy after he was found on the cliffs. He was only released when his townsfolk vouched for him.

On 22 September the l'abbé Délébecque was shot at the foot of the Danpierre Column in Valenciennes, France, executed by the Germans as a spy. He had been found in possession of a number of letters from French soldiers to their families. He was said to have been the seventh priest to be shot in the vicinity of Cambrai since war was declared. In Abo, Finland, the German consul was shot as a spy by the Russians.

Colourful stories abounded. One British officer told *The Times* of a German spy found wearing a British officer's uniform under which he wore a French officer's uniform—and under that his own. 'He was sent back to be tried. The French would have shot him where he stood,' he said happily.[5]

There were also more sobering reports. On 7 August 1914 two German spies were caught and shot at Louvain in Belgium, and two days later two more, who had disguised themselves as French officers, were captured and shot by the Allies. The next day a man and his nephew were found at Ghent sending pigeons to Germany. They were shot at dawn. Four other suspected spies were arrested in Ostend and shot.

The British were similarly ruthless in France. On 12 August two German spies, one dressed as a French artillery officer and the other as an NCO, were arrested after a long chase through northern France. Their car was found to contain enough melinite to 'blow up the biggest bridge in France'. They were executed at Tours. Other German spies dressed as nuns were arrested in Malines late at night and shot at dawn. And on 21 September 1914 a French farmer who had been given 50,000 French francs by the Germans was found to be telephoning the movements of troops to the Germans. He was shot, as were another 15 others, over a three-day period.[6]

In Antwerp 50 spies were taken in one day, and on 12 August the *Etoile Belge* reported that 2,000 spies had been arrested. It is more likely, however, that many of those hunted down as spies were Germans who had lived in Belgium, often for years, and were now refugees.

On 14 August, 100 Germans and Austrians were arrested in Dublin, and Germans in England were detained in Olympia, west London, where, *The Times* reported, they were perfectly happy, smoking, playing cards and, naturally, reading *The Times*.

The international press was full of spy fever, which inspired some unlikely spy detective heroes. Georges Leysen, an 18-year-old Belgian boy scout from Liège, was singled out as a scout of whom 'boy scouts all over the world will be proud'. He had 'already a bag of 11 spies, all of whom had been shot'.[7] And in Brussels an old man no longer fit for active service, but who spoke German, volunteered as a spy-catcher. He would approach men in bars and after ascertaining they were German would ask, 'Where do we meet tomorrow?' He would then signal to waiting policemen who would arrest both the spy-spotter and his prey. Back at the barracks, the spy-spotter would, of course, be released for further duty.[8]

The British papers reported hundreds of German spies sent in advance of the army. They were clearly cannon fodder:

Invariably in British uniforms, unable to speak English or French and allow themselves to be captured without the slightest attempt to resist or defend their identity. They are shot without exception but their loss does not affect the working of the system in the least. Ten may be found in one place and will be shot one day; there will be twenty there the next.[9]

On 4 October *The Times* reported that eight spies had been shot in Soissons in France. Some had telephones in their cellars, while others signalled to the enemy from chimney stacks.

The first woman spy exposed, whose name was never published, was shot by the French in August 1914. She was the wife of a forester from Schliebach. Executed at Belfort, she was described as a 'veritable monster', having 'sawed open' the throat of a wounded French soldier.[10]

Given the prevailing hysteria, two women—Juliette Zarlowska and Selmar Gibbs—were fortunate to survive. Zarlowska, the divorced wife of a German officer, dressed as a Red Cross nurse and, using the name Mrs Booth, met wounded British soldiers at the Gare du Nord. Over dinner she quizzed them about troop movements and tried to discourage them from fighting. In November 1914 she was fined 1,000 French francs and sentenced to two years' imprisonment. Four months later in March 1915, 62-year-old Selmar Gibbs was convicted at Perpignan of sending messages to German agents in Spain and imprisoned.[11]

Chapter Four

The Intelligence Corps was seen as a temporary and laughable bunch of amateurs to be suffered and made use of in various background intelligence functions perhaps, but not to be taken seriously.
Archibald Wavell [1]

THE INTELLIGENCE CORPS

In 1910 the then Colonel George Macdonogh, the staff officer in charge of MO5—created for a variety of duties including protective security and censorship of the post and telegraph—began to compile a list of suitable recruits: lecturers, artists, journalists and schoolmasters, but mostly people who spoke French and German and preferably another language. He did not approach them until the beginning of the war; to their surprise each received a telegram inviting them to join an ad hoc Intelligence Corps. There had been plans for the development of such a Corps from 1904, but nothing had been done about it.

Later the GHQ General Staff officer Major Walter Kirke wrote:

> I was ordered to take charge of Secret Service arrangements for the Expeditionary Force and to organise an Intelligence Corps forthwith. The page here was completely blank and the puzzle was how to fill it. [2]

The new Corps in its first few weeks seems to have been almost as amateurish as the pre-war British spies. The first commandant was Major T.G.J. Torrie, a relative of Macdonogh. Formerly of the Lucknow Cavalry, Torrie simply wanted to be in the action, and was afraid that if he returned to India he would miss the war which both sides were confidently predicting 'would be over by Christmas'. He had no experience in intelligence—who had?—and lasted a bare six weeks before requesting a transfer back to the front to command the 2nd Life Guards at Ypres. [3]

The Corps' initial membership consisted of the commandant and 20 senior officers, 25 officer scouts with motorcycles, 6 drivers, 4 cooks—paid one shilling and sixpence daily—and 25 detectives from Scotland Yard, mostly from Special Branch. The appointment of the detectives was not as odd as it may seem; they turned out to be very useful, for example in the Corps' work in France flushing out German agents, work which later spread to Italy, Salonika, the Middle East and then Russia.

The Corps' recruitment process was haphazard. A working knowledge of cars and motorcycles was deemed useful in potential officers, but in the last resort they were 'required to remain on a horse for a reasonable length of time'. It was not just any horse on which proficiency was to be shown: those used had been 'bluffed out' of the Grafton Hunt. Major Walter Kirke found that 'Modesty as to their attainments was not a characteristic of many of the successful competitors'.[4]

The recruits came in all shapes and sizes. Lieutenant Dunkels had one of his family's Rolls-Royces especially armour plated. Major Malcolm Henry Mortimer Lamb had been the governor of Shrewsbury Prison. A man for whom card indexes and lists were all-important, he compiled an index of 'Undesirable Prostitutes'; there is no surviving index of desirable ones.[5]

One recruit, Captain W.L.R. Blennerhasset, arrived armed with his father's sword and two spare shirts. He might have known how to hunt, but he proved to be a hopeless motorcyclist. When Lieutenant James Marshall-Cornwall, who expected to be astride the Grafton gelding Sunbeam, was told he had instead to use a motorcycle, he admitted he did not know how to ride one. Blennerhasset then allowed him to ride pillion on his vehicle: completely out of control, their journey lasted 50 yards. Another motorcyclist, Lieutenant Fairburn, managed to catch his rifle in the spokes, and off he came.[6] A. J. Evans had no time to get measured for a uniform and bought a Middlesex Regiment uniform he had seen on a dummy in a shop window in Regent Street.

Major John Lawrence Baird, later Viscount Stonehaven, wrote in his diary of 12 August: 'After breakfast it occurred to me that it would be well to take Jilling, my steward, as batman.'

At the time this decision was made for him, Jilling was hard at work dismantling his master's yacht *Gertrude*. Later Baird would write 'Torrie approved, Jilling willing'.[7]

Baird thought the sacking of 12 officers even before they sailed for France 'unfair'. They had already bought their kit and taken an examination in French. After all, the War Office knew their qualifications 'before taking men on'. But the Corps did not have time for a lengthy elimination process. Some who survived were described as 'unreliable', 'useless', 'unbalanced' and 'neurotic'. Some, including Lieutenant Mark Arthur Blumenthal, were bounders; indeed just the sort of men who could leaven the Corps. Blumenthal joined in October 1914 as a major. Rather unsportingly, his former employers then disclosed he had been convicted of fraud and he resigned his commission. In March 1916, still in the Corps, he was promoted to lieutenant, but in October the next year there were reports that he was spending his nights in Amiens with a lady from the French Mission. Despite his appeals he was obliged to resign his commission a second and final time in December 1917.[8]

However, the surviving recruits were full of initiative. One exchanged his motorcycle for a car and later exchanged that and their successors, always upgrading during the retreat from Mons until he ended with a Rolls-Royce, which was expropriated by General Staff. He was then given another motorcycle.[9]

The Intelligence Corps, by then consisting of 12 regular or reserve officers and 42 scout officers, sailed for France on 12 August 1914. By 21 August the Corps' duties had been established at GHQ. They were to examine prisoners of war, undertake cipher work, and control passes and permits. They were also required to spread false rumours. Officers not engaged were attached to the Royal Flying Corps or cavalry regiments where, given their command of French, they were used as despatch riders.

The first member of the Corps to be decorated was 2nd Lieutenant Roger Rolleston-West, then attached to HQ 19th brigade, who was awarded the DSO. He arrived in France on 13 August and had already been captured by the Queen's Own Cameron Highlanders and held as a spy for two days. On 31 August it was discovered that, with Von Kluck's First Army advancing, only two of three bridges at Pontoise-le-Noyen had been destroyed. Rolleston-West, in what his brigade commander considered a suicide mission, returned to blow the bridge, riding miles over the bad and congested French roads with Sapper

Lieutenant J.A.C.Pennycuick on his pillion carrying the boxes of explosives. Pennycuick was also awarded the DSO.

The first officer to be killed was Julian Horace Martin-Smith, who had earlier helped save the guns of the 9th Lancers when they were under attack. He was shot at Pecy on 6 September 1914 and died two days later.

Many of the roads in France were neither tarmac nor paved; they were pitted ruts which quickly became bog-like when it rained—which it did that autumn. On 7 September Macdonogh, Torrie and Major Walter Kirke went into a ditch after their driver failed to negotiate a bend and hit a tree. Macdonogh broke his collarbone and Torrie was knocked out, but Kirke borrowed a bicycle and pedalled off for help.

A fortnight later an incident occurred on which legends are founded. Mansfield Cumming and his son Alastair, a lieutenant in the Corps, were driving in a Rolls-Royce near Meaux when the car hit a tree. Alastair was killed and Mansfield Cumming lost a foot. By 1916 the story told by the novelist Compton Mackenzie was that Cumming had taken a penknife and hacked the flesh off his trapped foot before crawling over to put a coat over his son.[10] The playwright and agent Edward Knoblock, who later also worked for Cumming, described Cumming hacking off the remains of his leg. Back in England in a *procès d'impressment* and to test the nerves of applicants, Cumming used to stab his cork leg with a penknife and if the applicant jumped, Cumming would tell him, 'Well, I'm afraid you won't do'. Whether that is true, Cumming certainly made a great recovery. He later obtained a sort of motorized scooter which he rode at speed through the corridors of Whitehall.

Torrie was replaced by Archibald Wavell, who was appointed temporary major on 24 September 1914. Wavell had initially been 'left behind' at the War Office, with tasks being handed to him there by Macdonogh and Kirke at ten minutes' notice. In his new role he immediately displayed great initiative by changing a compromised cipher without referring to superior officers. But, in fact, he was not interested in intelligence work:

> Once I got a grip on the purpose of the Intelligence Corps, got it organised, cleared up one or two minor scandals, and dismissed one or two unsuitable types, I found there was only one or two hours work a day.[11]

Another officer, Sigismund Payne Best, whose accounts are rarely less than self-serving, described a more chaotic scenario:

> They had no maps of France to use. By chance I had taken with me a Michelin Guide of France and that became the bible of GHQ. It was the only clear map they had. They hadn't any idea what the country was like.[12]

It was not immediately clear to those in charge what to do with the 25 Scotland Yard detectives. They had no experience of the army and regulations had not been agreed with the French so, with nothing for them to police, some became VIP bodyguards, a job they kept throughout the war. Others were joined at Le Cateau-Cambrésis near St Quentin by men from the Sûreté and began a study into the control of the civilian population which formed the basis of a counter-espionage system.[13]

Some of the detectives proved their worth in examining prisoners. During a battle a series of 'cages' held captured men. Nearest to the dressing station was the divisional prisoner-of-war cage, so that the interrogating officers could examine wounded prisoners without wasting time. Farther back came the Corps cage, where there were facilities for a more exhaustive examination. But the best results were thought to be obtained at the casualty clearing stations. Frederick 'Boots' Hotblack found that German prisoners responded better when treated well. Half a tin of bully beef and a biscuit worked wonders. Often as they walked back to the Corps cage shelling would be audible, and the prisoner would comment proudly, or adversely, on the capacity of the German artillery. Hotblack found that Bavarians did not think much of Wurtembergers or Saxons, and that the Prussians despised everybody.

So far as interrogating Germans was concerned it was thought that persistent repetitive questioning did no good at all; a more inventive and fluid approach was required. However, repetitions produced satisfactory results with Latins. S.T. Felstead gives the example of the Argentinian Conrad Leytor, detained in the middle of 1915, when the ship on which he was sailing was held at Falmouth, and sent for investigation to London. He was broken down by repetitive questioning by Admiral 'Blinker' Hall. After every explanation which did not answer the question and which took several minutes, Hall repeated 'Tell me, señor, why are you going to Spain?'Then after another series of explanations, Hall asked 'Tell me, why are you going by such a roundabout route?' Worn down, Leytor finally admitted he was carrying despatches to Prince Ratibor, the German ambassador in Madrid. As Leytor had not come voluntarily to England there was no question of any spying charge, and he was interned.[14]

The intelligence gained from German prisoners was soon to prove significant. In October 1914 during the 'Race to the Sea' to liberate Antwerp, Sir John French ordered an advance into the heart of Belgium. Macdonogh, from information obtained by questioning German prisoners, deduced that the Germans had brought three Reserve Army Corps units to be directed against the British left flank, which would have been exposed to a devastating attack if French's plan had been carried out. As a result French cancelled the plans and took up defensive positions around Ypres.[15]

Wavell was gone by 14 November, when he became brigade major of the 9th Infantry at Hooge. (On 16 June the next year he was badly injured, losing an eye.) Now the adjutant J.A.Dunnington Jefferson replaced him in the Corps, first promoted to major and then appointed commandant on 7 December 1914. He remained in command until 17 February 1916. On 2 March that year Captain A.A. Fenn was appointed commander, and he remained until the Corps was disbanded in September 1919.

At the end of August the second batch of the Intelligence Corps disembarked at St Nazaire, collected their motorcycles and were told to report to the Grand Hôtel in Paris. They proved to be not much more expert on the motorcycles though, in fairness to the riders, the vehicles were still fairly rudimentary.

Gradually the Corps' duties expanded:

> Their duties in the first exhilarating months of mobile warfare ranged from interpreting for the cavalry, interrogating German prisoners, organising civilian work parties, obtaining food for retiring infantry, translating claims for damages from French and Flemish peasants and, on one occasion at least, supervising a party of Royal Engineers seeking to blow up a bridge after their own officers had been killed or wounded.[16]

Within six months the value of the Corps had been recognized.

Officers were attached to other regiments and some joined General Henderson's Royal Flying Corps. The Corps was also involved in some significant developments in modern warfare. In September 1914 the use of aerial recognizance was proved decisive for the first time. The bivouacs of all the corps of von Kluck's First Army across the Marne were photographed and, from this, his order of battle could be constructed. The failure of the Germans at the Marne was a key turning point in favour of the Allies in the early weeks of the war.

At that time air recognizance was a thoroughly hazardous operation. At first a hole was cut in the bottom of the cockpit and a folding bellows camera pushed through. Then came a procedure that was significant, if hazardous under fire: the photographer held the camera and the pilot held the photographer's belt as he leaned out to take pictures. By the following summer, techniques had been improved and the camera was fixed to the plane.

The Corps was also involved with the collation of information flown in by pigeons from behind German lines. The service was organized by Captain Alexander Waley in 1914; by January 1915 there were 500 trained pigeons. Six months later 1,500 birds were in full training, which included desensitizing them to gunfire.

From March 1917 balloons carrying pigeons in wicker cages were being released in the early evening across the trenches. A fuse burned through a wire which released the cage and dropped the pigeon by parachute. Attached to the bird's leg was a questionnaire asking details of German installations, troops and so on, sometimes as long as eight pages, which was to be filled in by any patriotic French or Belgian recipient. The pigeons also carried part of an up-to-date Paris newspaper intended to show that this was not a trap. Once completed, the questionnaire was to be reattached to the pigeon, which flew back to its loft, often horsedrawn. The birds could fly 50 kilometres at just over 60 km an hour; very often pigeons dropped around 11 o'clock at night had reported back by 9 o'clock the following morning. Forty per cent of messages got through; a five per cent success rate had been expected.[17]

Unfortunately, there was a high mortality rate among the pigeons, many of which were shot down—German soldiers being given leave for a successful 'kill'—or sometimes simply eaten. One estimate of the casualty rate was seven out of eight.

There was also a high casualty rate among those French and Belgians found with the messages or even with the pigeons. One such instance occurred on 4 October 1915, when Paul Busière, a miner in Liéven, was shot for having a bird in his possession.[18] Matters were not helped by a blunder in March 1918, when questionnaires were despatched with pencils clearly marked 'Stationery Office'.[19] By the end of the war it was estimated that 20,000 birds had been used. In one two-month period pigeons had carried 4,500 messages.[20]

As the Corps grew, so the other ranks became more ethnically diverse, many of them 'mere idlers who pick up a variety of languages from their penchant for travel'. One was a showman known as 'The Little Corporal' or 'Artful' who had previously run a travelling circus of Russian bears. Another, an Anglo-Armenian sergeant born in France, was said to be able to read every European language with ease with the exception of Basque, Magyar and Albanian.[21]

The Intelligence Police, a branch of the Corps, was founded in 1916. By the end of the war it totalled some 80 officers and 460 other ranks. This branch was not involved in the general behaviour of the troops; that was left to the Military Police. Their task was counter-espionage—pure if not simple. It is difficult to understand how these men were able to act quickly if they discovered a spy. Norman Shaw wrote that an Intelligence Policeman had to carry:

> Iron rations, a water bottle canteen, first field dressing and iodine ampoule, box respirator and smoke helmet, waterproof cape, second pair of boots, blanket and pack, road map of forward area, an Assistant Provost Marshall's pass with photograph, notebook with carbon sheets and pencil, 12 field service envelopes, special equipment as laid down including revolver and ammunition, compass, electric torch, chain and padlock for bicycle, red and green identity discs and for those using motorcycles, overalls, gaiters, goggles and mitts.[22]

The Intelligence Police was particularly concerned with *estaminets* and brothels as well as with civilians repatriated by Germans. They obtained information from refugees as well as by keeping a watch on strangers in the area. In the last months of the war some apparent German deserters were found to be double agents who would hope to join a labour unit and then desert again, taking with them what information they had accumulated. The Intelligence Police also investigated the mutiny at the Étaples transit camp in September 1917 and rounded up the deserters including Percy Toplis, the so-called Monocled Mutineer—although he escaped again.[23]

In 1917 the so-called Suicide Club, devised in part by Walter Kirke, 'Lives in their hands, pistols in their pockets', was formed. These were volunteer agents from the Corps, who would go on to enemy territory (on foot, horse or motorcycle) when the cavalry breached a line during the Somme push. Other troops did not like them, and although there were a few opportunities it was difficult to assess the right moment for the agents to 'go'.[24] In charge was an Anglo-South African, Captain R.G. Pearson, who was attached to the Cavalry Corps. He spent July, August and September with the cavalry, but the Suicide Club fell through; the agents were disbanded and Pearson returned to London. Eventually, when open fighting recommenced in August 1918, members of the reassembled Club began to supply interesting if limited information and, as a result, hostility towards them began to wear off. But, overall, the initiative was not a success.

Early in 1917 General Hugh Trenchard, then commanding the Royal Flying Corps, decided that landing agents behind enemy lines was too expensive in terms of both men and machines. The RFC restricted drops to 15 miles behind enemy lines; weather and moon conditions further restricted the number of agents put over. Silence was not golden: if Germans heard planes but no bombs they would know an agent had been landed. An alternative method had to be found. One idea was to land agents by the 'Guardian Angel' parachute.[25] Sigismund Payne Best is credited with having the idea in the autumn of 1916 of using free balloons.[26] After trials and lessons run by a solicitor balloonist known as 'Pink Tights' Pollock, so called because when his trousers split he was seen to be wearing pink long johns, it was decided that it was feasible to land agents by these balloons.

At first, the agents took pigeons with them, by which they were to send back information. Then Captain Round, chief inventor at Marconi, produced a portable continuous wave radio set weighing 60lbs, believed to be incapable of detection by position-finding techniques. However, once an agent was captured and executed, its use was discontinued.

Three agents, Faux, Lefebre and Jules Bar, were selected for the first flight and trained at Wormwood Scrubs.[27] There was almost a week of waiting before a favourable westerly wind allowed Faux and Lefebre to be sent up. The men came from near Valenciennes and the intention was that they would be dropped near there, make their way to safe houses and go into hiding. They would then organize an espionage service in communication with Major Ernest Wallinger through Holland.

At night the balloon with a launching crew was moved close to the front line to reduce the length and time of the flight as well as the margin of error in direction. Later, when the balloon was inflated, the agent was summoned from a nearby estaminet, hands were shaken and, depending on his nationality, either the Marseillaise or the Brabançonne was played on a wind-up gramophone. At the end of the flight balloonists had to sit on the edge of the basket until it neared the ground and then jump. A major problem was controlling the balloon and where it landed.[28]

The first flights were not a success. Faux and Lefebre lost their nerve after landing and did little beyond sending one pigeon message. Jules Bar, who broke a leg, was captured and shot. Seven other agents went over by this method and four were caught. Only one, an officer in the Belgian army, proved to be a success in providing reports in Luxembourg. He was awarded a DSO.

As the war dragged on so the Intelligence Corps expanded. The British Expeditionary Force, which had begun in 1914 as two corps of two divisions plus a cavalry unit, had by July 1916 become five armies, and in each of them there was now an intelligence unit. The men employed permanently on intelligence work joined the Intelligence Corps, now controlled by the head of the Intelligence Branch at GHQ. In December 1917, from the 24 officers and men who had sailed for France three years earlier, the personnel had grown to 1,225 including 12 WAACs.

As it expanded, so it was employed in other theatres of war. For example, in Turkey at the time of the Gallipolli disaster in 1915 there had been no effective intelligence in the area. Later, General Sir Ian Hamilton commented:

> Beyond the ordinary text books these pigeon holes were drawn blank. The Dardanelles and the Bosphorus might be in the moon for all the military intelligence I have to go upon.[29]

In late 1917, a separate corps was formed for the Macedonian front. Once again it seems to have been beset with inter-bureau rivalry. It also seems to have been a hand-to-mouth existence, for on one occasion, Compton Mackenzie's subordinate, Edward Knoblock, had to put in £200 from his own pocket to keep the mission going.[30] Mackenzie did, however, recruit a talented if disparate collection of agents, including the bell porter at the German Legation who was code-named Davy Jones. He worked closely with the French service under Capitaine de Rocquefeuil countering the German intelligence headed by Baron Schenk. Mackenzie's agents turned up evidence of espionage by both the German and Turkish attachés in Athens and in one coup in January 1916 there was a wholesale arrest of lawyers, Bulgarian nobility and 'ladies of the town'. In all, 22 spies of Macdonian nationality—although their names suggested a Turkish heritage— were tried at military courts martial in Salonika and Kiraissi between May and August 1917. Nine were executed while four had their death sentences commuted.[31]

One of the most successful agents of the Egypt office was Agent 4th class Alexandr Aaronsohn. In the Near East, Zionists wanted to build a Jewish state of Palestine, and Turkish-born Aaron Aaronsohn, whose education had been financed by Edmund Rothschild, believed that if the Jews proved capable of running a network providing information on Turkish movement in the area then, with the war won, the British would be under an obligation to help establish a Zionist state. Together with his sister Sarah, his brothers Alexandr and Ziv and a close friend, Avshalom Feinberg, he established a network known as Nili, an acronym of The God of Israel Doesn't Lie, which was a spiritual parent of Mossad.

Feinberg was sent to contact the British. In August 1915, travelling on a false passport, he managed to reach Port Said where he met up with the archaeologist Leonard Woolley who was working in intelligence there.[32] The network, which totalled around 40 agents, ran for a year and a half with Alexandr Aaronsohn penetrating Turkish lines in Judea and Samaria. Nili also organized train-watching on the Anatolian railway around the Gulf of Alexandretta, including the Affulah rail junction in Syria. Feinberg later disappeared during a mission to Egypt.

On 31 October 1917, using intelligence collected by T.E. Lawrence before the war and with information from Nili, Edmund Allenby took the Ottoman Turks by surprise in a decisive attack at Beersheba in today's southern Israel.

There are varying accounts of the end of Nili. One is that in September 1917 a pigeon carrying a message which confirmed relationships with the British was intercepted by the Turkish police. Another version is that it was betrayed by Perl Applebaum. Yet another is that one of the group, Naamannd Belkind, was arrested; drugged and beaten, he began to talk. He was later hanged at Damas. Another to give up names was Josef Lishansky. Aaronsohn's sister Sarah endured three days of torture before she managed to kill herself on 9 October 1917. She had, it seems, been allowed to return to her parents' home before being transferred to a prison in Damascus. She shot herself with a pistol she took from a bedroom drawer and died four days later.[33] Her father was also killed. Alexandr Aaronsohn was awarded the DSO.

Aaronsohn's controller had been Major Richard Meinertzhagen of the Royal Fusiliers who, along with Major P.J. Pretorius, had run espionage in what is now mainland Tanzania but was then German East Africa. Over the four years of the war they had several hundred informants and a number of local big game hunters as agents. In July 1915 it was Pretorius, who had been a big game hunter himself, who tracked down the cruiser *Königsberg* where it was hidden in the Rufiji river after breaking a piston crosshead and running out of coal.

In a classic example of 'waste not–want not', Meinertzhagen carried the wastepaper bucket emptying—which had done for the infamous Dreyfus—to an extreme. Because of the lack of lavatory paper, the previous day's messages were often used as a substitute by the Germans, and this produced a steady supply of messages and notes on coding.

Meinertzhagen also claimed to have devised the 'rucksack hoax', the deliberate loss of a haversack of false British plans which led to the British victory over the Turks at the Battle of Beersheba and Gaza in October 1917. Despite his boasts, recent research has shown he was not its creator.

Rather more genuine was Colonel Gerard Leachman, a political officer before the First World War, who rode on a mule from Baghdad to Aleppo and discovered the Wadi Khar. With dark Semitic looks he could pass as an Arab. In March 1916 he dominated the Bedouin of Turkish-occupied Mesopotamia by force of character, obtaining information for the British. Children, whom he paid in small amounts, were used as couriers. 'No information was too trivial for him'.[34]

After he had sneaked into the Turkish redoubt at Dujaila, Leachman reported that it was held by only 40 soldiers. His brigade commander, Brigadier General Kemball, passed the information up the line to Lieutenant General Aylmer, who refused to make any alteration to his battle plans. By the time he attacked Dujaila it had been reinforced and Aylmer lost 3,500 men.[35]

Obtaining intelligence is one thing, getting the authorities to act upon it is a completely different matter.

Chapter Five

'To England!' I would smile, raising my glass.
'To Germany,' he would reply, clinking his against mine.
Then we would leave the café and do our best to get the other fellow
ruined. James Dunn and Captain Raeder[1]

IN HOLLAND AND BELGIUM

By November 1914 the German Secret Service had established itself in Antwerp, the largest of Germany's three western espionage bureaux. It was directed by Captain Kefer and had been established with the help of Heinrich Grund, a German who had lived in Antwerp before the war. He was also the bureau's first agent and was given the codename SAS1. The bureau was divided into two sections: the English under the control of Captain Stumpff, and the French supervised by the legendary Fräulein Doktor, who also ran the spy school. There were other such schools at Lorrach and Baden-Baden, but Antwerp was for the élite.

Apart from Mata Hari, Fräulein Doktor has become the best known German spy of the First World War — but which of the known spies was she? Was she the elderly, bad-tempered but quite brilliant Elizabeth Schragmuller or the attractive and daring Anneliese Lesser (sometimes referred to as Annemarie) from the Tiergarten quarter of Berlin, who ended life a morphine addict in a mental hospital? Certain sources have it that there were two Fräulein Doktors. Others believe that she was Norwegian.[2] Did she even exist? Some feminist writers believe she was simply a male-inspired bogeywoman.[3]

Magnus Hirschfeld wrote of her:

One of the most famous of all German spies was ruined by intoxicants, morphine and cocaine, and now lives on, a pitiful wreck, in a private

> Swiss sanatorium. This is the legendary Fraulein Doktor, a woman
> with nerves of steel, a cold, logical engine for a mind, well-controlled
> sensuality, a fascinating body and demoniac eyes.[4]

The romantic Anneliese Lesser version is that she was Berlin-born
and thrown out by her parents when she had a child by an army officer, a spy who had trained her himself in espionage. He was shot, and
she gallivanted over Europe captivating army officers young and old.
After a series of adventures worthy of any E. Phillips Oppenheim
heroine, disguised as nurses, peasants and artists, she became a key
figure in the German Secret Service. Hair-raising escape followed
hair-raising escape until:

> … she was especially famous for the utter mercilessness and
> unscrupulousness with which she made the German secret service
> agents toe the mark. Everyone had to obey orders and prove his mettle
> or he was driven to suicide and occasionally assassinated.[5]

In 1916, following repeated failures in the German Secret Service she
apparently again took to the field, trapping the Greek spy Coudouainis
and re-establishing the service in Paris. She escaped capture in
Belgium, shot three men before reaching Switzerland, and finally
made it home to Germany where:

> [she] then broke down, not least because she herself had seen her
> impending doom. Her breakdown was so complete that she not only
> had to leave the service but to withdraw from the world of normal man
> altogether. Together with her chief she destroyed all her documents just
> before the terrific breakdown came, and then fell into mental darkness.[6]

This is clearly a fine melange of the Mata Hari and Marguerite
Francillard stories with additional colour; other stories describe her
being shot by Russians at Tannenberg. Allegedly she had been a spy in
Vienna in 1908 and had been recognized shortly before the Germans
took the town. The British police officer Edwin Woodhall claimed he
had met her twice.[7]

The other story is that of Elizabeth Schragmuller, a woman with a
doctorate from Freiburg University who had written her dissertation
on medieval stonecutter guilds. On joining the German Secret Service, she was initially employed in the censorship department, then put
in charge of the French section by Major Walter Nicolai, the German
spymaster who had taken over from Steinhauer.

The students at the spy school at Rue de la Pepinière in Antwerp were said to have been terrified of the Fräulein. They were given rudimentary training lasting, for the first students, three days, later expanding to six . The régime was extreme: the Fräulein made the students wear masks to keep their identities secret from each other, identified them only by numbers, and kept them locked in their rooms. They were only allowed to leave the school at the end of the day at three-minute intervals. On graduating, agents were given the equivalent of 1500 German marks on which they were expected to survive for a month. They had been trained in the use of invisible ink and were supplied with cover addresses.

As time went on German intelligence became more professional, and by the middle of 1915 the Fräulein had the students for 15 weeks. She was said to have approached espionage from a wholly academic point of view, believing that success was a matter of training, not of character and resourcefulness. At the end of the students' training, there was now a test run, often to contact a 'traitor' and to evade 'arrest' by German agents.

After the war evidence was given at a court martial in Lille that the Fräulein had a chateau near Antwerp (later moderated to a hotel on the Boulevard de la Loi) where she kept a bag of gold, the contents of which she strewed on the carpet to tempt potential candidates. There she was assisted by a man who posed as an English 'fop with a monocle' and a journalist. Other helpmates included a German NCO nicknamed 'Pipo' who had escaped the Allied clutches and Corporal Raymond Corbeau who later served a 20-year sentence for spying near Grenoble.[8] Of these 'facts', we know at least that Corbeau existed.

Vernon Kell certainly believed in the Fräulein's existence, and thought highly of her:

> She must have been a woman of some ability from the many accounts received, for she inspired respect, and her identity was concealed for a considerable time, in spite of many attempts to discover it. We have reason to suppose she is since dead.[9]

It has been estimated that by mid-December 1915 Nicolai had 337 agents operating in the west. The largest group was run out of Holland, headed from early 1915 by Fräulein Doktor. She controlled 62 agents, most of whom were active. By March 1916 the number was around

120 and three-quarters of them were active.[10]

To counter German activity, Vernon Kell used James Dunn, a journalist from the *Daily Mail*, whom he sent to Rotterdam to track down German agents. According to his own memoirs, Dunn was sent to Rotterdam by his paper as a cover after the fall of Antwerp. He was in the city by Christmas 1914:

> After complaining his department was facing substantial ruin he [Kell] granted me a substantial fee for expenses. I became an official counter-espionage agent, while acting as correspondent for the *Daily Mail*.[11]

Dunn found that Rotterdam was pro-German. Contraband channelled to the Germans including petrol in hollow tombstones and copper anchors painted to look like iron—much of which came from Birmingham—was rapidly changing hands among young clerks for between £20 and £30, a large sum compared to their usual salary of £1 a week. Young Dutchmen were being offered huge fees by the Germans to travel to England as representatives of Dutch gin. They met their paymasters at a café in The Hague, but the main centre of political intrigue was in a café on the outskirts of Scheveningen.

Dunn claimed that the chief of German spies in Rotterdam was Captain Raeder, formerly of the Prussian Guard, 'one of the most charming men and best sportsmen I have ever met'. Spying, as described by Dunn, was conducted on gentlemanly lines:

> 'To England!' I would smile, raising my glass.
> 'To Germany,' he would reply, clinking his against mine.
> Then we would leave the café and do our best to get the other fellow ruined.[12]

For a time Dunn was helped by the *Daily Mail's* Rotterdam correspondent Van Ditmar until, in one of the rare Dutch police purges, both were arrested in August 1915 at the insistence of the German Ministry at The Hague and charged with infringing the neutrality of Holland. Dunn was deported.[13] As a result of Dunn's deportation, Kell was forced to use the Cumming organization for reports.

Journalism was an excellent cover for any kind of intelligence activity. On 4 November 1915 an American journalist called Donald Thompson was sent to Germany, also by the *Daily Mail*, with pro-German articles in his pockets and a remit to collect news and photo-

graphs. On the other side William Bayard Hale, the Berlin correspondent for the American newspaper magnate William Hearst, was
under contract to the German Embassy in Washington (at a very substantial annual salary of $15,000) to advise on propaganda.

Tinsley also employed Leonhard Kooyper, war correspondent of
Nieuwe Rotterdamsche Courant, who made at least four trips to
Germany and another eight to theatres of war in Belgium and north-
ern France.

When war was declared, British espionage was already established
in Belgium and Holland: Cumming had Henry Dale Long as his
agent in Brussels and Richard Tinsley was established in Rotterdam.
Soon after, two further networks were established, so that almost from
the outbreak of war there were three separate and often competing
British spy networks operating in Holland.[14]

After the first few weeks of conflict, when the front had stabilized, it
became clear that the only way of getting information from behind the
British battle lines was through Holland. GHQ in France obtained
authority to establish a supplementary and parallel organization
responsible directly to the commander-in-chief in France.

On 22 November 1914 it was agreed by the British, French and
Belgian intelligence services that a central bureau should be established at Folkestone for as long as the Dutch–Belgian frontier was in
German hands. There were great advantages in choosing Folkestone.
It was an arrival point for refugees from Flushing; there would be no
need to travel on a time-wasting journey to GHQ; information could
be easily checked and sorted; a large number of ships docked there
and, as a result, a large number of professional and amateur agents
met there.

One officer was to represent each nation; they would meet once or
twice a day and pool information. Each officer would keep his office
distinct along with his own agents. Major Cecil Aylmer Cameron
(working as CF: Cameron Folkestone) was appointed to head the
British GHQ.

And then politics intervened. Because of the Boy-Ed case in New
York, Colonel John French—later British commander-in-chief—
informed Major Laurie Oppenheim, the military attaché in Holland,
that the Foreign Office wished to have its hands clean, and so on 12
April 1915 Major Ernest Wallinger (WL: Wallinger London) was

appointed in London by GHQ to ensure closer touch with Tilbury, where refugees arrived, than was possible from Folkestone. Wallinger was helped in no small part by Captain Sigismund Payne Best, on behalf of GHQ at St Omer in France. Cameron stayed at Folkestone.

So the three networks were established. Throughout the war, members of the Cameron, Wallinger and Cumming networks feuded constantly, poaching each other's agents and undermining each other as best they could.

Ernest Wallinger and Cecil Cameron were very different men. Wallinger, a gunnery officer who, through his wife's family, had private money, had lost a foot in the battle of Le Cateau. He was given an office at 7 Lincoln House, Basil Street, Knightsbridge, over which he lived with a batman and housemaid. His staff then consisted of Sigismund Payne Best, who acted as number two; a secretary typist; Emile, alias Joseph Ide, the first Belgian interpreter; and Werner, alias Thuysbeart, the second Belgian interpreter.[15] In April 1916 Ivone Kirkpatrick, who had been wounded at Gallipoli, joined Wallinger at Basil Street on a fortnight's probation and was then sent to Holland as a spymaster.

Cameron, who ran his operation from Folkestone at 2 The Parade, not quite overlooking the harbour, was a curious choice. One of the Camerons of Lochiel, he was the son of the acting head of MI5's precursor, the Victorian Intelligence Branch. He had a young wife, Ruby, who was a morphine addict. In June 1911 both of them had faced a charge of attempted fraud. Ruby Cameron had claimed that a £6,000 necklace which had been given to her by an elderly admirer, Billie Walker, had been snatched from her neck while her husband was buying a hypodermic syringe in a nearby shop. Sadly for the Camerons no one could find any trace of Walker and the jury convicted them in less than 25 minutes. Ruby was released after three months on the grounds of ill health, but Cameron served his full sentence before, perhaps surprisingly, he obtained a pardon, submitting that the reason he had not given evidence was in order to protect his wife. For a time he was sent to work under another name in Europe, but overall the fraud conviction does not seem to have done his army career any great harm. In fact, he gained social credit from standing by Ruby, even though there is little doubt of his guilt in the scam.[16]

Ivone Kirkpatrick takes what might be described as a generous view of the rival British services, which were also in competition with the French and Belgians and possibly the Russians.

> This division of the British effort into three water-tight compartments seems highly unpractical but it was due to undue nervousness in regard to the Dutch government. It was feared that the latter might attempt to suppress foreign secret services in Holland and that we should therefore be unwise to put all our eggs in one basket.[17]

In fact, the division was counterproductive: 'Denunciations, buying of other services' agents, duplication of reports, collaboration between agents was not uncommon. This led to apparent confirmation of news emanating in fact from the same service.'[18]

As Kirkpatrick indicates, spies of all sizes walked a thin line in Holland. Henry Landau, who was sent to Rotterdam by Cumming in 1916, thought that:

> At all costs we wished her to remain neutral, for even if she were drawn in to conflict on our side, we knew she would be immediately overrun by the Germans.
>
> In their attitude of tolerance to both sides the Dutch prevented acts of violence between the German Secret Service and ourselves which would undoubtedly have occurred if both sides had been forced underground. We would have raided the headquarters of the German Secret Police in the Witte Huis in Rotterdam. They would have done the same to us.
>
> On the whole, both sides should be grateful to the Dutch; they kept order and refereed, as it were, the conflict in Holland between ourselves and the German Secret Service.[19]

One who was undoubtedly delighted with this precarious arrangement was François van Sant, the head of police in Rotterdam, to whom Richard Tinsley was said to have paid £25,000 over the duration of the war. They lived diagonally opposite each other, which led to the (correct) allegation that van Sant was being bribed.

Ivone Kirkpatrick also cultivated the head of the Rotterdam police as a way of keeping in with the Dutch authorities. He invited him to dinner once a week and, during the evening, gave him the latest German order of battle, for which the police chief would get credit for passing on. The relationship came in useful for crisis management: for example, when Kirkpatrick was told by his agent, Emile Vandervorde, that a

Dutchman named Harmont, who posed as a *passeur*, carrying messages through boundary wire and frequenting border cafés, was in German pay and had betrayed part of a network. 'What should I do?' asked Vandervorde. 'Bump him off,' replied Kirkpatrick negligently. He was, he claims, horrified to hear that the agent had done exactly that in a café in San van Gent, putting five bullets in Harmont's stomach. Kirkpatrick asked advice of the police chief, only to be told that matters were worse than expected: Harmont had lived for two days, long enough to identify his killer. Eventually, Kirkpatrick negotiated a 12-hour amnesty which enabled Vandervorde to board the Harwich boat. He does not say how much it cost.[20]

Cumming's network in Brussels was initially headed by the long-serving Henry Dale Long. In 1914 he had three other agents working with him and a fourth in Dinant.[21]

Long seems to have escaped from Belgium in the first few months of the war, because he took Melville to meet his former housekeeper, Mme Curtois, at Victoria station on 10 February 1915.

After Long left Brussels, Mme Curtois had been repeatedly questioned and imprisoned over several weeks as the Germans tried to make her disclose his whereabouts. Finally Captain Reuter changed tack and offered her money to get Long to return. Mme Curtois then pretended she was willing to work for the Germans. The terms offered were simple: if she could persuade Long to come to Holland or Belgium they would give her 5,000 French francs and him 25,000. They merely wanted him to sign some papers and give them some information. Mme Curtois did not fall for this; she believed that they wanted Long back to shoot him. They gave her £24 to come to England and said that if she carried out the mission successfully she would be sent again. She was also given a questionnaire concerning the British fleet to memorize; when she said she had a bad memory Reuter gave her a written *aide-mémoire*. She was told to go direct from Folkestone to Edinburgh, where she was to stay at the best hotel and note any news. She was then to travel to London, Sheerness and Folkestone 'with the same effect'.

Instead Mme Curtois went straight to Long in England. Melville thought 'She would be delighted to avenge herself on the Germans and is undecided as to going to Edinburgh. She is a sharp intelligent woman and I think could be made use of.' A copy of Melville's report was sent to Cumming on 11 July 1915. Unfortunately, there is nothing in the file to show whether Mme Curtois ever did go on to work for the Allies.[22]

Espionage in the cinema involves grand feats of daring, like the theft of military secrets from the ambassador's safe. In real life, it mostly concerns minutiae. A great deal of espionage in the First World War was train-watching, which enabled the Allies to learn about German troop movements. GHQ chiefly wanted to know about large movements from the Eastern Front to the Western or vice versa, and movements along the Western Front which might presage an offensive.

There were two problems with train-watching. The first was collecting the information, and the second was getting it back to headquarters. Suitable personnel were relatively easy to find. The German invasion had dispersed thousands of Belgians; some to Britain, but most to France. By 1916 they had scattered all over the country in communities presided over by *aumoniers* or leaders, very often priests, of the displaced community. The task of Intelligence Corps officer Lieutenant S.H.C. Woolrych was to get the *aumoniers* to identify members of the flock who might be suitable for train-watching in Belgium—those who lived in houses backing on to the railway or had a good excuse to be there.[23]

Once recruited, the prospective agent was trained in Paris in conditions of great secrecy. The training consisted of a brief course on the German army to recognize badges and helmets and the different kinds of trains.[24] An infantry train had few horseboxes, but included cookers on platforms at the end of the train; cavalry trains were almost all horseboxes; artillery trains had guns on open platform trucks. Train-watchers were also to note the general appearance of the troops, clean or dirty, and their apparent morale. Between 40 and 52 trains a day meant a divisional move.

The work was very dangerous and food was short in Belgium; it required considerable courage to give up the safety of France. Families worked on a 24-hour basis and

> Their reports had to be written through a magnifying glass on very
> small bits of the thinnest and toughest tissue paper we could procure,
> by mapping pens in Indian ink, and then rolled into a tiny package
> which could be secreted almost anywhere about the human body.[25]

It was said that Paul Bernard, a member of the Bettignies network, could write 1,500 words on the back of a postage stamp. Messages were also written on scraps of contraceptives and swallowed, or inserted in bicycle valves.

One of the great *réseaux* or networks, *La Dame Blanche*, named after the spectral figure whose appearance, it was believed, would signal the end of the Hohenzollern régime, was under the supervision of the South-African-born, Cambridge-educated Henry Landau. Landau was both an adventurer and a lucky man. In early 1916 he had had a three-day leave from the trenches and on the morning he was due to return he caught measles. While convalescing, on the recommendation of a friend he applied to the War Office for a position, and since he spoke Dutch, German and French fluently he was accepted immediately. Landau was indeed fortunate; his battery was wiped out on the Somme and every officer killed.

Interviewed by Cumming, Landau was sent the same day to Rotterdam, accompanied by the roguish but able Lieutenant Hugh Dalton. Tinsley would give him cover and, within reason, would finance him.

Landau's first agent, M82, was Henri van Bergen, who had been an interpreter at the Belgian legation in China. He set up a fine network of train-watchers, but made the mistake of recruiting a German sympathizer, Wouters (then a police inspector at Antwerp), and introducing him to members of the network. On 4 August 1917 van Bergen was arrested with l'Abbé Moons and Mlle Ballenger. He, Moons and four others, but not the girl, were shot on 16 March 1918.

Through Landau, *La Dame Blanche* was run by two electrical engineers, Walthère Dewé and Herman Chauvin from Liège.[26] Edward Aimable, the Hirson village priest, agreed to set up a watching service on the Hirson-Mézières line which ran parallel to the German battlefront with an observation post at Fourmies. This was run by Aimable's long-standing friend Felix Latouche, his wife and their two teenage daughters, whose cottage overlooked the line. Starting on 23 September 1917 and working in shifts to cover the 24 hours in each day, they counted who and what was in the passing trains, using chicory for horses, haricot beans for soldiers and coffee beans for guns. Their reports were kept in a hollowed-out broom handle for collection by an agent.

Members of *La Dame Blanche* wanted legitimacy: to be soldiers in the British army. With Landau's urging and that of Cumming, the Army Council finally approved the network's militarization in February 1918. The benefits worked two ways. At the end of the war there would be some recognition for the 'soldiers'—and in turn they produced fuller and more accurate reports. By the end of the war it was the most successful intelligence network on the Western Front. Dewé and Chauvin were later awarded the CBE and other members were given citations and medals.

Methods of passing messages included plugs for the anus and vagina, false bottoms to tins, hollow basket handles, adapted packets of chocolate, and silk paper which could be sewn into clothing and did not crackle. Messages were carried in bars of soap, in walking sticks, in soles of shoes. Women carried messages in their hair. Messages could be inserted into a beet and thrown to someone on the other side of the boundary wire. An attempt was made to shoot arrows across the wire. In Flanders German soldiers could sometimes be persuaded to pass reports in invisible ink which appeared as harmless letters, in return for butter, bread or soap.

Payne Best gave morphine to the fence guards. Reports also came from Danish cattle exporters to Germany; their drovers carried them back to Denmark for onward transmission.

One long-standing method of getting messages through was via the *passeurs*, of which there had been whole families, very often smugglers. But gradually the Germans wired the border and a 10ft high, 200-volt electric fence was erected along the Dutch–Belgian border from the sea to the German frontier. It was patrolled by sentries every 100 yards who at night time sent up Very lights. *Passeurs* often went to the wire with two companions, one on either side, attached to them by 50 yards of string. When it was the optimum moment, so far as the position of the sentry was concerned, a companion would pull his string. When both strings were pulled simultaneously—which might not happen for two or more nights—the *passeur* made his run.

To get through the fence, some agents wore thick rubber gloves, while some had barrels with no tops or bottoms which they thrust between the strands and then climbed through. The return journey was not so dangerous for a *passeur*. He could cut the wire or shoot the sentry and make a bolt for it. He knew the country and could easily find shelter.[27] Nevertheless, the risks were significant: it has been estimated that, apart from those arrested and shot, up to 3,000 *passeurs* were electrocuted.[28]

The short-lived *réseau* Marié was run by pimp, smuggler and small-time criminal Victor Marié, who dealt with the problem of pigeon drops by hanging out his washing only when the weather was suitable.[29] Lord Haig, who thought him to be 'a bold, plucky fellow', had awarded him a DCM. But when Marié was captured he gave up the members of his *réseau*, and his defection caused the fall of the Grand St Pierre network.

Among those young women who helped *passeurs* were Leonie Rameloo and Emilie Schattemann, who lived in the Belgian–Dutch border village of Bouchaute. After the fences went up, along with Isidore van Vlaanderen they continued to pass people and messages to Holland as well as collecting information from Ghent. Eventually, in September 1917 they were caught and shot.

Perhaps the single most important act of a train-watcher concerned the German spring offensive of 1918. An agent reported an abnormal number of artillery formations undergoing special training; train-watchers saw troops returning from the Russian front and, as a result, General Macdonogh could almost pinpoint the area of the proposed offensive.[30]

Ivone Kirkpatrick supervised a series of train-watching networks, the smallest of which was Venus. This worked well for the whole of 1918, and was run by a mother and daughter in Ghent from where reports were otherwise scarce. Kirkpatrick wrote smugly, 'Tinsley had practically no information from there at all.'

The oldest service, M.S., was started in Hasselt in 1916 by some railway workers who were rowed across the river Mass. When two members were arrested on suspicion, the head of the group, the one-legged Visser, had to flee to Holland but not before he had appointed a successor. Even though German suspicion caused a suspension of operations, by the end of the war this particular service had sent in 130 weekly reports.

Kirkpatrick's network Moise was very speedy. On one occasion, information of the arrival of a German division in the early morning was received in Holland before lunch. Then there was Hadrian, run by the burgomaster of Schnellebelle, and Felix, a group of prostitutes who reported clients' pillow talk and whose reports were accurate and swift. Payment by Kirkpatrick to Latouche and a German sub-agent was in cash or drugs obtained from England. After the war the agent escaped to Holland to avoid falling into the hands of the Germans. 'When I last heard of him he was editing an anti-Bolshevik rag for a living. A picturesque rogue.'[31]

A similar operation was Negro, run from Charleroi by René Dumonceau. He was arrested and condemned to death in Belgium after the war. Kirkpatrick last saw him in prison in June 1919. Also under Kirkpatrick's aegis was Alice, which he thought was a relatively unimportant service but through which a large number of recruits for the Belgian army were smuggled into Holland.

Cumming's station chief in the Netherlands was the consul general in Rotterdam, Ernest Maxse. He was the son of Sir Henry Maxse, a colonel in the Coldstream Guards, and an Austrian mother. In his youth, Maxse, an Old Harrovian with a dyed and waxed moustache and a monocle, had served in the Prussian cavalry.

The character of Tinsley, Cumming's spy controller in Rotterdam, was just as colourful. Major Walter Kirke of MO5 distrusted him, thinking that he might be smart but that 'no really high class agent such as Ramble [Louise de Bettignies] would work for him'.[32] Nor did he think that Tinsley would inspire much patriotic fervour. True to the British education system, Tinsley spoke neither German nor French; not, one might have thought, much in the way of qualification for running a train-spotting service behind enemy lines. He had, however, mastered a little Dutch.[33]

Tinsley had been recruiting agents since the first month of the war; two of his men, Willem Both and J.M. van Gelderen, had earlier received prison sentences of five years and a year respectively for espionage in Holland. In 1915 Tinsley's operations cost £3,000 a month, with railway-watching accounting for £2,000.[34] By the end of 1916, Tinsley had a total of 27 British, Belgian and Dutch agents. At one time he employed over 300 people and his operation had four departments: naval, German army, technical (which provided false papers), and press. He also formed close links with Carl Minster, the socialist journalist, to help him with the dissemination of propaganda.

For the first year Tinsley's right hand man was Arthur Frankignoul, who ran the train-watching service in Belgium and northeastern

France. Unfortunately, Frankignoul had tied 200 agents in the interior to one solitary channel of communication with the outside: the tram which ran daily across the Belgian border to Maastricht. Early each day the Belgian reports were hidden in the tram and retrieved by Frankignoul's agents when it arrived in Holland. This method worked so smoothly that he believed it could last for ever; worse, he had also made the mistake of allowing the Belgian agents to know the names of others. So, when it went wrong and Frankignoul was arrested by the Germans in early 1916, the whole service collapsed like a house of cards. Ten members of his network were executed. Thereafter, the tram was stopped inside Belgium and passengers walked across the border to Holland.

Co-operation seems to have been at a premium. Tinsley was not at all happy with the rival CF and WL networks. All intelligence went back to the tall, scholarly Major Laurie Oppenheim, described as retiring in disposition and highly strung, neither of which can have helped matters; nor does he seem to have had much idea of the life of an agent in the field. However, he was a brilliant staff officer with an analytical mind.

> He got every scrap of information there was to glean from them [my reports], and in the examination of train-watching reports he was an expert in gauging the exact volume of each troop movement.[35]

Ivone Kirkpatrick recalled that Oppenheim once received reports that train movements had been normal for the first five days of the week, but there had then been two trains on the sixth day and two more on the seventh. Oppenheim had telegraphed that the 14th Reserve Division was almost certainly arriving in Belgium from Romania. Asked how he could be so certain, he replied:

> It's perfectly simple my dear Watson. The circumstance that the division is arriving at the rate of two trains a day shows that it's coming from a theatre where conditions prevent a speedier movement. The only such theatre at the moment is Rumania. A study of the German order of battle in Rumania shows the only division there fit to fight on the Western front is the 14th Reserve. You'll see that next week your agents around Ghent will report the arrival of elements of this division.[36]

That year, 1915, the Dutch commander-in-chief complained that Maxse and the German consul C.R. Kneist had set up espionage systems in Rotterdam. Maxse had already set one up in the northern town of Delfzjil on the left bank of the Ems estuary which forms the border with Germany.

On the night of 4 May 1916 Tinsley's accountant, J.F. Cowie, who acted as a courier, was arrested for public drunkenness; later in the month Tinsley's cover was blown in *De Telegraff*. A month later, some of his reports were captured when the Germans seized the *Brussels* in the North Sea. Amid protests, its cigar-smoking captain Edward Fryatt (who in March the previous year had rammed a German submarine, for which he had been given a gold watch) was court-martialled at Bruges and executed on 27 July as a *franc-tireur* or guerilla.[37]

There was worse to come for the Dutch bureau. The reports captured from the *Brussels* identified some of the Belgian train-watchers, who were arrested. Almost inevitably, the network broke down. By August that year no further reports were coming through and there seemed little likelihood of any being forthcoming in the near future.

In November 1916 the Flushing–Folkestone ferry was intercepted by a German destroyer and ordered into Zeebrugge. Agents and couriers threw their bags overboard to avoid a repetition of the *Brussels* fiasco, but since the bags had not been provided with sinkers they were only partially successful. One British bag was retrieved by Germans using long boathooks. Its contents would have dire personal repercussions for Maxse. All Allied subjects of military age and 40 Russian escaped prisoners were landed. As a result, the owners of the Flushing to Tilbury service decided to close it for the duration of the war. Later, the British reopened the Harwich–Hook of Holland ferry. There was a daily service, but ships sailed fairly frequently under escort, and the service was later to tail off; in winter 1917 only one or two ships sailed a month, and sometimes none for six weeks.[38]

The intelligence historian, Christopher Andrew, has described Maxse as looking like a stage villain and his behaviour certainly merited the description. In a letter in the captured bag, Maxse had described the commercial attaché at the Hague, Francis Oppenheimer, as a 'typical Boche Jew' who was playing the enemies' game. He had also helpfully added a few suggestions on how to end Oppenheimer's career. At first Maxse maintained the contents of the letter were privileged and he only climbed down after the threat of legal action. With men like Maxse on one's side, was there any need for an enemy?[39]

According to his critics, Tinsley was capable of even worse behaviour. Cumming had ordered him to give Payne Best as much help as possible, but had also told Best that Tinsley was 'an absolute scoundrel'. On his arrival in Rotterdam, Best claimed that he was met by Peter Peterson, one of Tinsley's men, who drove him to an hotel. While Best was having a bath, his room was searched—on Tinsley's orders, Best thought. He also claimed that Tinsley had manhandled Lieutenant Bennett, Best's deputy, who had a withered arm. Best moved into a flat and set up an independent office.[40]

Best may have been a little harsh on him, at least on the subject of the search of his room, but there was certainly plenty of ambiguity surrounding Tinsley. He also owned an hotel, known as the Uranium, on the waterfront which was run for him by Gottfried and Thérèse Huber. The Hubers may have been acting for German interests, for it seems that Thérèse provided the German agent Walter Schwäbsch, known as Patent, with the names of Germans suspected of betraying the Fatherland.[41]

There was also a firm belief that Tinsley was not above a little blackmail. The British legation in The Hague kept a list of Dutch firms that had dealt with the Germans and were therefore not permitted to deal with the Allies. Tinsley was thought to be taking money from firms to keep them off the list. Best was convinced that on one occasion he caught Peterson in flagrante taking money from a Dutch ship-owner. In his papers, Best notes, 'Being blackmailed by a consortium consisting of our military attaché and C's representatives.' On 17 May 1915 Oppenheim was warned about Tinsley's agents bribing other agents. But there was also a suspicion that in their turn Oppenheim's agents were bribing French and Belgian agents.[42]

Landau, however, rated Tinsley highly:

> T's outstanding quality was that he was a fighter; he was ever ready to fight with the Belgian authorities when we complained of interference with our agents, and even with the British war office at times. Since he was living as a citizen in a neutral country, with ample private means, the Chief in England always had to handle him carefully.'[43]

Best was not necessarily as sparkling white as he may have thought himself; in the autumn of 1917 there was a falling out with Kirkpatrick over Best's involvement with the wife of a Belgian officer.[44]

Tinsley seems to have been inviolate; it was Best who was recalled in November 1917. Not that Tinsley got on any better with Best's successor, Kirkpatrick, who reported that Tinsley was a 'liar and first class intriguer with few scruples',[45] a description Kirkpatrick later tried to play down. Just the sort of man one would want as a spy if not spymaster. A later investigation found there was no evidence that Tinsley was either an embezzler or a blackmailer, but reported that 'he was difficult to get on with'.[46] But Tinsley's agents were providing good information and, when his position was discussed at the regular meetings over the service in Holland, the participants went to lengths not to offend him and bring about his resignation.[47]

Nor was the bureau itself free from penetration. To the annoyance of both Tinsley and Henry Landau, Cumming sent over assistants on a fairly regular basis. In early 1918 he sent a Dutchman, Manen, who was related to a well-connected family. He was attached to Oppenheim's office to assist with coding telegrams, but on 22 March 1918 was seen putting carbon copies of telegrams in his pocket and later handing them to a German agent. He had been blackmailed over a homosexual affair. He was immediately put on board a boat for England where he was held in custody until the Armistice. The damage was said to be 'fairly minimal', but Cumming sent no more assistants.[48]

With all this intriguing and in-fighting it is difficult to understand how any useful information got through.

In January 1918 it was agreed that the Paris bureau, also run by Cecil Cameron, was no longer justified. In early 1917 his reports had been excellent, but now his train services were at a low ebb and in fact nothing worthwhile had been received since the previous October. His health, he felt, made him incapable of reviving them. The London and Folkestone bureaux now merged under Wallinger, a step nearer the goal of one Allied service in Holland. That left Paris. Could Cameron's subordinate, George Bruce, justify its existence in another form? Certainly he could.

What GHQ now wanted, and what Bruce was able to do through his contacts in Paris, was to establish posts in Luxembourg, an important railway centre, with a view to reporting train movements by means of intermediaries in Switzerland. He succeeded in this not only through his contacts but also the bravery of Lise Rischard who established not only a train-watching service but also the insertion of coded messages in the newspaper *Der Landwirt* which cut delivery time of the messages to five days.[49]

Bruce also turned his attention to escapes by British prisoners of war. He was helped by the recently escaped Lieutenant Buckley who volunteered to be recaptured so he could instruct his new fellow prisoners. It was decided that he was too well known to the German authorities; he had been in a camp for 18 months and had made four unsuccessful attempts. Bruce and Buckley gave lectures to the British Expeditionary Force and supplied maps and compasses to be smuggled into the prison camps. Particular attention was paid to members of the Royal Flying Corps and the Tank Corps:

> who from the nature of their employment were more liable to capture than the average officer and were from their small numbers and the expense of their training more desirable objects of attention than the average officer of a fighting unit.[50]

Unfortunately, after a number of escapes, the Germans began to make things more difficult and the smuggling ceased when they threatened, at a conference in The Hague, to stop food parcels.

Also working in the Paris bureau was 29-year-old Charlotte Bosworth. Charlotte, whose father was a music publisher and who was educated abroad, first worked as a deputy assistant censor in London. She was recruited with Lilian Brooking and left for Paris in December 1916 via Southampton and Le Havre. 'Germans didn't torpedo this route because they used it for their spies,' she later wrote. She worked with Captain Camena d'Almeida of the Deuxieme Bureau and, through a study of captured German paybooks, which were delivered in sackfuls after important battles, she could work out the attrition rate of German troops. Each German soldier was given a company number and when he was killed or invalided out a succeeding number was awarded to the new replacement, showing the wastage for each unit. When Lilian Brooking resigned in early 1917, Charlotte's 20-year-old sister Sylvia took her place. They were both able to read German and were horrified when an American, who had not the faintest idea how to do so, joined the bureau.[51]

The Paris office was finally wound up on 15 March 1919.

SPIES IN THE TOWER

'I suppose you would not wish to shake hands with a German spy?'

'No. But I will shake hands with a brave man,' replied Lord Athlumney, the Provost-Marshall, who had come to fetch him from his cell.[2] It was the first execution in the Tower of London for 150 years. The prisoner was said to be the only one who was calm. When the chaplain leading the small procession was about to take the wrong turning, the spy touched his elbow to put him right. He was taken to the miniature rifle range to face a firing squad composed of men from the 3rd Battalion of the Grenadier Guards. And so Carl Hans Lody passed into folklore as the exemplar of both the 'good spy' and how a man should die.

Lody had never stood a chance. His ill-prepared 'spying' activity arose out of national desperation. At the beginning of the war - Germany's main intelligence interest was in the navy and the naval dockyards. With the British authorities' wholesale round-up of suspected German agents, there was something approaching panic in the German intelligence ranks: it was crucial to get men, able or not, properly trained or not, over to England to find out what was happening. The first spy, Lody, a junior lieutenant in the German reserve navy, was sent almost immediately after the outbreak of war, and he lasted barely five weeks.

Lody had lived in America where, in Nebraska, he had married the wealthy Louise Storz, the daughter of Gottlieb Storz, who was prominent in the Omaha brewing industry. The marriage does not seem to have been welcomed by her family; it lasted only a year and it seems that Lody was given a $10,000 pay-off by his father-in-law. He then worked as a travel agent and for a German shipping line. Lody had also known Arthur Tapken, first director of 'N' (Nachrichten Bureau der Rechsmaine), who had been his commander in the navy. It was only natural for Lody, who spoke English with a strong American accent, to be approached and, however reluctant he may have been, he later told the British authorities:

> I have never been a coward in my life and I certainly would not be a shirker …When it was put before me I must admit I felt uneasy; I felt I was not a fit man for a job of that kind.
>
> My services were considered absolutely as an honour and free, because I happened to go there, and they know I am in so-called well-to-do circumstances. Or I do not think they would ever have dared to approach me with such a proposition.[3]

So keen were the Germans to get a man into England that no real effort was made to train Lody. He was given cover addresses to write to in Christiana, Stockholm, New York and Rome, and off he went.

Lody arrived in Newcastle from Bergen on 27 August 1914 and made his way to Edinburgh. He was travelling as Charles Inglis, an American whose passport had been 'mislaid' by the passport bureau in Berlin when he had gone to obtain an extension. Lody was naive, unfortunate and ill-prepared, as was soon proved by his actions: three days after his arrival he sent a telegram to Adolf Burchard at Trottingatten, Stockholm. All telegrams had to pass through the censor and Burchard was known to be suspect. Lody also drew attention to himself by using an incorrect telegram form and only signing it 'Charles'.

If Paul Daelen, the talented German agent who survived multiple trips to England, had managed to contact Lody in time, things might have been different. As it was, by the time Daelen was in a position to give Lody a new cover address, Lody had already gone to Ireland. It was only a matter of time before he was scooped up.

The only report of Lody's which was allowed to go through was one which erroneously said there were Russian troops in England. After that he was followed, and arrested on 2 October in the Great Southern Hotel, Killarney. His room was searched and details of cruisers sunk in the North Sea together with an address book in cipher were found. Dr John Lea, travelling with Lody and also claiming United States citizenship, was arrested at the same time but, after questioning, was released and allowed to travel to America. He was fortunate. There was a note circulating which recommended that he should be arrested and, if found guilty, shot. Then, as now, communication between the authorities was not what it always should be.

Lody was brought to London, where he was questioned by Sir Basil Thomson, Assistant Commissioner of Scotland Yard. Because MI5 had no power of arrest, the Special Branch had to be called in. Interrogation was usually undertaken by Thomson, which caused jealousy in Kell and Cumming, who thought that he was getting their share of the kudos.

Qualified as a barrister, Thomson, the son of the one-time Archbishop of York, had been in the Colonial Service. On returning to England he became the governor of Dartmoor and Wormwood Scrubs prisons before being appointed assistant commissioner to Scotland Yard in 1913.

Hugh Hoy, confidential secretary to 'Blinker' Hall, Director of Naval Intelligence, thought of Thomson: 'His manner was charming, quiet and sympathetic, and no one could extract so much information as Sir Basil did with such apparent guilelessness.'[4]

Others thought his interrogation techniques may have left something to be desired. He is said to have opened the questioning of the Irishman Sir Roger Casement:[5]

T: What is your name?
C: You know it.
T: Ah, yes but I have to guard against impersonators.[6]

Thomson later wrote:

About the examinations in my room there was never anything in the nature of what the Americans call the 'Third Degree' which, I understand, consists of startling or wearying the suspect into a confession. If they preferred not to answer questions they were detained until further inquiry could be made about them. In many cases it was the detention that influenced them. They were not sent to prison unless it was clear their detention would have to be prolonged.[7]

Lody's trial began on 20 October 1914 in what was then the new

Middlesex Guildhall in Parliament Square, now the Supreme Court. The evidence against him was overwhelming and the result a foregone conclusion. Nevertheless, Lody maintained his principles. Asked who had sent him to England he replied:

> I have pledged my word of honour not to name that name. I cannot do it. Although names are discovered in my documents, I do not feel that I have broken my word. But that name—no, I cannot give that. I have pledged my word.[8]

Found guilty, he was invited to speak before sentence was passed and declined to do so.

Executions of spies were carried out at the Tower of London, both because it was held to be the most convenient place and because its impact as an execution site would have more effect on the country at large, and possibly on Germany, than would an ordinary prison.[9]

As with everything, some spies were better than others and some died 'better than others'. Lody was one of the latter, writing to his relations, 'I have had just Judges, and I shall die as an Officer, not as a Spy'. He also asked that his guards be thanked for their kindness towards him.[10] He was shot on the morning of 6 November 1914. Thomson thought he died, 'as all Englishmen would wish to die'.

As far as the authorities were concerned, even after the war Lody's behaviour was a benchmark against which the conduct of other captured spies was set.

The 58-year-old Carl Frederick Muller was the next German spy to be shot. He spoke Russian, Flemish and Dutch as well as English with only a trace of an accent. It seems that after the Germans entered Antwerp on 8 October 1914 following a bombardment of the city, Muller, as an agent for a German factory, had been allowed to go to Germany to buy machinery. He was arrested on his return to the Goch railway station at the end of November and taken to Wesel where he was held for a month. Here he was recruited by German intelligence as a linguist and a man with some knowledge of shipping.

Muller arrived in Sunderland on 11 January 1915 claiming to be in ill-health and posing as a Russian on his way to America. For a time he lodged with people he had met two years earlier in Antwerp but then he came down to London, booking into a boarding house in Guilford Street, off Russell Square in Bloomsbury.

Within days he left for Rotterdam, returning to Guilford Street on 27 January. He wrote letters full of pious hope about the end of the war to his friends in Sunderland but, using the name Lempret, he also sent a letter to Rotterdam from Walden Street in Whitechapel, east London, a name and address he seems to have chosen at random. In invisible ink it gave details of troop movements, as did his next letter in the name of Cohen, sent from Deptford High Street.

Back he went to Rotterdam, returning on 13 February. By now residents of the boarding house were becoming suspicious and Muller was reported to Scotland Yard. A police search turned up nothing. He sent a third letter to Rotterdam, again with details of troop movements. He also tried to recruit John Hahn, a baker from Deptford whose father was a naturalized German whom Muller knew vaguely, to help him with his letters. Hahn's bakery was doing badly and the promise of extra money was a temptation. Unfortunately for Muller, Hahn decided to send a letter of his own. This time the part in invisible ink told of 4,500 men being assembled at the Manchester canal to go to Boulogne. It was complete rubbish, and it was intercepted. Hahn was arrested and his blotting paper revealed Muller's address. On 25 February Muller was arrested and this time a search of his room turned up a lemon (which, with formalin, was a standard combination for making invisible ink) and a list of major seaports.

Muller and Hahn were tried at the Old Bailey, where Muller argued that the proof he needed to show he was not a spy was in Antwerp. The jury convicted them both within 20 minutes. Hahn received a prison sentence of seven years. Muller was shot on 23 June. He broke down the night before but had regained his nerve on the morning of his execution, shaking hands with each member of the firing squad in turn. His death was kept secret and, for a time, false messages were sent in his name to Antwerp. In return German spy chiefs sent him some £400 and, much to the delight of the Security Service, he was awarded an Iron Cross. Inevitably, his employment was terminated. The letter read: 'Owing to a sequence of wrong information coming from you which has much misled us, we are herewith dispensing with your services.'

Part of the £400 went toward buying a car for one of the British intelligence officers. It was named 'The Muller'.[11]

Anton Kuppferle avoided both the firing squad and the hangman.

Born in Germany but taken to the US at the age of nine, Kuppferle served on the Western Front in the early days of the war and then pestered von Papen, the German military attaché in New York, to allow him to work as a spy.

He came to England on the White Star liner *Arabic* on 4 February 1915, claiming to be a United States traveller in woollen goods, but he was ignorant of both the niceties of spoken English and the American accent. He wrote a message about war vessels he had seen on the boat coming over, and on his return from a trip to Dublin he was arrested. In his possession were lemons and formalin.

Kuppferle appeared at the Old Bailey, pulling his black frock coat around him in the dock. On the first night of his trial he hanged himself with a silk scarf, leaving a letter in good English on the slate provided in his cell, giving his real name, admitting he was a German soldier and wishing he had been shot. 'I am not dying as a spy but as a soldier.' Unlike the spies shot in the Tower (who were buried in the East London cemetery), he was buried at Streatham Park cemetery.[12]

In October 1914 the German Haicke Petrus Marinus Janssen received a medal for saving lives on the British ship, the *Volteria*, when it was burned in the Atlantic. On 12 May 1915 he arrived at Hull, staying at Percy's York Hotel and telling the owner he was a Dutchman travelling in cigars on his father's behalf. He travelled quite legitimately but ten days after his arrival he was in Southampton sending telegrams to Dierks & Co in The Hague, an address known to be used by German intelligence. The contents were easily decipherable. He was arrested at the Crown Hotel; in his possession were telegrams from Dierks saying that money was on its way and a certificate of his employment by Dierks.

The day after Janssen's arrival, Willem Johannes Roos, another sailor, had landed in Tilbury, and his telegrams to Dierks were also intercepted. He was allowed to move round the country sending telegrams from a variety of ports including Aberdeen and Inverness. Roos was another 'cigar salesman' but, when asked to produce the goods, he told the Scotland Yard officer, Herbert Fitch, that he had smoked them all because there was no longer a British market. Nor was he able to explain why Dierks & Co should employ a sailor to sell their cigars. His coded messages, this time using scent as invisible ink, were sent to the same Hague address. He was arrested on 2 June at the

Three Tuns Hotel in Aldgate and taken to Scotland Yard where, interviewed by Thomson, he denied knowing Janssen. On his way to Cannon Row police station Roos smashed a pane of glass and tried to cut his wrists.

On 16 July Janssen was convicted. Roos was convicted the next day, expert witnesses having been called to show that he knew little or nothing about the cigar trade. Roos also claimed to have been in a series of mental hospitals. Both were sentenced to death. Janssen said he had information to give about the German Secret Service, but it was not of sufficient value to save his life. All the addresses he gave were already known, as was the trick he disclosed that messages could be hidden in the spines of books. Nothing came of Roos' claims of insanity.

Both were executed on the morning of 30 July 1915. Janssen went first at 6 o'clock. It was said, 'his iron nerve held'. Roos, shot ten minutes later, asked to be allowed to finish a last cigarette. 'His courage could evoke nothing but admiration,' wrote Thomson.[13]

Ernst Melin followed them two months later. The 49-year-old son of a member of the Swedish Parliament who also owned a steamship company, Melin had visited Britain in 1887 and had also lived in Hamburg. Later he worked in Russia, but when war broke out this one-time alcoholic lost his job. He told his father he would go back to Hamburg. It was while lunching with a Swedish commission agent there that he was recruited as a spy and sent to Britain specifically to look at naval ports.

The British authorities had noted that Melin had been to see the spymaster Hilmar Dierks in Antwerp, where he was given rudimentary training in ship identification, a code, a copy of Baedeker, £30 and sent on his way to London's Strand Palace Hotel. From there he moved to a boarding house in Belsize Park.

Melin reported on details of searchlights, Zeppelins and troop insignia. He went back to see Dierks and asked to do more, and over the months he was sent around £200 in return for information about the sinking of the *Royal Oak* and other British ships. His letters to his spymaster, addressed to 'Uncle' and signed 'Kate', included messages in invisible ink.

Melin seems to have been a rank amateur, putting dots in his copy of Baedeker against ports he had visited. He claimed the lemon juice he kept in his room was an aftershave lotion for his sensitive skin, but the owner of the Belsize Park boarding house, Flora Milligan, had noticed he went to a barber every day.

When he was arrested on 14 June and interviewed by Thomson, 'Blinker' Hall and Lord Herschell from the Admiralty, Melin maintained that he had refused to travel to ports in England. At his third interview he made a full confession. He was shot at the Tower on 8 September and died 'like the gentleman he once was'. Before his execution, he, too, shook hands with his guards.[14]

Augusto Alfredo Roggen, a tenant farmer from Montevideo married to a German woman, spoke reasonable English but otherwise seems to have been wholly unprepared for life as a spy. At the outbreak of war he travelled to Switzerland and then to Frankfurt, where it is likely he was recruited. He arrived in England on 30 May 1915, and stayed at the Bonnington Hotel in Southampton Row, Holborn. In an attempt to establish his cover he went to a horse dealer in Hanover Square to buy ten high-quality hackney mares, a huge order worth £3,900 which immediately aroused suspicion.

His technique, such as it was, seems to have been to question everyone with whom he came into contact. He stopped in Lincoln on 4 June where he went to discuss another huge order, this time for agricultural equipment but really as a cover to try to establish troop numbers. The next day he travelled to Edinburgh from where he sent a give-away postcard to Heinrich Flores, a German teacher of languages in Rotterdam, who worked for Dierks, assisting him in the recruitment of agents.

On 9 June Roggen went to the Tarbet Hotel at Loch Lomond. The loch had been used as a torpedo testing range. He bought a map of the area, but did not get a chance to use it. By the time he was arrested at 5 o'clock that afternoon, he seems only to have reached the stage of letting his spymaster know he had arrived, and trying to contact another German agent, George Breeckow, who was already in custody. Secret ink was found in his room.

At his trial on 20 August Roggen did not give evidence, for which decision he blamed his solicitor and counsel. An appeal for clemency by the Uruguayan minister failed. Lord Kitchener noted that it was a matter for the Foreign Office if they wished to do a favour to the Uruguay government. They did not. When Roggen faced the firing squad on 17 September he refused a blindfold and marched to his chair.

There is a curious postscript to Roggen's story: the next year, the ship on which his brother, Dr Emilio Roggen, was sailing from Holland to South America was intercepted. He was interrogated and provided the satisfactory explanation that he had been interned by the Germans at the outbreak of war and forced to work as a medical officer. He had just been released. Apparently he did not know of his brother's death.[15]

The next spy to be caught was a 24-year-old violinist, Fernando Buschman, born in Paris, the son of a German who had become a naturalized Brazilian. An instrument maker whose business had collapsed at the outbreak of war, Fernando Buschman had been friends with a German woman who was going to Holland. She told him he could not write directly to her but that Flores, the known German spymaster who worked from Dierks & Co., would forward any mail. Buschman was later introduced to Flores in Rotterdam. Unlike Roggen, Buschman was short of money and repeatedly telegraphed his spymasters in Rotterdam. The wires were intercepted and from then on Buschman's days of freedom were numbered. He seems to have supplied only very basic intelligence and wrote *Impressions of London*, jottings which were found in his papers at Harrington Road, Kensington. He was arrested on 4 June 1915, six weeks after he arrived in London; part of the evidence against him was his use of invisible ink. He played the violin throughout the night preceding his execution. He, too, refused a blindfold. Buschman is reputed to have kissed his instrument saying, 'Goodbye, I shall not want you anymore.'[16]

The only German spy convicted of treason who was not shot was Robert Rosenthal, sentenced at the Middlesex Guildhall on 6 July 1915. He had first arrived in Britain in November 1914, went back to Holland, returned and was arrested in Newcastle on 12 January 1915 prior to attempting to go to Bergen. His trial was held in camera and the case against him was that he had come to England to obtain military intelligence which he was taking back to Germany. He had also sent a telegram to George Haeffner at 20 Kirkgarden, Christiana, Norway, giving the disposition of ships.

When questioned, Rosenthal refuted the evidence against him; he denied that he knew a man named Kulbe in Berlin or elsewhere; claimed that James Willers was a friend from Copenhagen; the man

Salomon was his agent; and he had been employed by Major Ryan of the American Relief Committee. He didn't know of the address Belzigerstrasse 19. He was not interested in gas lighters, which had been mentioned in an intercepted letter sent by him to Norway.

The letter was read to him in English. Half way through, Rosenthal leaped to his feet, clicked his heels, saluted and said, 'The game is up. I am a German, I confess everything'.

After his trial Rosenthal wrote to Lord Kitchener asking for clemency and giving details of his contacts in Berlin, claiming that Melton Feder of the American Relief Committee in Berlin was a master spy; Franz Kulbe was Korvetten Kaptain von Prieger; and Belzigerstrasse 19 was their Secret Service address in Berlin. He added, 'I have a clear conscience and am at heart not a German nor a spy. I am a Jew and am very sorry to be in the condition I am today.'[17] But this declaration was not sufficient to save him.

Rosenthal was sent to Wandsworth prison where he was guarded by soldiers rather than warders. He attempted to strangle himself with his bedclothes. He was hanged on 16 July by Thomas Pierrepoint, assisted by Robert Baxter, a lay preacher.[18]

In the same year, 33-year-old piano salesman George T. Breeckow was arrested. His father, a Russian, had become a naturalized German. Breeckow, a fluent English speaker and naval volunteer who had been educated in America, had been sent to the spy school in Antwerp. He arrived in London on a foreign passport and moved into the Ivanhoe Hotel in Bloomsbury Street under the name of Reginald Rowland. He had been told to contact Louise Emily 'Lizzie' Wertheim, and an arrangement was made to meet at the Waldorf Hotel in Aldwych. He was to wear a lavender sweet pea in his buttonhole.

Lizzie Wertheim was born Klitzke in Stargatt in German Poland. She came to England where, in 1902, she married Bruno Wertheim, whose father was a naturalized British subject. It was not a happy marriage, and a deed of separation was filed in Berlin in May 1913. By then Bruno Wertheim's father had died, leaving him a substantial inheritance and Lizzie obtained a very decent allowance of over £500 a year. On 3 October 1914 she travelled to Amsterdam just as the Germans were bombarding Antwerp, but intending to go on to Germany to see her mother. Instead, Lizzie, well spoken and well travelled, was recruited to the German cause. She lived at 32 Coptic

Street in London where she was visited by another German lady, Mrs Schwartz. Both were thought to have had German agents as lodgers.

Wertheim and Breeckow became romantically involved; they stayed in Bournemouth from where Breeckow sent messages in invisible ink to Flores in Rotterdam. Whether he was quite as involved as she is another matter, because he wrote to his employers: 'She is extraordinarily obstinate and must be treated gently… Never mind, gents, I am some Bear, when it comes to the ladies.'[19]

The pair decided that Breeckow would visit Westcliff, from where he sent more information to Flores. Wertheim arranged to go to Scotland with Mabel Knowles, an American friend who had once given her English lessons. As an American alien, Knowles had to produce a passport at the Edinburgh hotel where they were staying. She could not do so and returned to London.

Unfortunately, Wertheim's English lessons had not eliminated her German accent and she drew attention to herself by making a number of trips to the naval bases in the area and quizzing the locals. As a result, she was questioned at her hotel by the local police—but was allowed to return to London where she was kept under observation.

George Breeckow was not much more discreet. Booking in at the Westcliff Hotel, he wanted a room with a sea view and asked the proprietor for a spyglass. A letter to Flores was intercepted and inevitably found to have writing in invisible ink. He was arrested in London on 4 June. Rice paper with details of British warships was found in the top of his shaving brush. When his room was searched and his passport seized it was found to be forged.

Lizzie Wertheim was arrested at Mabel Knowles' home on 9 June. She spiritedly tried to throw a piece of paper from her window, but when it was retrieved it was found to be a letter from Breeckow, in the name of Rowland, thanking her 'ever so much for your news'.

Because of complications over whether Lizzie Wertheim was actually English, instead of facing a court martial, she and Breeckow appeared in front of a jury at the Old Bailey on 20 September 1915, charged with the intention of assisting the enemy. The evidence was overwhelming and the jury convicted them in a bare eleven minutes. At the trial Breeckow did the decent thing and made admissions which were designed to save Wertheim.

I want to confess, my Lords, that I have never received a word of information of Mrs Wertheim about the Fleet or Navy of England. It is merely a coincidence that I could fit her in my report of the German Naval Intelligence, and I am very sorry for the miserable unfortunate position she is now in.[20]

To an extent he succeeded. He was sentenced to death, but Mr Justice Bray was at pains to point out that, while the death penalty was an option, the English did not hang women spies, and he sentenced Wertheim to ten years to be served in the women's prison in Aylesbury. Another of her friends, Miss Brande, was interned.

In the five weeks before his execution Breeckow, who had been in a state of collapse as he left the dock, broke down completely. His appeal and a petition for clemency were rejected. His last request was to have a woman's handkerchief used as a blindfold as he faced the firing squad; whether it was Wertheim's is uncertain. There is a story that, despite the cause of death being given on his death certificate as gunshot wounds, he died of a heart attack before he was shot.[21]

On 29 September 1915, small, bespectacled Irving Guy Ries, aged 55, appeared before a court martial. Born in Chicago, he had arrived in England from New York on 4 July 1915, travelling from Liverpool to London to stay at the then very grand Hotel Cecil in the Strand. His cover was that he was a representative of two corn merchants. Almost immediately he came under suspicion when a money telegram was sent to him apparently by an N. M. Cleton from Rotterdam. This was the nom d'espionage of Dierks' wife.

Ten days later Ries was on the road again, following what had become the recognized spy trail from Newcastle to Glasgow to Edinburgh. He called on various corn merchants en route but did no business, and when he registered with the police, as was required as an alien, he told them he wished to travel to Rotterdam to collect money owed to him. It was noted that more money arrived from Holland, and when Ries took his passport to the American consulate they sent it to Scotland Yard.

Ries was arrested on 10 August at the Hotel Cecil. The charges were that he had communicated with Cleton; possessed a false passport; collected information which might be useful to the enemy; and intended to assist the enemy. The case against him was the reverse of the usual. Instead of his communications to Holland being intercepted, it was their communications to him which were the basis of the case. It was clear he had been writing to his spymasters. The prosecution was unable to show he had actually sent any information. As the Advocate General told the court martial, Ries was accused 'of doing an act preparatory to collecting information'. That act was coming to England and visiting the towns. Ries' case marked a change in tactics. For him secret ink was out. Spies would now be sent on flying visits and be required to report when they went back to Holland.

Ries refused to provide his real name. His parents, he said, were Dutch and Scottish and he had bought the passport on a New York street for a bet. He had not been collecting information, but he could give no real explanation of why he was in communication with Cleton. He claimed he was a diamond smuggler, not a spy.

He was found guilty after eight minutes. Shortly before he was shot on 27 October, he made a full confession giving his real name. He shook hands with the firing squad, saying, 'You are only doing your duty as I have done mine.' Thomson agreed that Ries' parents should never be told of what they would have considered a dishonourable profession for their son.[22]

Only two more spies were shot in England during the war. The first was Albert Meyer, described by Sir Basil Thomson as 'a despicable character', who was executed on 2 December 1915.

Meyer had arrived in England in 1910 and had been employed as a cook and a waiter. At the outbreak of war he was detained at Folkestone but, claiming to be a Turkish subject, he was released six weeks later. In April 1915 he obtained permission to go to Holland, from where he wished to go to Denmark, by now claiming to be Danish. He was back in England by the second week of May.

He was arrested after the interception of a letter sent to an address in The Hague, giving details of ships in Chatham and signed Svend Person, but without the correct address of the sender. Other letters and postcards in the same handwriting followed—one signed 'Lopez' giving details of torpedo boats—and eventually one signed 'Tommy' from an address in Margaret Street off Oxford Circus. When the police went to the lodgings, they found Meyer and his wife Catherine Rebecca Godleman (whom he had married on 20 May 1915 at St Pancras Register Office). A typewriter which matched one of the letters was found. Kitty Meyer was released without charge.

Either Turkish or German but certainly not Danish, Meyer was not one of nature's gentlemen. He was a pimp and a fraud, sponging off cafés and restaurants in Soho. He had also been cheating his German paymasters, sending them wholly false information. His defence after his arrest was to try to blame an innocent man who had been at the same lodgings. According to S.T. Felstead, when Meyer was taken to be executed on 2 December, after singing 'It's a Long Way to Tipperary', 'He burst into a torrent of blasphemous cursing reviling his Maker and calling down the vengeance of Heaven on those who had deserted him.'[23]

The last of the spies to be shot in the First World War was 35-year-old Peruvian-born Ludovico Hurwitz-y-Zender. He left Peru in August 1914, apparently coming to Europe via New York to sell food, paper and handkerchiefs. It is not clear when he first arrived in Britain but, during a period of ten days in May 1915, he sent five telegrams from an address in Glasgow to August Brochner, who was a post-box for the German Secret Service in Christiana, where Zender had probably been recruited. The codes were simple. Instructions to 'ship anchovies' meant that a boat or boats had left a British harbour. 'Buy immediately' meant that one or more had arrived.

An arrest warrant was issued, but Zender had sailed from Newcastle on 28 May, three days after the last intercepted telegram. He was arrested on his return to Newcastle on 2 July. When he was questioned it was apparent that the fish he claimed to have ordered were out of season and unavailable. His trial was delayed at the request of the Peruvian legation and did not take place until 20 March 1916. He was shot on 7 April, showing what was described as 'a fair amount of calm'.[24]

And so, despite the fact that the Germans continued to shoot spies until the end of the war and the French did so afterwards, and despite Vernon Kell's complaints that a failure to execute female spies was an act of false sentimentality, Zender had the doubtful privilege of being the last spy to be shot in the Tower of London.

Chapter Seven

The information I wrote is not worth a hang. It is not worth anything, you can see for yourself. Only give me a fighting chance; send me to the front. Kenneth Rysbach[1]

SURVIVORS

For a variety of reasons, including luck and mismanagement as well as clemency, some German spies caught in Britain during the First World War escaped the firing squad. Bad timing on the part of the British saved one early German spy, Frederick Parker Dunbar, who was arrested because the authorities stepped in too soon when in 1914 he was found in the north of Scotland. Of American origin, Dunbar had served in the German navy for over 20 years; according to his story he had resigned his commission and come to Britain to see his 16-year-old-son who was being educated in Scotland. However his passport was in the name of William Culden. Fortunately for him he was arrested before he had been able to send any information, and as a result he was interned as opposed to interred.[2]

Careful checks were not always made on volunteers. One man who got away completely unscathed was a German posing as a Scot and calling himself John Maclinks. He claimed to be both a music hall artist and a newspaper correspondent, and in early 1915 proposed to Valentine Williams at the War Office that he should go to Germany for the *Daily Mail* and then on to Kiel to see what he could find out about the High Seas fleet. He said he could speak a variety of German dialects. Williams demurred but, when Maclinks insisted the risk was all his, gave him £25, apparently never expecting to hear from him again. Williams later received two letters from Maclinks, the first saying that he had ended up in Germany after he had fallen asleep on the train going through Holland. He told the authorities he was a waiter trying to rejoin his regiment. The second said that he had reached Kiel. Williams thought that Maclinks had subsequently been interned in Ruhleben camp, outside Berlin.

The story did not end there. After the war Henri Beland wrote more about Maclinks and the damage he caused at Ruhleben. Maclinks, who was already there when Beland arrived in June 1915, now claimed to have been *The Times'* pre-war Vienna correspondent.

> According to all initial appearances, Maclinks was a loyal British subject. He associated with the British prisoners, who in turn would visit him in his cell. He had great talent and intelligence.[3]

Also at Ruhleben was a young man, Russell, who had been arrested in Brussels. The two became close friends. One day Russell was taken away. On the same day one of the *kommandantur's* officers, Captain Wolfe, had visited the jail, and it was known that while there he interviewed Maclinks, who was now ostracized.

Later Maclinks confessed to another British internee, Kirkpatrick, that he had denounced Russell as a spy in the employ of the British government in Belgium. Maclinks apparently was an Austrian officer, which accounted for his command of German dialect. He was transferred and apparently spent the rest of the war undercover in other prisons.

After the outrage caused by the execution in Belgium in October 1915 of the English nurse Edith Cavell, despite complaints by Vernon Kell of misplaced sentimentality, the British authorities decided not to execute women spies. This was partly an attempt to win the propaganda war and obtain the sympathy of neutrals. An immediate beneficiary was Eva de Bournonville. Arrested on 5 November 1915 on arrival at Newcastle on 29 September, de Bournonville, a Swede, admitted from the first that she was in the pay of the Germans.

Her father was a naturalized Swede and, born in Denmark in 1875, she went to Stockholm at the age of seven where she learned six languages. Of French extraction, she was in turn a governess, an actress and a secretary before she was recruited, a decision which was generally attributed to her living beyond her means. She began working for a man called Schmidt after she got into debt.

Once in England she spent a good deal of time asking people about anti-aircraft measures; how many guns there were in London and so forth. She put up at a private hotel in Bloomsbury where young officers were known to take their leave, and tried to develop friendships with as many of them as possible. She had been supplied with secret ink and her letters were intercepted from the first week in October. In her short stay she worked hard. She had already given details of anti-aircraft guns and an air raid at Croydon as well as trying to obtain a position in postal censorship.

When she was arrested, she told Basil Thomson she had been paid £30 a month and been promised large sums if she provided worthwhile information. But, she claimed, she disliked the Germans and would rather have worked for the British—and wanted to work the double cross. She was sentenced to death on 19 January 1916 at the Old Bailey and in the following February her appeal was dismissed. The sentence was later commuted to penal servitude for life, and she ended up in the women's prison at Aylesbury.

The harsh conditions there were not to her liking. On 5 April 1916 she told the prison governor that she had information to give; her intention was to harm Schmidt rather than to help England. She also wanted to improve the conditions under which she was kept. In return, she offered to reveal Schmidt's secret code and the name of his 'cleverest agent' who travelled to and from England, but she wanted an undertaking that the agent would not be arrested. She was told there could be no bargaining but, that if her information was useful, the authorities would be informed. She gave up the code but not the name of the agent.

A most unlikely potential spy came in the form of May Higgs, a young British girl who wrote to her mother for transmission to the German spy bureau in Holland in 1915, offering her services to Germany. Her letter was intercepted; it was thought that because of her age and what was described as 'mixed parentage' she was deemed not suitable to be tried. First she was placed in the custody of her relations, but she escaped to Europe. On her return she was sent to a convent for the duration of the war.

Louise Herbert, the German-born wife of an Englishman clergyman, was leniently treated when she was convicted of attempting to obtain information about munition factories. When her letters to

Switzerland were intercepted and she was questioned, she claimed that she would have spied for Germany but had not managed to do so. As a propaganda exercise the judge's approach was clearly worthwhile. When Herbert received a prison sentence of six months in October 1915, the *New York Times* commented favourably on her sentence, saying that it was 'a far more serious matter than Miss Cavell's transgression'.[4]

Marie Edwige de Popovitch, allegedly a Serb, was arrested in Malta and sent to England for interrogation in 1916 after sending a series of telegrams to Switzerland. She had been suspected of noting the names of vessels passing through Malta for destruction by submarines. After she tried to seduce the ship's captain on the journey to England, she was deemed to be insane and kept in Aylesbury, where she quietened down when she was allowed to keep in her cell the two canaries which had travelled with her from Malta. Eventually, she was sent to an asylum.

In September 1918 64-year-old Martha Earle received a year's imprisonment under the Defence of the Realm Act for writing to her sister in Germany in what she called a family code. A German by birth, she had moved to Britain in 1908 when she married an English headmaster. She sent no information of military value.

The British courts were determined that the trials of spies should not be simply show trials; adjournments were granted to the defence and the best solicitors and counsel were made available to them. Nor were the trials foregone conclusions. In January 1916 the Danish-born Johann Christian Zahle Lassen, a commission agent in wine and whisky, was acquitted at Guildhall. The evidence against him was slight. He certainly knew Germans but there was not much more against him, and he was repatriated.

The Government was keen not to upset its allies by executing those of their nationals who were spying for Germany. When J.B. Sterndale Bennett took up guard duties at the Tower of London, a Dutchman and a Swede were there under sentence of death. Affairs were managed in some style and Bennett remembers that when the Dutchman was reprieved the announcement was made to him one evening by a neutral diplomat wearing a fur coat with an astrakhan collar, evening dress and top hat.[5]

The spy in question was Leopold Vieyra, who had a slight cast in one eye and a moustache—in fact he looked rather like the 7th Lord Lucan—and had been an acrobat in the music halls. He had first come to England before the war, bringing the Midgets, a troupe which included the Gondins, a famous Brazilian act. The troupe played barracks and naval towns such as Aldershot, Salisbury and Portsmouth, instead of larger and more lucrative venues, and there was a suspicion even then that Vieyra was spying. One dwarf, Little Mary, was suspected of stealing military documents for him.

After that, he managed the Bijou cinema on the Finchley Road in Hampstead, under the name Leo Pickard, and lived with a Mrs Annie Fletcher in Acton Vale, from where he ran Pickard's Film Agency. He returned to Holland and then, on 6 May 1916, came back to England, ostensibly to buy films. Vieyra's mission was doomed from the start because MI5 had good information that he was on his way. He was seen hanging around railway stations in London trying to get into conversation with men returned from the front. His letters to Sophie Blom in Amsterdam—she was the sister-in-law of Philip Dieche who had earlier sent money to the spy Frank Greite—were intercepted, and when Vieyra's rooms were searched ammonia and absorbent wool (essential ingredients for writing in invisible ink) were found on the mantelpiece. The letters contained the words Sheerness, Plymouth, Newcastle and Glasgow. Vieyra was also using a ballpoint pen, desirable for spies because it apparently did not leave an impression on paper. Annie Fletcher did what she could for Vieyra, explaining that she had bought the wool to try to get rid of surplus hair between his eyebrows. Whether she would have tried as hard if she had known that there was a Mrs Vieyra in the form of Josephine Jensen in Holland is not recorded. In his interviews Vieyra admitted he was a German spy, and after the war his name was found in the records of the German Admiralty Bureau. Condemned to death, he was reprieved and sentenced to life imprisonment on 11 November 1916.

Kenneth Gustav Triest, an American who had a German father but did not speak German and had not been to Germany, had told friends just before the war that the Kaiser had invited him and his father to visit the country. In the autumn of 1914 he entered Princeton, but had left by January 1915 when, claiming Canadian citizenship, he enlisted in the Royal Navy and was sent to HMS Eagle.[6] In March he volunteered to do signal work and was sent to Chatham. He was caught when he wrote to the German banker Baron Bruno von Schröder asking how to escape to Germany. There was some suggestion that the young Triest was not fully responsible for his actions which, if it is correct, meant entry standards to Ivy League universities were not at their highest. The British decided to court-martial him and so began a political battle, with his father seeking the help of the US Secretary of State Robert Lansing and later President Theodore Roosevelt to prevent a trial.

By October 1914, coverage in the American papers was running strongly in favour of Triest. His father came to Britain to retrieve him on the perhaps dubious grounds of insanity. When, together, they returned to America in November the British decision not to try Triest was widely praised. In return, Roosevelt published an open letter thanking the British and contrasting their mercy favourably with the case of Edith Cavell.[7]

Another case where a father influenced his son's fortunes was that of journalist and employee of the Brazilian consulate in Rotterdam, Jose de Patrocinio, who arrived at Gravesend in September 1917 with instructions to conduct an intelligence mission. Already anxious about being caught, he confessed all when he landed. To make doubly sure, the English agent Tinsley arranged for a burglary to take place at de Patrocinio's Amsterdam premises to seize supporting evidence. He had been tempted with the considerable sum of £1,000 to find out where the next offensive in France would take place. His father, who had been instrumental in freeing the slaves in Brazil, was something of a national hero and to execute his son would have caused serious political trouble. De Patrocinio was repatriated in 1919.[8]

Some spies did rather well for themselves when arrested. Captain Hans Boehme was awarded officer status and detained in Brixton prison under the title 'military lodger', a designation he apparently liked. In 1914 he had been involved in sabotage in America and the next year was in Ireland fomenting trouble. In March that year he was in Scotland on behalf of Walter Nicolai, but then his nerve seems to have failed him and he declined a mission in April 1915. However, he was back in action in January 1917 when he was arrested immediately after his arrival in England from New York, giving the name of Jelks Leroy Thrasher. He had been caught out when he bowed from the waist after telling the authorities how he had been raised in Quitman,

Georgia.[9] He had done sterling work while in New York recruiting, among others, William MacCully, a Scots-American who came to Scotland and was in England for two months in 1915 before working in Karl Boy-Ed's New York offices. Boehme also recruited Anthony Brogan who co-ordinated German sabotage in Britain from both Madrid and Lisbon.

Frank Lauritz Theodore Greite was born in Brooklyn on 5 July 1885 of a Dutch father and Danish mother. He was educated in Berlin and earned a living selling oil, cotton and grinding machinery. Married to a German wife who lived in Hamburg, he had a French mistress, Suzanne Dupont, who lived in the *département* of the Meuse. Recruited as a spy, Greite came to England in October 1915. He was tracked after posting letters in a south coast town to a known address in Sweden. During his time in England he received £400, of which £250 came from Holland. According to the not wholly reliable detective Herbert Fitch, when Greite was arrested on 25 March 1916 at Tilbury, he tried to sandbag the policeman. He had invisible ink in his tie.[10] On 19 August 1916 he received ten years' penal servitude and was a pain in the side of the Home Office for the next eight years.

The spy Adolpho Guerrero posed as a Spanish journalist representing the Madrid paper *Lirbal*. He had been promised £50 for every ship sunk as a result of his reports. He managed to get a passport for his mistress, Raymonde Amondarain (known as Aurora de Bilbao), but she was arrested on landing in England. In turn, he was arrested in Whitfield Street, off Tottenham Court Road. Condemned to death, after representations from Madrid he was reprieved and given ten years. Aurora was deported.[11]

Some spies simply lost their nerve. Joseph Marks was arrested when he disembarked at Tilbury on 18 July 1915 from Rotterdam, travelling on a Dutch passport. He was happy to tell all he knew and was rewarded with a five-year sentence.

Carlos Kuhn de la Escosura was arrested when, after a tip-off, officers boarded the SS *Gelria* in January 1916, which was on its way from Holland to Spain. He was travelling on a forged passport and was brought to Ramsgate for questioning. He said he was a sales representative in films and produced a few one-reel love stories to back his story. He claimed he had gone to the German consulate in Rotterdam to get a passport and outside he had met a man selling ready-made passports. Without realizing he had committed any offence, he had bought one. In fact he had long been connected with the German Secret Service. He could not be tried since he had not landed voluntarily, so was sent to Reading gaol from where he escaped on 3 November 1917. He reached London and sought asylum at the Spanish Embassy. He was, however, handed over and re-interned.

In November 1916, the 28-year-old American-born journalist and spy George Vaux Bacon was arrested, caught in London after letters to Holland were intercepted. When his bags were searched, the substance Argyrol was found in the tops of his socks; he was to have rinsed them in water to make invisible ink. Bacon always claimed 'it was a fantastic story designed to produce an exclusive story on espionage' and that he had simply been playing the Germans along. The Argyrol, he said, was to be used to cure venereal disease. In January 1917 he was sentenced to death but immediately reprieved so that he could go to New York to give evidence in the trials of his spymasters there, Albert A. Sander and Charles Wunnenberg, who had paid him £25 a week. In March the pair received two years apiece and a fine. Bacon served a year in a prison in Atlanta and then tried to join the American army; he was rejected because of poor eyesight.[12]

One spy for whom it is possible to feel at least a grain of sympathy is the Belgian diamond-cutter, Leon Francis van der Groten. When war broke out he went to Breda in Holland, from where he assisted in the escape of French and Belgians from German-occupied zones. He also supplied Richard Tinsley with information. Van der Groten's greatest mistake was to assist a man called Theunissen who had been helping French intelligence and who was having an affair with Groten's wife. In early 1917 Theunissen told Tinsley that Groten was about to betray the Allied Services. Tinsley promptly hired Groten and, equally rapidly, Theunissen persuaded a friend to pose as a German agent to recruit Groten to carry out a mission in England. In June 1917 Theunissen and Groten went to Hull together where Groten was immediately arrested — while Theunissen returned to Holland and the matrimonial bed. Van der Groten was sentenced to death, but this was commuted after strong representations by the Belgian government.[13]

There was a considerable amount of politicking over the fate of Alfred Hagn, a Norwegian who was arrested on 27 May 1917. He was, wrote Basil Thomson, 'one of those young people who write novels,

German Espionage in Essex

PHOTOGRAPHING THE SITE OF THE SECRET MAGAZINE
AS SEEN BY A RESIDENT OF EPPING

THE HOUSE, NOW TO LET, OCCUPIED
BY THE PARTY OF THREE. THEY
WOULD GO OFF WITH CYCLES & CAM-
-ERAS SOMETIMES TOGETHER, OFTEN ALONE

HORSES FODDER, ETC.
THE HARMLESS FOREIGN
GENTLEMAN, WHO PHOTOGRAPHED
PICTURESQUE BARNS ETC. & WHO COLLECT
-ED MUCH USEFUL INFORMATION WITH
A GLASS OF MILK

A FAVOURITE EVENING RENDEZVOUS, YE OLD THATCHED HOUSE HOTEL
WHERE THEY CHARMED AND AMUSED THE FREQUENTERS

The full story of these three Germans, who left the neighbourhood at the end of June, after a residence of six months, is told on the opposite page.

How the Military Spies Who Have Been Staying at Epping Conducted their Operations

1. Illustration from the *Graphic*, 18 July 1908.

Above, left to right
2. James Edmonds (1861–1956), head of MO5, the forerunner of MI5.
3. William Melville (1850–1918), who in 1903 became head of Britain's new secret intelligence agency and was later described as MI5's 'master spy'.
4. Mansfield Cumming (1859–1923), left of frame, the first head of what was to become MI6, c.1907.
5. **Left** Basil Thomson (1861–1939), assistant commissioner of the Metropolitan Police and head of Special Branch, who interrogated spies on MI5's behalf, c.1925.
6. **Below** British Intelligence Corps officer taking down the names of wounded German prisoners brought in from the war front.

7. **Right** One of many Berlin to Washington cyphers decrypted by Room 40.
8. **Below** Official memo concerning the decrypted Zimmermann telegram which helped to bring America into the First World War, from Walter Page, the US ambassador in London, to the US Secretary of State.

SECRET.

L.W.   February 24th 1 p.m. 1917.

HW 3/179

Balfour has handed me the translation of a cipher message from Zimmermann, the German Secretary of State for Foreign Affairs, to the German Minister in Mexico, which was sent via Washington and relayed by Bernstorff on January 19th.

You can probably obtain a copy of the text relayed by Bernstorff from the cable office in Washington. The first group is the number of the telegram, 130, and the second is 13042, indicating the number of the code used. The last but two is 97556, which is Zimmermann's signature.

I shall send you by mail a copy of the cipher text and of the decode into German, and meanwhile I give you the English translation as follows:-

"We intend to begin on the 1st of February unrestricted submarine warfare. We shall endeavour in spite of this to keep the United States neutral. In the event of this not succeeding we make Mexico a proposal of alliance on the following basis:-

'Make war together - Make peace together'. Generous financial support and an understanding on our part that Mexico is to reconquer the lost territory in Texas, New Mexico and Arizona. The settlement in detail is left to you.

You will inform the President of the above most secretly as soon as the outbreak of war with the United States is certain and add the suggestion that he should on his own initiative invite Japan to immediate adherence and at the same time mediate between Japan and ourselves.

Please call the President's attention to the fact that the ruthless employment of our submarines now offers the prospect

of

9. **Above** Edith Cavell's grave at the Tir National in Brussels.
10. **Below** Letter from Vernon Kell to Cavell's mother, enclosing photographs of her grave.
11. **Inset below** Portrait of Edith Cavell in her youth, *c.*1890.

M.I.5.

Personal.

4 December, 1917.

Dear Madam,

I have been directed by the French Authorities to forward you the enclosed photographs which, they consider, you would like to possess in memory of your daughter; and I have no doubt they will prove to you a sad but precious link with Miss Cavell's memory.

The large photographs were sent by the French but I had copies made in case you would like to make use of them.

I have the honour to be,

Madam,

Your obedient servant,

Mrs. Cavell,
24, College Road,
Norwich.

12. **Above** Execution of a German spy by French troops, *c.*1916.
13. **Below** French soldiers monitoring telephone calls for espionage at the Allied communications centre in Aisne, France, *c.*1916.

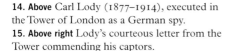

London Tower
November 5ᵗʰ 14

To the Commanding Officer of
the 3ʳᵈ Battallion G Guards
London.

Sir

I feel it my duty as a German officer to express my
sincere thanks and appreciation to the guards and sergeants
being and having been my guardians.

Although they never neglected their duty they have
shown always the utmost curtesey and consideration
towards me.

If it is within the frame of reglements I wish
this may be made known to them

I am, Sir, with profound respect
Carl Hans Lody
Sr Lieutenant Imperial German
Naval Reserve II

14. Above Carl Lody (1877–1914), executed in
the Tower of London as a German spy.
15. Above right Lody's courteous letter from the
Tower commending his captors.

16 Below Passport of German spy Carl Muller,
who was shot in the Tower of London in 1915.

Ministère Impérial
des Affaires Étrangères.
Consulat Général
de Russie dans les
Pays-Bas.

Rotterdam, le 30/12 Janvier 1915
/12 Février

Nº 166

Le Consulat Général Impérial
de Russie prie les Autorités compéten-
tes de bien vouloir accorder au sujet
Russe Charles Frederic Muller se
rendant en Angleterre, toutes les
facilités compatibles avec les Lois
et Règlements en vigueur.

Le Consul Général

17. **Above** The different faces of Mata Hari (1876–1917), the Dutch seductress shot by the French as a German spy.

18. **Right top** Franz von Rintalen(1877–1949), the German spy working in America.

19. **Right below** Fritz Duquesne (1877–1956), the German master spy (figure standing).

20. **Far right** Marthe Richard (1889–1982), the French spy and aviatrix.

21. Sheet music of the song 'The Ladder of Love' with messages in secret ink between the bars, posted to the Germans by naturalized British subject Kenneth Rysbach.

paint Futurist pictures, compose poetry and prose for magazines and fail to arrive anywhere'.[14] Thomson was being a bit unkind. Hagn, educated in the United States, was 34 years old; he had devotedly nursed his invalid mother, published a novel, *Skindirer*, and was quite well thought of as a painter.

He arrived in England on 9 October 1916 as the correspondent for the Norwegian newspaper *Dagblader*. He returned to Norway and came back on 13 April 1917, landing in Hull. His aim was to get to Paris, although he signed a declaration that he would not try to leave England for the duration of the war. He was now also representing the *Bergens Tidende*. He took lodgings in Tavistock Square in Bloomsbury and an Italian professor at the same boarding house denounced him. A letter to Julie Hagn was intercepted; no invisible ink was found on it, but there was a trace of cotton wool on the paper. (German agents were taught to damp paper with cotton wool and an ammonia solution.) A second letter dated 15 May was intercepted, and this time there was invisible ink. The information was purely about British morale. Hagn's room was searched and a bottle labelled 'Throat gargle' was found to contain the invisible ink.

Immediately after his conviction on 27 August 1917, Hagn wrote a petition for clemency, which was backed by representations from the Norwegian ambassador in London. For propaganda purposes it suited the authorities to have his sentence reduced to life imprisonment, and his death sentence was duly commuted. Two years into his sentence he began to starve himself in Maidstone prison believing that 'such a wretch as he had no place on earth'. He was repatriated on health grounds on 13 September 1919.[15]

Horst von der Goltz, adventurer, fantasist and syphilis sufferer, arrived from Holland on 3 November 1915. He landed at Harwich, was interviewed and allowed to go to London. A tail was put on him in the form of Sergeant Harold Brust who, in his memoirs, describes how he followed him from Liverpool Street station to an east coast town and then on to the dunes, where Goltz simply disappeared. Goltz was back in his hotel the next morning and on 13 November gave himself up to the Foreign Office. He claimed later that during the night he had eaten 2lbs of incriminating evidence which, if discovered, would have hanged him. Interviewed by Thomson, Goltz said he had been seen in Holland by Ernest Maxse and that he could give details of times of Zeppelin raids as well as the sources of the Emden and Leipzig supplies. He handed over keys to a safe deposit box and was charged, initially with espionage, and also with the lesser charge of failing to register as an enemy alien. Goltz thought of himself not as a spy but as a secret diplomatic agent:

> a man who directs spies, who studies their reports, who pieces together various bits of information and who, when he has the fabric complete, personally makes his report to the highest authority or carries that particular plan to its desired conclusion.[16]

It was decided that there was insufficient evidence to proceed on the espionage charge and Goltz presented an elaborate defence to the charge of failing to register. He had been born in San Francisco and, on the death of his father, had gone to Germany at the age of 12; he left five years later and became a Mexican citizen in order to join the Mexican army. As a Mexican officer on leave he was not required to register. The Mexican authorities wrote to the Home Office to say there was 'not a vestige of proof to support that statement'. In fact papers were found showing Goltz to be a major in Pancho Villa's army, with a leave of absence signed by Madero. The magistrate took the view that Goltz should have registered, and sentenced him to six months' hard labour at Pentonville prison. At the conclusion of his sentence he was to be deported. In fact he stayed in Brixton and Reading prisons for the next fifteen months.

There was more to Goltz than first appeared. He wrote to 'Blinker' Hall telling him that he had valuable information to offer. Hall replied that, before he would make a trip to Brixton, Goltz would have to give at least an outline of what he had to volunteer. Then a doctor called Robert Emerson wrote from Mexico that Goltz was a 'professional spy' who claimed to be a relative of the field marshall of the same name. He could be identified by a scar in his left groin incurred when the doctor had treated him for buboes. If Goltz was deported, 'a most dangerous, well trained German spy will have escaped'.

What Goltz could say was that he had been involved in the conspiracy led by Franz von Papen to blow up the Welland canal. When papers were taken at Falmouth from von Papen they showed payments to Goltz, alias Bridgeman Taylor. At the end of the month, in return for indemnities against prosecution, Goltz made a series of affidavits setting out his part and that of the others in the Welland canal and other conspiracies. In April 1916 Goltz was sent, with Brusch as his minder, to America to give evidence against his co-conspirators.

The voyage was not a success. The idea was that Goltz should pose as a Manchester cotton broker and Brusch as his secretary, but secrets are difficult to keep on board a liner, and unfortunately there were no provisions for keeping Goltz away from the other passengers. Worse, by mischance he met a *New York World* journalist to whom he gave his version of his life, including spying at an early stage for the Russians, amorous adventures on the Riviera and how he had duped the British Home Secretary.[17] Later, Brust claimed to have asked him how he disappeared on the East Anglian coast. Goltz told him that he had been picked up by submarine and dropped off in Kent.

British nationals convicted of spying generally got long sentences. They included the son of a naturalized British subject, Kenneth Rysbach, also known as Kurt Herlot de Rysbach and Charles Courtenay, who was born in the Singapore Straits Settlement to a French mother. In 1935 he told a *Daily Express* reporter that his father was Swiss and that he had been educated at Harrow and the Lycée Commerciale in Paris. Rysbach, a music hall juggler, claimed that he been dancing in Germany when war broke out and was denounced or deserted, or both, by his partner. He said he had been interned on 4 August. He was released and told to report to the authorities three times daily. He was rearrested on 6 November 1914 and detained in Ruhleben, where he was recruited as a spy. He arrived in England on 27 June 1917 and sent messages to August Brochner in Christiana, to whom Ludovico Zender had been writing. These took the form of sheet music of the songs 'On the Way to Dublin Town' and 'The Ladder of Love' with messages in secret ink between the bars.

Part of the information supplied was relatively innocuous and dealt with morale and the promise of things to come:

> I shall soon be one of the interpreters at the war office in London and
> have promised my brother some money and he will tell me all the news
> of the fleet so I await your orders and can do nothing without money.[18]

But the remainder gave the position of a munitions factory in Richmond. Rysbach was traced to Stockwell Road, Brixton, where he was living with his fiancée Ena Graham, a music-hall trick-cyclist. He had just got work at £5 a week dancing at the Princes Theatre, Glasgow.

His story was that he had never intended to spy for the Germans and had kept a tube of secret ink merely as a souvenir. During questioning, he agreed that he had received £130 from a German spymaster, but that he was merely playing his master along. He told the arresting officer: 'The information I wrote is not worth a hang. It is not worth anything, you can see for yourself. Only give me a fighting chance; send me to the front.'

He nearly got away with it. The first jury at his trial could not come to an agreement but, at the retrial in October 1915 with Mr Justice Darling and the hanging judge Mr Justice Avory in charge, a second jury convicted him. Asked if he had anything to say before sentence was passed, Rysbach said he would die ' singing God Save the King'. In the end he did not need to. Avory said the death penalty could have been imposed but, because there was no evidence to contradict his story that he had been interned, he would be sentenced to life imprisonment. During his sentence he volunteered to work for the British Secret Service, an offer which was declined. His brother, a leading stoker, was cleared of any suspicion of involvement.[19]

On 14 August 1914 Robert Blackwood, a lodging-house keeper, was arrested in Liverpool. Incredibly, earlier in the year he had written to the German Embassy asking whether they needed his services, and he heard from Leo Sirius in Berlin setting him some simple questions about defences in the Mersey. Blackwood replied correctly using Abel Heywood's Almanac, freely available in the city, to tell Sirius the number of guns at New Brighton Fort—and was rewarded with two £1 postal orders. He received a set of more demanding questions and failed in his replies. Sirius had known the answers to the first questions already and was merely testing Blackwood. He wanted much more detail but, before Blackwood could reply, the police came knocking.

In 1915 Sir Joseph Jonas, German-born former Lord Mayor of Sheffield and owner of one of the largest manufacturers of crucible cast steel, wrote to the papers:

> I am doing everything that lies in my power to bring about the glorious triumph of the British Army and so do away with that system of militarism in Germany which I have consistently opposed from my earliest youth.[20]

Jonas had come came to Sheffield at the age of 21. He gave up his German nationality in 1872 and was naturalized three years later. He was the first German consul in the city.

In 1918 he and his clerk Charles Vernon, who had changed his name from Karl August Hahn, appeared at the Old Bailey charged with conspiracy to obtain and communicate information useful to the enemy as long ago as 1913. He had obtained information regarding the manufacture of rifles by Vickers for the British government and passed it on to one of his largest customers, who also wanted to know about British aircraft and a new steering process for British warships.

Jonas' defence was that he was merely obliging a good customer. There was a story, however, that Jonas had made a bet in his club that, 'We shall be in Paris in three weeks', although his supporters maintained that he had refused the bet. Acquitted of the felony charge, Jonas was convicted on a lesser misdemeanour and on 16 July he was fined £2,000. Vernon was fined £1,000. A fortnight later Jonas was stripped of his knighthood — but his disgrace did not prevent the Lord Mayor of Sheffield and the Master Cutler attending his funeral when he died on 24 August 1921.[21]

One man who lasted until 1916 was Albert Bright, a Rotherham iron merchant. In April that year he was sentenced to penal servitude for life. He was thought to have been obtaining information from Ben Brooks, a munitions worker at Vickers, from as early as 1905. When Brooks died, Bright approached his son Harry at the old man's funeral and asked him to get information about armour plate, lyddite guns and shells. Bright said he would pay £100 for information, but Brooks junior told some of his fellow workers, who suggested he report the matter to his manager. There was, however, no hard evidence that Bright had actually passed on the information, which probably saved him from the gallows.

One of the more curious of spies was Ignatius Timothy Trebitsch Lincoln. Hungarian-born and Jewish, he converted to Anglicanism and was a curate in Appledore, Kent, before he became a journalist. He was elected Liberal MP for Darlington in 1910, but lost his seat in 1914 and was then given a position as censor of Hungarian and Romanian correspondence. It was not long before he was asked to resign and, worse, also to resign from the National Liberal Club. It seems this humiliation turned him and he offered his services as a double agent. When this was rejected he went to Rotterdam and agreed with the German consul, General Gneist, to hand over spurious information to the authorities in England. On his return he was arrested and effectively deported to America. In 1916 he was arrested in New York for earlier forging the signature of the Quaker philanthropist, Seebohm Rowntree, on a £700 draft. On his return to England, Lincoln received three years' penal servitude.

The last of the First World War spies to be tried at the Old Bailey was Louise Matilda Smith, whose case was heard on 4 March 1918. Born in 1867 at Heidessorf with one brother who was a staff officer in the German army and another in the submarine service, in February 1913 she had married John Henry Smith, a chemist who had lived in Zurich for 20 years. They came to England in 1915 and lived in Manchester until John Smith died in 1917.

In April that year it was discovered by the censor's office in Cape Town that Smith had sent, in a parcel containing tea, cuttings from pro-German Swiss newspapers whose publication was banned in South Africa. It happened again that month and later in August after which the authorities took action. A letter to Smith's mother in Germany sent to an accommodation address in Switzerland was intercepted. Two more followed, containing information in code about Zeppelin and submarine activities:

> On Sunday I went out to see the place where the big birds roost. It was full of birds and some of them are very big indeed. It is said that they will soon take longer flights. I do not think that the great eagles that fly over us are frightening these birds; they only make them angry.[22]

Her explanation at her trial that the letters were to her uncle who was a keen ornithologist was not received well. There was, however, no evidence that Smith was an agent, simply that she was pro-German. It was agreed that her attempts were amateurish. Mr Justice Avory, while pointing out that the death penalty was an available option, sentenced her to ten years' penal servitude. Her daughter was fined £50 and recommended for deportation.

Just how many spies were caught? Churchill gave the number as 30, James Edmonds as 43. War Office records suggest there were 28 tried by court-martial in England, of whom two were acquitted. Additionally, 40 were tried at a military court abroad and ten at a general court martial abroad. Of those convicted, nine were executed and the death sentence commuted in another six. Other penalties ranged from 28 days imprisonment to penal servitude for life.[23]

These men and women were the tip of the iceberg. Most spies were never caught. During the First World War, the Admiralstab (German Naval staff) sent at least 120 agents to Britain, some on several missions. The largest number by far were Germans. There were also 19 Dutch and 14 German Americans. Five of the naval agents were women.

Paul Daelen completed five missions and was later awarded the Iron Cross. He spent the war reconnoitring Liverpool, Cardiff and Glasgow as well as Plymouth and Falmouth, unhindered. Paul Brodtmann, the managing director of the Continental Tyre Company who had actually been named in Edmonds' largely spurious list in 1909, survived until the end of the war, making his way backwards and forwards to Europe.

Another of the long-serving spies who went unmolested was Maria de Styzinska Brett-Perring, the widow of a British officer who had committed suicide in dubious circumstances in Monte Carlo. Probably recruited by Despina Psycha (or Storch), over the years she had spied for at least six countries. In the war she claimed to have worked as a nurse in France and, as she had certainly been the mistress of a German officer in Berne, was under a high degree of suspicion when she volunteered to work for Britain. She was allowed to go to Pontarlier in France, with the authorities there being given strict instructions that she should not be allowed into Switzerland.[24]

Perhaps the most important of those who got away was Jules Silber, who had worked for the British in South Africa but then came to England where he acted unsuspected as a spy in the Censor's Department throughout the war. Towards the end of the war, through a combination of restrictions and ill-health—he found himself too weak to swim to a boat which had agreed to take him out of England—Silber remained in England until 1925, at one time working for a film company. By then British citizens were allowed to go to Ostend for the weekend without a passport and he escaped into Holland under the wire at Eschen on Whit Sunday that year.[25]

There could, however, still be gentlemen's agreements among spymasters. Some spies were allowed to come and go under a *laisser-passer*, so to speak. Cumming, for one, still believed it was possible to conduct espionage on a civil basis. When told that Colonel von Ostertag —the former military attaché at the German Embassy and now director of German espionage in England with his HQ at The Hague—had been seen in Bond Street, he replied:

> It is quite possible. The Colonel's mother is English. She lives at Kew. I heard the story and sent him word that he needn't have any hole and corner business with me. I told him if he merely wanted to come over unofficially and see his mother and not to spy, it could probably be arranged.[26]

Later, when Cumming heard von Ostertag had died in Holland, he is said to have remarked: 'Yes, but what does he mean by it?'[27]

Chapter Eight

I don't believe Wilson will go to war unless Germany literally kicks him into it. Ambassador Walter H. Page, 12 February 1917[1]

ROOM 40 AND THE ZIMMERMANN TELEGRAM

On the first night of the war, the British ship *Teleconia* sailed to Emden, near to where the Dutch coast joins the German. Using grappling irons, the crew ripped up German communication cables which ran on the sea bottom through the Channel — one to Brest, another to Vigo, the third to Tenerife, and two to New York. Brought to the surface, the cables were cut and let sink again. That left the British-owned Eastern Telegraph cable in the Mediterranean, which presented no problem, and one more cable to which the Germans had access. This ran between West Africa and Brazil and was principally owned by America. After some delicate negotiations, which excluded America, the cables were pulled by Eastern Telegraph. Germany was now obliged to rely for its communication on its wireless station at Nauen, outside Berlin.[2]

The significance of communications was starkly brought home when one of the great cryptographic errors occurred in the first weeks of the war. In August 1914 the Russian army was deployed in an attempt to trap the entire German force in a pincer movement at Tannenberg in East Prussia and then move on to Berlin. Unfortunately, an order found on the body of a Russian officer killed on 20 August spelled out the Russian aims. The Russian general Samsonov had allowed some messages to be sent unencoded. The messages were intercepted, and as a result, on 31 August the Russian Second Army was effectively wiped out. Up to 30,000 men were killed and another 90,000 taken prisoner—the worst defeat of the Russians since Borodino in June 1812. Samsonov later shot himself.[3]

During the first month of the First World War code-breaking by British Naval Intelligence, if it existed at all, was amateurish in the extreme. After Germany's overseas cables were cut, its services had to resort on a daily basis to wireless messages or foreign cables, all of which could be intercepted. Signals in code were brought to the Admiralty, but the Director, Sir Henry Oliver (known as 'Dummy') had no one on his staff who could break, let alone interpret, them.

It was more or less by chance that Oliver recruited Alfred Ewing, then the Director of Naval Education, during lunch in mid-August at the United Services Club. The idea that Ewing—one time Professor of Engineering at Cambridge, with knowledge of radio telegraphy as well as an interest in codes and ciphers—might be his man apparently came to Oliver while walking across St James's Park to his club.[4]

The old boy network contributed information. Ewing heard from a barrister friend and amateur radio ham that he and another friend had been able to pick up German signals from Nauen. Eventually 14 listening posts were established in Britain—the first in Hunstanton, with three others in Malta, Otranto and Ancona in Italy. Ewing faced some stiff challenges: at the beginning of the war he had been given a completely bogus code-book with which to work. Nor did his initial recruits help much. A.G. Alastair, a language teacher to the Admiralty, came along with three others during their summer vacations. They may have known German, but they knew nothing of code-breaking. But, by early 1915 Ewing managed to recruit men from King's College, Cambridge, including Alfred, known as 'Dilly', the brother of Monsignor Ronald Knox and regarded as the most brilliant member of the team. Other Cambridge men included the Reverend William Montmorency, a translator of early German theology. Later, men from outside academia, including the publisher Nigel de Grey from Heinemann, were recruited.

So gradually, for a time at least, the cryptology department came together. The War Office had established its own code-breaking unit under Brigadier F.J. Anderson, who had rudimentary experience of communications intelligence derived from the Boer War. Ewing sent Alistair Denniston, who would become head of Bletchley Park during the Second World War, to liaise with the unit. But there was no progress until 1 October, when French cryptanalysts broke the main German military code and generously handed it to the British. Progress lasted only a fortnight, with rivalry intensifying between Anderson's men and those of Ewing; seemingly it was easier to fight each other than the supposed enemy. By mid-October all co-operation had ceased, probably after Winston Churchill from the Admiralty told Lord Kitchener of a military intercept before the Field-Marshal heard of it from Anderson. Co-operation was not resumed until 1917 and even then it was on a strictly limited basis.[5]

Back in the autumn and winter of 1914 the naval cryptographers were not only ignorant of the subject, they were working in extremely poor conditions. Lacking dedicated premises, they could not all use Ewing's office at the same time so they worked a shift system. If Ewing had visitors, the cryptographers were packed off to his secretary's boxroom until the meetings ended. This situation lasted until November when 'Dummy' Oliver was promoted to Chief of Staff and Captain William Reginald Hall, known as 'Blinker' because of a facial twitch, was appointed Director of Naval Intelligence.[6] His first act was to move the cryptology department to the more spacious Room 40 in the Admiralty Old Building. Even more valuable was his decision to appoint Commander Herbert W. W. Hope to analyze the German intercepts. Hope knew neither German nor the art of cryptology, but he did have consummate seamanship and 'the ability to read the enemy's mind'. His appointment was, thought one of his underlings Nobby Clarke, 'a stroke of genius'.[7]

As well as the appointments of Hall and Hope there were three quite separate strokes of luck for naval intelligence. The first occurred on 11 August 1914 when, unaware that war had been declared, a German-Australian steamship was boarded near Melbourne by the Royal Australian Navy, which confiscated the Handelsverkehrsbuch (HVB), the code-book used principally by the German Admiralty to communicate with merchant shipping but also used by the High Seas Fleet. The Australians did not realize the HVB's importance and so it did not arrive at the Admiralty until the end of October. Despite its capture, the Germans continued to use the HVB, albeit in limited circumstances, for another 18 months.[8]

On 6 September the German cruiser *Magdeburg* was wrecked in the Baltic. Winston Churchill was informed by the Russian naval attaché that the body of a German officer had been picked up with the Signalbuch der Kaiserlichen (SKM); 'clasped in his bosom by arms rigid in death were the cypher and signal books of the German Navy'.

A week later these 'sea-stained priceless documents' were in the hands of Churchill and Prince Louis of Battenberg, the First Sea Lord.[9] After a number of false starts, caused mainly through Ewing's failure to grasp the principles involved, the SKM was eventually deciphered by the Fleet paymaster, Charles Rotter. When the Germans changed the code he broke the new one in short order.

The final stroke of luck that year was the recovery by a British trawler fishing off the island of Texel in the North Sea, of a lead-lined chest containing a copy of a third German naval code-book, the Verkehrsbuch (VB).

In fact within the year there was a fourth discovery, which without doubt would turn out to be the most important of them all. This was a code-book owned, and lost in the spring or early summer of 1915, by the German vice-consul Wilhelm Wassmuss, the so-called 'German Lawrence of Arabia' or 'Wassmuss of Persia'.

But before then, in early 1915 a new German transmitter began operating from Brussels using an indecipherable code. The Germans had discovered a disabled station when they entered the city in the first days of the war. Alexander Szek, a Croydon-born Austrian, had made it fit for use. Szek and his father had moved to Brussels in 1912; he had stayed there when his father went to Vienna, but other members of his family still lived in the Croydon area.

'Blinker' Hall was told that the code might be got from Szek, and after a great deal of pressure the authorities agreed to try to persuade him to help. The first plan was for Szek to steal the code and bring it to England. This would have been worthless: no code and no Szek would mean that the code would be changed almost overnight—so Szek agreed to copy it piecemeal, column by column. These fragments were sent to Major Laurie Oppenheim in Holland, but after three months Szek apparently baulked at finishing the job, refusing to copy the final part until it was agreed that he and the British agent working with him could leave together for England. The code duly arrived in England, but Szek was never seen again, and there is no coherent account of what happened to him.

One story is that the unfortunate Szek was arrested in Charleroi in September 1915 and executed by the Germans on 10 December 1915 —but 'Blinker' Hall is said to have told the Admiral of the Fleet, Sir Henry Oliver, that he had paid £1,000 to have Szek disposed of. This would have been in character: it was said by Edward Bell, the American attaché in London, that Hall was 'The coldest hearted proposition there ever was. He'd eat a man's heart and hand it back to him.'[10]

The sad thing is that Szek, like so many others, probably died in vain, because within a matter of weeks Wassmuss lost his copy of the code.

Wassmuss was born in 1880 in Ohlendorf, 60 kilometres southeast of Hanover. He was described as a short, broad and heavy man with a high forehead, blue eyes generally looking upward and a slightly melancholy mouth. He entered the German Foreign Office in 1906. Sent first to Madagascar, he was promoted to vice consul and assigned to the German consulate in the Persian Gulf port town of Bushehr in 1909. For the next years he studied the desert and its tribesmen. In 1913, he returned to Persia. At the start of the First World War, Wassmuss realized his ambition to incite a revolt against the British and lead the Persians in a guerilla war. His plan was accepted by his superiors, and he became one of the world's first covert action operatives—an agent who does not specifically try to collect information but who functions in a foreign country to obtain a definite result.

In early February 1915 Wassmuss sailed a river steamer, the *Pioneer*, down the Tigris to a point below Kut al Amara in Mesopotamia. From there he and his party moved eastward into Iran where he began work to end Anglo-Russian domination in the Middle East.

A fervent patriot, Wassmuss was also a mystic, a megalomaniac and, like Lawrence, a man with a deep love for the Arabian desert and its peoples, their customs and languages. Wearing the flowing robes of a desert tribesman, he became known as Wassmuss of Persia, and successfully organized the Tangsir and Qashghâi tribes to revolt against the British in the south of the country. This was the zenith of Wassmuss's career. The local police at Shushtar tried to arrest him as a spy. Wassmuss was warned of the danger he was in and managed to escape, travelling south to the town of Behbahan. The apparently friendly local chieftain invited him to dinner, then promptly placed him under armed guard. The plan was to sell Wassmuss to the British but, during a lengthy discussion of the price to be paid, Wassmuss escaped, leaving behind his luggage and the German diplomatic code-book.

Like Lawrence, Wassmuss was an inveterate liar, and his version of his escape is romantic in the extreme. He claimed that he told his guards that his horse was sick. As a result, every hour he was escorted under guard to the stables. By the early morning the guards had tired of taking him and he was allowed to go on his own. Seizing this opportunity, he leapt on his horse, and with one amazing bound was off into the desert. His bags were found by the British in the chieftain's courtyard.

However successful he was in organizing the tribesmen, Wassmuss was in urgent need of his lost luggage and went as far as seeing the governor of Shiraz to make a formal demand for its return. This was impossible as it was now held by the India Office in London. The German code-book was later found in one of his bags and sent to Room 40.[11]

The lost code enabled Hall's team to read German diplomatic communications throughout much of the First World War and, over the next 18 months, the intelligence gleaned, when heeded, was to have immense and most favourable repercussions for the Allies.

Room 40 had already made a significant contribution to the war effort. Broken codes had enabled it to warn of an attack by German battle-cruisers on 14 December 1914 on Scarborough and Whitby, in theory undefended ports and so protected by the Hague Convention. Unfortunately, as with later information on the Germans' position in the North Sea, the warning was not followed, and the raiders fled unharmed. Along with an attack on the protected Hartlepool, 122 civilians were killed and more than 300 wounded.

On 23 January 1915 Hall's team had decrypted ciphers showing that the German Admiral Hipper was leaving the Jade estuary with his Dreadnoughts. Although Admiral Beatty sailed at once and destroyed the *Blücher*, the Admiralty had failed to pass on Hall's information that there were no submarines in the area. Beatty thought he saw a periscope and turned 90 degrees to port. A further series of blunders and mis-signalling took place allowing three German battle-cruisers to escape.

In the spring of 1916 Hall's team decoded the German naval commander Admiral Rudolph von Scheer's messages communicating his intention to lure the Grand Fleet into a battle in which he would then produce the entire *Hochseeflotte*—but once again Room 40's excellent intelligence was wasted by the Admiralty.[12]

The Room 40 team continued to expand, and once again success bred infighting between Ewing and Hall, who wanted the code-breakers subsumed into the Intelligence Division. It would end in victory for Hall and in 1916 the return of Ewing to academia. He continued to visit Room 40 once a week until May 1917, when he left the Admiralty.

In January 1917 the German Foreign Secretary, Arthur Zimmermann, sent a coded telegram that made history. It was addressed to Johann von Bernstorff, the German Ambassador in Washington, to be forwarded to Heinrich von Eckhardt, the German Ambassador in Mexico.

In November 1916, at the age of 50, Zimmermann had been made Foreign Secretary, and, for a time, the appointment of this large, apparently good-natured, big-moustached, big-drinking, middle-class bachelor was welcomed by the Americans as a sign that liberalism was taking over from military autocracy; it was 'as if he were the sun that would begin the melting of the snows'.[13] They were wrong. Zimmermann was a hard-liner. It was he who told the American Ambassador James W. Gerard that there were half a million trained Germans in America who would join the Irish in beginning a revolution, only for Gerard to reply, 'In that case there are half a million lamp-posts to hang them on'.[14]

Just as von Papen had wanted to attack Canada in 1914 to tie up that country's troops, so in 1916 Zimmermann had negotiated with Roger Casement, the Irish patriot, about sending 25,000 soldiers (principally Irishmen captured on the retreat from Mons) and 75,000 rifles to Ireland to start an uprising. Casement got as far as landing from a submarine at Tralee Bay, County Kerry. But Room 40 knew of his potential arrival. He was captured and later executed.

Three days after Casement had landed, a German ship, the *Libau,* renamed the *Aud Norge* and flying Norwegian colours, was sent to Ireland loaded with 20,000 rifles, However it failed to rendezvous with the patriots and, intercepted by HMS *Bluebell,* was scuttled.

This was not Zimmermann's first attempt at global troublemaking; he had been involved in an attempt to foment revolution in India towards the end of 1915. And he had already been condemned for what was seen as his unbending attitude to the death of British nurse Edith Cavell in 1915, saying, 'It was a pity Miss Cavell had to be executed but necessary'.[15]

Zimmermann planned to bring Mexico and Japan into the war on the German side. His logic was simple. With U-boats carrying out unrestricted attacks on shipping and with American troops occupied in a war with Mexico, and possibly Japan, the Allies would be forced to surrender within six months. There was some prospect that the Mexican President Carrranza might react favourably to the plan; the American General 'Black' Jack Pershing was at the time leading a 12,000-strong punitive expedition into Mexico in reprisal for Pancho Villa's attack on Tucson. In fact Pershing's expedition floundered deeper and deeper into the country, ending in failure and a humiliating withdrawal. Meanwhile, Woodrow Wilson, 'the friend of all nations engaged in the present struggle',[16] was still valiantly trying to negotiate peace.

On 9 January 1917, Wilhelm II gave his authority for the unrestricted use of submarine warfare from 1 February. No announcement was to be made until the last possible moment. On 16 January Zimmermann sent his fateful telegram to von Bernstorff to be forwarded to Eckhardt. It stated that if the unrestricted submarine warfare did indeed threaten to bring America into the war he should approach the president of Mexico to enter the war on Germany's side. A second telegram was sent instructing the ambassador to take care of the first.

Zimmermann's telegram went via three separate routes. The first was the usual one from Nauen to Sayville; the second via the 'Swedish roundabout': Berlin to Stockholm and on to the Swedish embassies for onward transmission; the third was sent on an American State Department cable following an agreement which allowed the Germans to send confidential matter to their ambassador in New York. The telegram went through the State Department the next day.

All three telegrams were picked up by Room 40, and they began the work of decoding them. Meanwhile, von Bernstorff duly forwarded his telegram to Eckhardt, adding a line, 'Foreign Office telegraphs January 16, No. 1. Most secret, decode yourself ... End of telegram, Bernstorff'.[17]

When it arrived in Room 40, the Zimmermann telegram was handed to the duty cryptologists, the Reverend William Montmorency and

Nigel de Grey. The telegram was in rows of numerals in three, four and five groups. The only unusual thing was that the telegram was exceptionally long. The top group of numerals were 15042, a variant of the German code-book 13042.

It had taken a long time and much effort to obtain the code-book, but now the cryptologists were able to pick out words 'Japan', 'Mexico', 'For your Excellency's personal information', 'Most Secret'. Given that it was addressed to Washington, the telegram could only have been for von Bernstorff.

Two hours later there were still gaps, but it was clear that the message fell into two halves. The first announced that there was to be unrestricted use of submarines against merchant ships; the second that, if that failed to bring the Allies to their knees, then to propose to Mexico that she should form an alliance with Japan to fight America.

Montmorency and de Grey took the partially decoded result to Hall, who now had a problem: what should he do with it? The obvious course was to inform the Foreign Office, but he suspected there could be leaks in that department, and if the Germans discovered their code had been broken, a new one would be devised which might take years to break. The other problem was informing the Americans without them finding out that their telegrams were being read by the British. After all, if Britain could tap the traffic of neutral Sweden they might be doing the same thing with America—which, of course, they were.

Hall thought that using Lord Arthur Balfour, whom the Americans trusted, might be the answer—but that still left the question of disclosing the skill of the British code-breakers. He thought of stealing a copy of the telegram in Buenos Aires, one of the staging posts of the roundabout, but then there would be no proof that the telegram ever reached Mexico.

In the late afternoon of 31 January von Bernstorff gave notice to Secretary of State Lansing that all-out U-boat activity would begin in less than eight hours saying, 'I know it is serious, very. I deeply regret that it is necessary'. Three days later von Bernstorff was sent home and the exuberant British naval attaché Guy Gaunt, believing that America was now sure to enter the war, sent Hall a telegram 'I get drunk tonight'.[18]

On 3 February Woodrow Wilson broke off diplomatic relations with Germany, but was still shilly-shallying about a declaration of war.

Hall now went to the Foreign Office and within three weeks obtained a copy of the telegram with inside help from the Mexican Telegraph Office. By now it had been completely decoded and Hall showed it to Edward Bell of the American Embassy, who promptly denounced it as a fake. However, it was agreed that Balfour should take it to the American Ambassador Walter Page, a pro-war man.

The Americans would be told where they could find the Zimmermann telegram and the subsequent one from von Bernstorff. Code groups would be wired to London, and Bell would decode it at the American Embassy—technically American soil—with the help of de Grey. The American government could then say it had been decoded on American soil by Americans.

Wilson finally released the contents to the newspapers and the *New York Times* carried the banner headline 'GERMANY SEEKS ALLIANCE AGAINST U.S.'[19] The public reaction was one of disbelief, with the lawyer Joseph Choate, one-time ambassador to England, telling Gaunt it was a forgery. And then, on 3 March, despite advice from the propagandist Hearst newspaper man William Bayard Hale, Zimmermann admitted the telegram was genuine.

On 4 April 1917 America declared war on Germany, and American soldiers sailed for Europe.

Zimmermann, with a good deal of help from Room 40, had finally brought America into the conflict.[20]

Chapter Nine

Don't employ a bad character or a woman. Sooner or later they will fail you. Ferdinand Tuohy[1]

WOMEN SPIES FOR THE ALLIES

Nurses have, in general, always had a good press, described as angels or angels of mercy, ready to heal the sick and comfort the dying. In 1915 the English nurse Edith Cavell became a symbol of all that was good in her profession.

Often described as an English 'girl', at 49 Cavell was, in fact, approaching what was then late middle-age. Born the daughter of the rector of Swardston in Norfolk in 1865, she had trained at the London Hospital and had been a governess, a nurse and a nursing instructor before, in 1907, she was asked by Antoine Depage to run *École Infirmière Diplomier*, a nurses' training school in Brussels.

When war broke out, the school was converted to a hospital and, in November 1914, Cavell agreed to hide two English soldiers from the Cheshires, Lieutenant Colonel Dudley Bolger and Company Sergeant Major Frank Meachin, who had become separated from their unit after the Battle of Mons. For the next three months she looked after refugees and passed them on to couriers who would guide them to Holland.

In February 1915 her work expanded when she joined a much larger network based in Lille and Mons and which included Louise Thuliez, known as Alice, the network's most important courier. Thuliez, a schoolteacher from Lille, like Cavell is usually portrayed as a sweet innocent girl, but she, too, was a mature woman. Thuliez' second in command was Marie-Léonie Vanhoutte from Roubaix, known as Charlotte. Others in the network included Philippe Baucq, editor of the clandestine *La Libre Belgique,* the Countess de Belleville, and Princesse Marie de Croÿ and her brother, who used their houses —the Croÿs' chateau at Bellignes had a secret staircase—to hide the prisoners. Thuliez also distributed Baucq's newspaper and regularly passed on information about a munitions depot between Douai and Cambrai.

Cavell had been under suspicion by the Germans from early summer and on 14 June the nursing home was searched, but nothing was found. Then on 31 July Louise Thuliez and Philippe Baucq were found at his home with thousands of copies of *La Libre Belgique* and were arrested. Cavell lasted less than a week. On 5 August she was arrested and taken to St Gilles prison. In all, 35 members of the network were arrested in the following months.

Cavell was possibly tricked into making a confession after being told that the only way she could save the lives of Thuliez and Baucq was to come clean. Overall 7,000 refugees were thought to have slipped out of Belgium during the June, July and August of 1915 and Cavell accepted she had assisted 200 of them. The Germans would later say the number of escaped soldiers was around 20, 000.[2] Not everyone regarded Cavell as a heroine. The author Ferdinand Tuohy, a member of the Intelligence Corps in the First World War wrote:

> It was a woman who gave away most of the French espionage system in Belgium… Miss Cavell. It would be idle now to trace the cause of this collapse other than to where it belongs—to the trial of Miss Cavell, with its third degree revelations extracted by the Germans.[3]

On 11 October 1915 Cavell and Baucq were condemned to death. The Princesse de Croÿ saved herself by saying she did not know what had happened to the men after they left Brussels. The British authorities took the view that their intervention would not assist Cavell: 'I am afraid it is likely to go hard with Miss Cavell. I am afraid we are powerless,' wrote Sir Horace Rowland of the Home Office, while Lord Robert Cecil of the Foreign Office agreed that 'Any representation by us will do her more harm than good.'[4]

Appeals were, however, made by the Spanish and American ambassadors, who pointed out to the Germans that Cavell's death, added to the burning of Louvain and the sinking of the *Lusitania*, would simply cause their further alienation. Baron von der Lancken, leader of the political department of the Governor-General of Belgium, agreed that because of Cavell's work with German soldiers and her complete confession she should be reprieved—but negotiations foundered when the authorities moved so quickly that, along with Baucq, she was executed at dawn.[5]

On 11 October 1915, the night before her execution, Cavell took communion with Stirling Gahan, an English chaplain. He later told the world that Cavell had said: 'Standing before God and eternity, I realise this—patriotism is not enough, I must be free from hate and bitterness.'[6]

Just as in the case of Mata Hari, there were conflicting accounts of her death—all the soldiers had missed and an officer had applied the *coup de grâce* with a single bullet; the soldiers had deliberately fired high; Miss Cavell had fainted on the pavement and the soldiers insisted on shooting her now or never. There is also a story that a German soldier, Rammler, was executed for refusing to fire on Cavell, and that he was buried between Cavell and Philippe Baucq. The story is of doubtful provenance and seems to have been created by Reginald Berkeley in *Dawn,* his biography of Cavell.[7]

Joseph Ide recruited the Belgian Gabrielle Petit when she arrrived in Folkestone. She began her career as a spy helping her soldier fiancé, Maurice Gobert, cross into Holland to rejoin his regiment and then worked for Ernest Wallinger collecting information on troop movements in and around Tournai and distributing the underground paper *La Libre Belgique,* as well as being a leading figure in an underground mail service. The German agents Pinkof and Petermann were set against her, and she was betrayed and arrested in February 1916, tried in March and shot, at the age of 23, on 1 April. Curiously her death caused nothing like the outrage over that of Edith Cavell.[8]

Louise Frenay, or Derache, was another woman against whom German soldiers were said to be reluctant to fire when she was shot in Liège on 7 June 1915. She and two dozen others had worked for a network run by Justin Lenders. They had been denounced as train-watchers and one confessed, apparently after promises that they would all be treated leniently. The story goes that volunteers were called for the firing squads but, when there were none, a detail was selected. When, at dawn, the Belgians were lined against the wall at the Chartreuse fort and the soldiers saw they were to shoot a woman, they fired at her legs. She fell to the ground in agony and one report has it that a priest fainted. When the soldiers were ordered to reload, they refused. A non-commissioned officer was then said to have been ordered to administer the *coup de grâce*. The remainder of the prisoners was then shot.[9] Louise Frenay was one of eight executed that day including Lenders and Charles Simon, a British subject living in Namur. It was a bad time for those convicted of espionage by German courts.[10]

The War Propaganda Bureau run from Wellington House elevated Cavell's death into the War Crime of the Century.

> The execution of Edith Cavell 'a poor English girl deliberately shot by the Germans for housing refugees, will run the sinking of the *Lusitania* close in the civilised world as the greatest crime in history.'[11]

In November that year new breeds of chrysanthemums were named after both Cavell and Lord Kitchener.

At the time, propaganda was highly important. John Buchan headed the British War Propaganda Bureau, which produced pamphlets such as Conan Doyle's *To Arms!* and G.K. Chesterton's *The Barbarism in Berlin*. Other contributors included Rudyard Kipling, Ford Maddox Ford and John Masefield in a series which ran to over 1,150 pamphlets. Many were illustrated by the talented Dutch artist Raemaekers —who is perhaps best known for his depiction of the fallen Edith Cavell.

Reaction to her death can be contrasted with that towards two German nurses shot by the French for helping German soldiers escape. One German officer is said to have remarked 'What? Protest? The French had a perfect right to shoot them.'[12]

The Germans did what they could to deflect criticism, pointing out that the English killed suffragettes and that, earlier in the year, the French had shot the German women spies, Marguerite Schmitt and Ottilie Voss. The English press was quick to deny any similarities in the cases.

In the aftermath of the wave of outrage, all the other death sentences were commuted in England. Recruitment figures doubled. Even so, conscription had to be introduced the following year. From then on, Germany took a similar line and women condemned to death were generally reprieved. Not so German women spies in France.

Anne-Marie l'Hotellier, director of a hospice in Cambrai, helped hundreds of soldiers to escape. Caught in August 1916 by the Germans she was sentenced to 10 years' hard labour and was released at the end of the war. She continued working at the hospice until 1924.

The French-born Mme Fauquetot was sentenced to death after being caught spying by the Germans. The sentence was commuted to one of life imprisonment and she suffered badly in prison in Liège before being released by the Spartakistes. She was later decorated in England as well as in France.

Other Belgian women included Léonie van Houtte, who dressed as a peasant, spied behind German lines and was sentenced to 15 years' imprisonment; Marie Gervaise was shot in September 1914 for spying; Flore and Georgina Danel were executed together at Tournai; and Angèle Lecas was shot at St Armand after being convicted of carrying on a pigeon service. Mme Mailcet was condemned to death and reprieved because she was pregnant. Mlle Birel, arrested in 1915, ran a large *réseau*, and Henriette Moriamé continued to work after the execution of Louise Thuliez, helping Allied soldiers escape until she herself was arrested. She later joined a religious order and died on 28 August 1918.

Marthe Cnockaert McKenna's work as a nurse saved her life. She was trapped in her Belgian village when war broke out and she earned an Iron Cross for her efforts in the Roulers German hospital. She was then recruited into espionage by Louise Deldonck, a friend who was already working as a courier. McKenna first acted as a letter-box for a woman she named as Canteen Ma who sold vegetables and so had the freedom to roam the countryside. In turn she passed information on to another female agent, Number 63. From then on her involvement escalated.

McKenna was caught in 1916 after she and another agent dynamited a supply depot. Sentenced to death, her hospital work and the Iron Cross stood her in good stead, and she was reprieved to spend the rest of the war in prison in Ghent.

The 37-year-old Louise de Bettignies, whose code name was Alice Dubois or Ramble, was one of the spies recruited by the bureau at Folkestone that was staffed by British, French and Belgian officers.

She had been educated at Girton College, Cambridge, and had turned down the opportunity to be governess to Archduke Franz Ferdinand's children. After training in Boulogne and Flushing along with Léonie Vanhoutte (known as Charlotte), she began to work in February 1915 collecting and passing on information about troop movements and supervising a large network of both old and young workers. In all, she made nearly 20 visits to England. She and Charlotte were arrested in November 1915 when nine members of her network were swept up. For a time, British Intelligence hoped she might escape punishment because she had eaten the report she was carrying. Sadly, she did not. She was sentenced to death, although this was commuted to hard labour. Bettignies did not give up, organizing a strike in Siegburg prison in Germany against the practice of forcing women prisoners to assemble munitions. She developed a tumour in her chest and, after an operation in April 1918, died on 27 September.[13]

The Grandprez family from Stevelot—Elise, her sister Marie and brothers Constant and François—first helped escaped Russian soldiers hidden in the Ardennes and then became train-watchers and couriers, and ran a letter-box. Using invisible ink, Elise and Marie transcribed reports on to the pages of books and matchbox covers and sent them on to Lille. In March 1916, one of their group, Dieudonné Lambrecht, was caught and shot in Lille, but the network survived until January 1917 when Elise, her sister and brothers and two others, the Gregoires, were arrested. After being betrayed by Émile Delacourt, a double agent, she, Constant and André Gregoire were sentenced to death; while awaiting execution, Elise is said to have made small Belgian flags out of hair ribbon she had sent in, to wear before the firing squad at the Chartreuse de Liège. Delacourt was sentenced to death in his absence in 1922. The previous year another double agent Maurice Thielens was sentenced to death for his part in their betrayal.[14]

One of the great spy romances of the war was that between Marie Birckel, a schoolteacher living in Lorraine, and Emil Fauquenot. At the beginning of the war she had helped refugees, but then came to England, where she was questioned as a refugee herself on arrival in Folkestone. The Deuxième Bureau was impressed with her past work, and she was recruited. She was to join smugglers on the Belgian–Dutch border but she was arrested within a few days of arriving in Liège and imprisoned. Fauquenot, who had helped Marie get across the border,

lasted only a little while longer. In charge of the Maestricht information centre, he was betrayed and arrested on 1 July 1916. There was little evidence against Marie and it was not clear whether Fauquenot
had been arrested in Holland or Belgium. Both were sentenced to
death, but following the intervention of ex-King Alfonso of Spain,
they were reprieved. They were imprisoned in adjacent cells; she
counted German soldiers from her window, sending information to
the Allies through the nuns who staffed the prison. He escaped on 28
March 1918 and she was repatriated the day after the Armistice was
signed. They later married.[15]

Generally, women in espionage have been keen to make it clear
that, despite dangers and temptations, their virtue remained intact.
An exception was Georges Ladoux's protégée Marthe Richard, who
may not have been a *grande horizontale*, although she would no doubt
have liked to be considered one. In recent years Richard has rather
fallen from grace. Her exploits as a pioneer aviator have been down-
graded and, instead of a great spy, she is now regarded at best as a
one-mission woman (and not a terribly dangerous mission at that).

Born Marthe Betenfeld on 15 April 1889, Richard worked at a
dress manufacturer and on the streets of Nancy, where there were
complaints that she had venereal disease; she was given a card[16] and
spent some time in hospital. She then went to Paris where she again
worked as a prostitute for the Italian procurer Antonio Mazzini, who
claimed to be a sculptor, until she met and married, at the age of 18,
wealthy fish merchant Louis Richer. Their story was like a French
Pygmalion. He taught her grammar, diction and how to ride a horse.
She also became an aviatrix, although her stories about breaking
world records are spurious.

Richer was killed in 1914. Two years later, when Richard was having an affair with Jean Volain, a Russian who was working for the
Deuxième Bureau, she was introduced to Georges Ladoux. It was he
who sent her to Madrid to extract information from the naval ambassador, Hans von Khron, the nephew of General Lindendorff. According to Ladoux's story and Richard's own later memoirs, von Khron
set her up in an apartment in Cadiz and sent her on a mission to
Argentina with thermos flasks of weevils to poison a cargo of wheat
being shipped to France. With the help of a Deuxième Bureau agent
who was also on board, she drowned the weevils.

When von Khron found she was two-timing him, he thought of having her prosecuted, and ironically it was Mata Hari's lover Arnold Kalle from whom he sought advice. Kalle told von Khron to do nothing.

Later, Richard would admit to passing French secrets to von Khron, boasting rather proudly that she had done the same thing as Mata Hari but that while the unfortunate Dutch woman had been shot *she* was given the *Légion d'honneur*. Given that her memoirs were originally concocted by Ladoux, it is difficult to know just how much of her story is true.[17]

One of the great unsung heroines of the early days of the war was the 20-year-old nurse Marcelle Semmer, the daughter of the superintendent of a phosphate factory, who found herself left behind at Eclusier in the Somme. For a period of weeks after the French defeat at Charleroi, she obtained and passed on accurate details of the positions of German guns. She also pulled up a drawbridge over a canal at Eclusier and then threw the key into the water, so delaying the German advance for a day. She sheltered French soldiers in the tunnels of the mines in the area, helping them to regain their regiments. She was caught and escaped three times, once after being locked in a church. When sentenced to death (the first time) she is said to have told the tribunal 'Shoot me with French bullets and not Boche ones'. She was saved when the French artillery suddenly opened on the German post and she escaped. One story of her is that the French commander required his soldiers to salute her when she passed. Later she went to Paris and became a nurse. In March 1917 she was awared the Croix de Guerre.[18]

If Georges Ladoux had turned his attention to the small, dark, bespectacled *estaminet* keeper Mathilde Lebrun from Verdun, the widow of a non-commissioned officer with three children, he would doubtless have built her into a figure to rival Marthe Richard. But perhaps not. Wandering through No Man's Land behind the German lines does not have the same cachet as sleeping with the German naval attaché. Again, how much of Lebrun's exploits are publisher-made is now difficult to assess, but most versions of her story have her, a German speaker born in Lorraine, sent behind the lines after a court-martial as a way for her to prove her patriotism.

She claimed she had been in a shell hole under a barrage of shelling and about to be engulfed in 'liquid fire' when she decided she was safer surrendering to the Germans. She was questioned for a fort-night and finally pretended she would work for Germany. She was given the number R2. She claimed that over the next three years she made 13 trips across No Man's Land and was able to denounce Mata Hari (whom she alleged was at a spy retreat in Switzerland when she said she was in Spain) as well as the German spies Felice Pfaadt in Marseilles and Gimeno-Sanchez on the Riviera. She also claimed to be involved in the exposure of a dozen spies in Paris. How much is true and how much is a good story is, of course, another matter[19].

There were 11 women among the 332 Belgians who worked for escape or intelligence networks and were executed. This number does not include escapees shot or electrocuted trying to cross the border.[20]

Tuohy, never an unbiased observer—in his book *The Secret Corps* Germans are continually referred to as Huns and Boches—thought that the French used more women as spies than the British because French women were more intelligent. German women were simply 'scum'. A more likely reason was the language barrier.

Tuohy was not in favour of women spies at all, and in one diatribe wrote:

> In effect, women spies fail both in the head and in the heart, and also
> in character composition for the business on hand. Women are funda-
> mentally inaccurate. They experience a constant 'urge' to be working
> in limelight, jibbing at the patient compilation of dull details which
> forms the basis of spying. They talk… The root difference is, one
> supposes, that a woman, to be a spy, must be an adventuress by nature;
> whereas a man agent can just be any unit stepping from a train at
> Victoria Station each morning around 9 a.m.[21]

The train-watchers in *La Dame Blanche* and other networks counting their beans would not have recognized themselves. In Belgium women made up some 25 per cent of networks, rising to 30 per cent in the case of *La Dame Blanche*.

Chapter Ten

Now I have something to tell you that will surprise you. I thought it was too big a secret. This Captain, Captain Ladoux asked me to go into his service, and I promised to do something for him. I was to meet him in my house in The Hague. Mata Hari[1]

FRÄULEINS FOR THE KAISER

There is little doubt that the most famous of the First World War spies, male or female, was the Indonesian-born Margarethe Zelle, known as Mata Hari, who was executed at Château Vincennes on 15 October 1917. But was she an important spy? Was she even a spy at all? Was she simply an exotic *grande horizontale*, a consummate liar with a penchant for lovers who paid; who was careless of their nationalities, and possibly set up by a double agent?

Born in 1876, the daughter of the owner of a hat shop, at the age of 15 Zelle was seduced by, or at least became involved with, Wybrandus Haanstra, the headmaster of the nursery school where she was training.[2] At the age of 19, she married Rudolph MacLeod, twenty years her senior and a captain in the Colonial Army in the Dutch East Indies, after answering his advertisement in an Amsterdam newspaper seeking a companion while on leave. The marriage failed from the beginning because, according to her, MacLeod was not only a jealous wife-beater but also within a matter of weeks took up with prostitutes. In January 1897 they and their son, Norman John, sailed for the Dutch East Indies. In May 1898 she gave birth to Jeanne Louise, known as Non. In June that year, when the family was in Sumatra, both children became seriously ill and Norman died. One version of the death is that they had been poisoned by their nurse who, dying shortly afterward, confessed that her soldier-lover, who had been disciplined by

MacLeod, had ordered the poisoning. Other versions include an attempted rape by MacLeod of the nurse. The marriage further deteriorated and, with Non, they returned to Holland in 1901. On 26 August the next year MacLeod left his wife, taking Non with him. She did, however, manage to obtain a divorce settlement which required him to pay 100 Dutch florins a month towards her rent.

Margarethe Hari arrived in Paris from Amsterdam in 1904 as an artist's model. She failed at this, but on a second visit she took a position in a riding school, then a euphemism for prostitution, and was advised to become a dancer. The following year she made her appearance dancing at the salon of Mme Kiréevsky, first as 'Lady MacLeod' and then as 'Mata Hari', which translated as Eye of the Day. Opinion as to her talent differed, but she was beautiful and, at 5' 10", exceptionally tall, and it was thought that, in time, she might become a rival to Isadora Duncan. Her success grew: there was dancing at lesbian evenings for the American socialite Natalie Barney, engagements at the Folies Bergère and the Trocadéro Theatre and, importantly, an appearance at a *soirée* held by Baron Henri de Rothschild, which introduced her to *le tout Paris*.

For the next decade Mata Hari enjoyed a successful dancing career around Europe combined with that of a courtesan in the beds of politicians and high-ranking military, whom she particularly prized. In 1906 she became the mistress of Alfred Kippert, a lieutenant in the Westphalian Hussars, who took her to watch the Imperial Army manoeuvres in Silesia. In 1911 her lover was the financier Félix Rousseau, with whom she lived in Neuilly-sur-Seine and whose bank collapsed. After that there was General Messimy, who became the French minister of war in August 1914. In the summer of that year she renewed her liaison with Kippert. When they had broken up in 1907 he had given her 100,000 German marks and bank drafts for a similar amount for 1908 and 1909. Ten years later the payments would be used at her trial as evidence, however dubious, that she had long been a German spy.

In July 1914 while dining with her lover Griebel, a senior police officer in Berlin, she heard that Austria had invaded Serbia. A month later, trapped in Berlin without a travel permit, she wrote to another lover, the Austrian cavalry officer Baron Fredi Lazarini, that she feared she would not be able to get home to Neuilly. Once her papers were in order, she returned to live in Nieuwe Uitleg in Utrecht with yet another lover, the elderly Baron Eduoard van der Capellen, until on 27 November 1915 she obtained an English visa and prepared to leave for France, travelling first to England.

Detained at Folkestone when she arrived on the boat train for Dieppe on 3 December, she told the Police Alien and Military Authority that she was going to Paris to settle her affairs and then to sign for a professional engagement, she hoped in South America. The next day her story changed slightly. She was going to settle her affairs in Paris but then she would return to Holland and The Hague. Since the Baron had been called up that was the only place where he could visit her.

Her luggage was searched and she was allowed to catch the boat. But the next day a notice was circulated to all British ports warning them that she was 'not above suspicion and her subsequent movements should be watched'. This 'utmost unsatisfactory' woman was to be refused permission to return to England. The following year an MI5 notice, issued on 22 February, read, 'This woman is now in Holland. If she comes to this country she should be arrested and sent to Scotland Yard'.[3]

In April 1916 the British consul in Rotterdam refused to grant her a visa and when the Dutch Foreign Minister, Loudon, asked the British government to instruct the consul to overturn his refusal, the reply was decidedly sniffy: '[The] authorities have reasons why admission of lady mentioned in your 74 is undesirable'.[4]

By now Mata Hari was nearing 40 and was reduced to casual, if well paid, prostitution. As often happens with older *cocottes*, at least in fiction, she now fell in love with a younger man. In June 1916, she met 21-year-old Russian officer Vladimir de Masloff at what was euphemistically called a *salon* given by her friend Mrs Dangeville for officers on leave. On his return to the front, de Masloff lost the sight of an eye and his throat was burned in a mustard gas attack. He was sent to the Vosges to recuperate; Mata Hari was refused permission to travel to see him. Flushed with love, she seems to have had the idea of becoming a spy to raise sufficient money to pay off her debts and relinquish part-time prostitution. She approached a French Secret Service agent, the tall, chain-smoking, ash-spattered Georges Ladoux who, despite his claims, was never actually head of the Cinquième Bureau. He believed her to be a German spy already.

Mata Hari had the great idea that, through an introduction to General Moritz Ferdinand von Bissing, the officer in charge of the occupation of Belgium, she would seduce the Crown Prince. Quite what that would do for the war effort is not entirely clear. Ladoux's memoirs are so unreliable it is difficult to determine exactly what he had in mind, but it appears that he proposed she go on a mission to Belgium travelling via Spain and England.

During the intervening months notes were placed in Mata Hari's file (The National Archives MEPO 3/244) recording that she was suspected of having been to France on an important mission for the Germans, for which she had received 15,000 French francs, and that she was soon to be sent on another. In June 1916 a note was sent to Ladoux saying that, 'She has since been reported to us from Holland as being in German pay'. When in Paris, her movements were tracked on a day-to-day basis and her followers listed the men with whom she dined and slept, including the Marquis de Beaufort; English, Irish and Scots officers; a French general; and, slumming, an Italian captain of the military police.[5]

On 12 November 1916 she landed at Falmouth on a boat from Vigo, Spain, and was promptly taken into custody. Initially the British authorities believed her to be the German spy Clara Benedix from Hamburg, suspected of being a courier for the German consul in Barcelona. She maintained that she was Mata Hari, but accepted that she had met and travelled with Benedix. Clara, she said, was the same height as she but a little stouter. Curiously, both were said to have a drooping eyelid.

After a night at the home of detective George Grant (rather than in a police cell), where she had a bath but cried and refused to eat, she was taken to London where she stayed at the Savoy. Her 10 pieces of luggage were searched. When Sir Basil Thomson interviewed her she played what she obviously thought was a trick-taking card:

> Now I have something to tell you that will surprise you. I thought it
> was too big a secret. This Captain, Captain Ladoux asked me to go
> into his service, and I promised to do something for him. I was to meet
> him in my house in The Hague.

There followed an exchange of telegrams with the French office, which on 17 November replied that Ladoux had effectively denounced her, saying that he considered her extremely suspect and adding that he had not been able to gather definite evidence against her and therefore had pretended to make use of her in the hope of finding future proof.

She was, said the telegram, never an agent for the Cinquième Bureau 'who have always regarded her with suspicion'. At least they confirmed she was not Clara Benedix. She was released, but after applying to go to The Hague 'to marry Captain Vadince de Masloff' [*sic*] was refused permission to travel to Holland. She remained at the Savoy Hotel until there was a boat from Liverpool bound for Vigo. From there she left for Madrid on 11 December. She now had seven weeks of freedom left.[6]

Mata Hari now claimed that Ladoux was ignoring her. What she did not realize was that he was heavily involved in troubles of his own over treasonable plots for Paris newspaper proprietors to influence French opinion in favour of early peace with the Germans on less than favourable terms. When she found the name of Major Arnold Kalle, the German military attaché in Madrid, in the diplomatic register of the Ritz Hotel, she went to his home where she asked him why she had been confused with Clara Benedix—and went to bed with him before going back to the Ritz. So far, so good. If, so she thought, she could extract good information from Kalle, then Ladoux would reward her well.

She would later admit to pretending to be a German spy and telling Kalle that there would be a major offensive in the spring, and that a Greek princess had been urging the French to replace the neutral King Constantine with her pro-German husband. She also passed on news of low civilian morale in Paris. In return Kalle told her of an intended submarine landing in Morocco.

Men still fluttered round Mata Hari, including Colonel Joseph Denvignes, the French attaché in charge of espionage. Word got back to Kalle, who was extremely displeased. On their next meeting he passed useless information and gave her 3,500 Spanish pesetas, which she interpreted as a gift for her favours, and the French rather less kindly.

By the time she reached Paris on 3 January there had been rumblings of suspicion against her. A French agent had wanted to know why a Spanish senator and another man had been seen with her when she was known to be hostile to Britain and France.

In early January Kalle sent radio messages in a code known to have been broken by the French, which led to her being identified as a German agent H21. She was arrested in her hotel room on 13 February and, until her death, was lodged in the women's prison at St Lazare.

Mata Hari could not have been more unfortunate in the timing of her trial, which coincided with the collapse of the Chemin des Dames offensive, at which the French were estimated to have lost 118,000 men, which presaged mutinies in the French army as well as industrial strikes. An example had to be made of somebody.[7] Ladoux tailored his evidence at her trial to secure a conviction. It was certainly in his interests to promote his part in the trapping of a dangerous spy. There was also evidence that she had been controlled by Fräulein Doktor. In the climate that prevailed this was quite sufficient to convict her.[8] Ladoux thought that after she had been condemned she might make a confession to obtain a reprieve. He was wrong.

By the time of her arrest the police had ferreted through her friends. One, the cabaret singer Jeanne Druin, received 15 years with hard labour and another, Germaine d'Anglemont, came under particular scrutiny. She had once had an Austrian lover and in 1915 had made a number of trips to Switzerland. Before the war she had not a penny but during it she had money to splash around and was weighed down with jewellery. She was thought to have 2 million French francs in cash. At the time the police investigated her, d'Anglemont was living with a Pole, Maurice Zamösky. But nothing evidential was ever found. She may have been fortunate.[9]

Immediately after Mata Hari's execution, rumours began. The first was that she had been naked under her coat and at the moment before the members of the Zouave regiment were to fire she exposed herself to them. The even more entertaining story was that the Zouaves had been bribed to put blanks in their rifles. This accounted for her *sang-froid* in the minutes leading up to the execution. After they had fired, out of the woods rode her Spanish playboy lover Pierre Mortissac, who gathered her up and galloped off into a sunset already occupied by Robin Hood, there soon to be joined by the Swedish-American Joe Hill and later by Marilyn Monroe and John F. Kennedy. Other stories had her locked away in the Fort de Har. In August 1929 when a woman was washed up on a Bordeaux beach, there were rumours that she was Mata Hari; it turned out she was Benita Adamason from Riga.[10]

Mata Hari was the third woman spy to be shot by the French that year. First to have that dubious privilege was Marguerite Francillard, shot at Vincennes à la Caponnière on 19 January 1917; once again, conflicting stories about her life and death abound.

Originally from Grenoble, Francillard was less than average height, with reddish hair. She had been under suspicion in 1916 and had been questioned and kept under observation. She told a friend that her lover, Franz, was annoyed by men pestering her and that she was going to Paris from where she would write. In fact, she was a typical post-box, receiving and passing on messages to her lover. Arrested, she was sent to St Lazare where she was placed in Cell 12, which Mata Hari would later occupy.

Magnus Hirschfeld thought:

> With the greatest naturalness she confessed everything, but with such simplicity and genuine innocence that the court was divided. This was one of the few cases during the war when there was such a lack of unanimity about the guilt of a suspected spy. However, by a majority of one, the verdict of death was finally imposed.

Comte Émile Massard has the romantic story that, when giving Francillard absolution before her death, the priest made her promise to call out 'Pardonnez-moi la France et Dieu and Vive la France' before the firing squad. And, he says, she did so, facing the squad bravely and without a blindfold.[11]

Another rather less romantic and probably more accurate version is Hirschfeld's:

> It was a very edifying execution when this naive child was tied up against the wall on 10 January 1917. Someone had been clever enough to convince Marguerite herself of her guilt but this was small comfort for her. One heard her shriek *Je demande pardon* and a moment later she was hanging there, a bloody corpse. She was photographed in this condition and subsequently, the picture was described as that of Mata Hari. The firing squad now filed past the corpse while the bugles played their melodies. And in Geneva the German agent sought a new mistress and a new messenger.[12]

Hirschfeld was wrong in one thing. Francillard's controller, Franz De Meyerem, a former Danish officer who served in the French Foreign Legion, was shot five days later, walking briskly to the stake and also declining a blindfold.

The second woman spy executed that year was Antoinette Tichelly, who worked for the Germans as Z160. She had been born in Paris in November 1870 to a German mother and worked for a time at large hotels in Mannheim and Frankfurt. Recruited by spymaster Grüber in 1915, she worked as a maid in the Hotel de la Marine, 59 boulevard de Montparnasse in Paris, and later in a munitions factory.

She first came under suspicion when the authorities noticed that all her postcards seemed to go to relatives and friends in Switzerland. Further interrogation showed that she had been questioning people on the whereabouts in the army of their husbands and sons. Convicted on 20 December 1916, she was shot, also at Vincennes, on 15 March, still maintaining her innocence and seemingly uncomprehending that she had done wrong, complaining she had killed no one. 'I haven't spilled any blood—you oughtn't to spill mine,' she told Massard. 'They think because they haven't fired a rifle or thrown a grenade they haven't done any wrong,' he wrote scornfully.[13]

Whether the beautiful 19-year-old Rose Ducimetière was more fortunate is open to question. She was raised in a Paris orphanage and was soon turned out on to the Boulevard Sebastopol by a Swiss-German waiter, Walter X. Information from her soldier clients was passed back to her pimp. She also wrote to them and, the story goes, was later sent to nurse at the Italian front where she questioned her patients about their military experiences. On her return to Paris in 1916 she was arrested at the Val de Grâce hospital.

Earlier, there had been previous Presidential commutations of death sentences on women spies including Catherine Weber, 'The Spy of Gizancourt', sentenced to death at Chalons on 15 November 1915 but whose sentence was commuted to 20 years forced labour.[14] But as the war dragged on, the French President, Raymond Poincaré, made it a principle to affirm every death verdict so that the courts would know that he would not interfere with the machinery of the law. On 24 April 1917 the court sentenced Ducimetière to death but then reversed it, substituting life imprisonment with hard labour. She died, still in prison, in 1933.[15]

It is difficult to know exactly how many women spies were shot by the French during the First World War. Émile Massard claimed there were only four—Aubert/Loffroy was the fourth—in Paris, and two in the provinces. He is certainly wrong. Sir George Aston claimed there were nine and these refer only to official executions. J.M. Spaight suggests there were nine with two prior to October 1915; F. Baumann puts the number at 14; while K. Baschwitz has it at a massive 81. There were, no doubt, many unrecorded ones.[16]

The two in the provinces to which Massard referred were most likely Marguerite Schmitt and Ottilie Voss. On 17 February 1915, 25-year-old Schmitt, born at Thiaucourt of French nationality, was arrested in Nancy. She had travelled via Switzerland from Anoux near Briey, then occupied by the Germans. She admitted, under questioning, that she had been sent to obtain information on troop movements in the area as well as the strength of troops camped between Bar le Duc and St Menehould. In her possession was a book of questions prepared by a German officer. When tried before a Council of War she simply said, 'I'm sorry'. She had been paid £9. She was executed on 22 March, two days after she had been condemned to death.

The 33-year-old Ottilie Voss gave her name as Jeanne Bouvier when she was arrested near Bourges on 27 February 1915. German-born from the Rhine provinces, she was unmarried and for the seven years before the war had lived near Bordeaux where she gave German lessons. When war was declared she returned to Germany and was employed as a spy visiting southern towns such as Lyons, Montpelier, Nice and Marseilles, with instructions to report on troop formations, railway military transportation and the disembarkation of troops, particularly of black soldiers. On 11 February she reported back and was given £8. She was provided with a further £9 and returned to France. On 1 March she made a full confession and was condemned to death. A petition for a retrial was refused as was an appeal for clemency on 16 May, and she was shot the next morning.[17]

There were also executions in Marseilles. On 22 October 1916, 26-year-old Felicie Pfaadt (R17 in her German network) was shot[18] and in January two years later a Swiss singer, Regine Diane, was executed after an attack on port security. A Mlle Lamart was condemned to death in August 1915, as was Sidona Ductret in June 1918.

On 25 January 1918, two prostitutes, Josephine Alvarez (or Redoutte) and Victorine Francher, were condemned to death for passing intelligence. They had been obtaining low-level information about the American Expeditionary Force and passing it to a 'Swiss merchant'. They were shot on 6 May 1918 in Nantes.[19]

Marussia Destrelles, an actress who appeared in provincial theatres, apparently committed suicide in 1916 in Switzerland. One of her brothers had been convicted of being a German spy and she became one also. Believing she was being watched by the French Secret Service, she offered to work for them. As part of a trap she was left alone in a room with what purported to be a list of French agents, and was given time to copy part of it. A name near the top was of a man suspected of treachery by the French who three weeks later was shot by Germans. The story goes that the French leaked her; after she was taken to dinner by a German officer the pair went to her room, where he gave her Veronal and spread the bed with roses, creating the impression that she had staged her own death.

Another version of the story is that Destrelles was a Polish widow and had been the mistress of a Romanian theatrical agent whose brother was convicted by the Swiss for spying for the Central Powers. A letter was intercepted in which she wrote that she had to be in Geneva to study for a role in a play, of which he was to pretend to be the author. The French consul in Lausanne investigated the matter and fell in love with her. She applied for a visa to go to France; this was granted on condition she gave up all contact with the Romanian and his friends. She was found dead in her hotel room covered in flowers after having dined with a friend of the French consul.[20]

A not dissimilar story is told about Blanche Potin, a dancer and *soubrette* who had worked for French Intelligence since before the war. In June 1916 she was sent to Paris to gain information on German movements in Belgium and to report to an agent either in Brussels or Antwerp. Silence. She had fallen in love with a German officer and betrayed a number of Allied agents. She disappeared, possibly to Scandinavia, and a woman answering her description was strangled in a Copenhagen hotel at the end of the year.[21]

In his mildly pornographic work dressed up as sociology, *The Sexual History of the Great War*, Magnus Hirschfeld described one highly talented woman spy as:

> ...the stout lady known by the *nom de guerre* of 'Turkish Delight' who
> had an equal fondness for men, money, alcohol and paté de foie gras,
> and of whom it was known that she stood on the payroll of every land
> as well as on the suspicious list of every land. This lady had more
> names to her credit than anyone else... She was an efficient spy, being

able to influence women also, but her personality was so striking that during the war she could only be used in neutral territory. Towards the end of the war, however, she managed to reach America and this proved to be her undoing, for all the way from Madrid to New York, she was observed in the company of a couple and among them a sort of triangular relation. When they disembarked separately at New York, she was arrested, her baggage opened and a number of important papers found. She maintained a stubborn silence, but one morning in June 1918, she was found dying in her cell from the effects of poison.[22]

This clearly refers, if not wholly accurately, to 23-year-old Despina Storch (also known by a host of other names) and her involvement with the Count Robert de Clairmont, Elizabeth Nix and the Count de Belville. Probably born in Constantinople, with a German mother and Bulgarian father, Storch resembled the silent screen vamp, Theda Bara. She married an English officer, James Hesketh, and was known by his name for some time. A friend of von Bernstorff, she was in America in 1915, the same year she was arrested in Madrid under the name of Nezie. She was identified by the French Secret Service as Mrs Hesketh and only released after some serious string-pulling by Germany. She returned to America via Barcelona and Havana, but her network was infiltrated by a young American agent and, on 18 March 1918, she was arrested along with Nix and the Count de Belville.

All were to be deported to France when Storch died from pneumonia at Ellis Island. Early reports, however, said she had taken poison to avoid deportation and the firing squad. The *New York Times* thought it very peculiar that both Storch and Maria Kretschmann de Victorica, another spy on Ellis Island, could have independently contracted pneumonia when both were about to confess. The paper thought that either they had 'self-injected pneumonia germs' or had been 'infected by a scientific murderer of the Imperial German Government camouflaged as a person on Ellis Island'. Storch is said to have introduced Marie Brett-Perring, that most underrated woman spy, to the espionage game.

Plump, blonde, Argentinian-born Maria Kretschmann de Victorica, dubbed 'the beautiful blonde woman from Antwerp', was sometimes thought to be Fräulein Doktor. Born in Buenes Aires in 1882 to German parents, she was educated in Germany where she wrote a

number of silent films. It was there she met the German spymaster
Colonel Nicolai. In 1914 she became the wife of the Chilean Jose de
Victorica in what was seen as an arranged marriage so that she could
use her husband's neutral status to move freely during the war. In any
event, he disappeared shortly afterwards.

Over the years a number of disparate coups including Dublin's
Easter uprising and the loss of Kitchener and the HMS *Hampshire*
have, also quite wrongly, been attributed to Maria's attentions. In 1918,
along with another agent, Carl Rodiger, also known as Hans Wessel
(who replaced von Bernstorff in the spy system) and who was travelling
on a Swiss passport, she was sent as an agent of the Propaganda Division of the German Foreign Office to monitor South American relations with the United States and to help in sabotage work.[23] For a time
she lived at the Spencer Arms on Upper Broadway. She was then
traced to the Netherland Hotel, but by then she was gone. Under the
name of Miss Clark she had moved to the Hotel Nassau on Long
Beach. By now, the American code-breaker Herbert Yardley was inter-
cepting and translating the ciphers.

When Maria was arrested on 27 April 1918, a scarf impregnated
with secret ink was found in her hotel room. She was charged with
conspiracy to bomb British and American ships. In poor health
brought about, in part, by her drug addiction, she was transferred to
Bellevue hospital. This 'stout German lady', resplendent in a sable
coat with muff to match, two clusters of diamond rings and one set
with a large emerald, was brought to give evidence at the trials of the
Irish agitator Jeremiah O'Leary (who, she said, had helped her send
secret messages to Germany) and, in 1919, of alleged spy Willard
Robinson.[24] Although she was still under indictment she was released
at the end of the war, after which she lived at a Catholic convent in
New York. She regarded herself not as a spy but as a 'German propagandist caught and gotten stranded by the war'. She died on 12
August 1920 at Maluk's sanitarium at 41 East 78th Street and was
buried at the Gates of Heaven cemetery, Kensico.[25] The indictments
against Rodiger and ten others were dismissed on 22 October 1922.

Given the life-and-death nature of espionage there is not a great deal
of comedy in the business, but one amusing incident occurred when

the naked Lieutenant John William Spaulding of the Sixth United States Infantry, from nearby Fort Oglethorpe, a major army training centre, was found naked under the bed of the rich Baroness Lona Shope Wilhelmina Sutton Zollner in the Hotel Patten in Chattanooga on 13 December 1917. She was lying on the bed partially disrobed. Both were taken to the police court. The five times married 44-year-old baroness and Spaulding, half her age, were charged with indecent and immoral behaviour. They each paid a $10 fine.

But there was worse to come. The baroness faced an additional charge under the Espionage Act 1917. There was evidence that she had details of port departures in code. She was also married to a 'dangerous alien'. Her son, a midshipman at Annapolis, had learned to sing the German national anthem as well as a 'Prussian battle song'. She had visited the training camp, danced with the officers and apparently had 'more than one under her spell'.

Zollner's defence to the immoral conduct charge was that the lieutenant had come to her room to get an aspirin. She had certainly written him titillating love letters and they had discussed marriage, but there was no question of any immoral behaviour. She 'took a spell with her heart and fell asleep' only to be wakened by the house detective.

Unexpectedly, the judge ruled that her letters did not prove her immoral conduct, and, since she had not been found *in flagrante*, she was released on a bond of $2,500 with a condition that she did not contact any military personnel except her son; she was to live at her brownstone on Madison Avenue and report her movements twice a week. She was never obliged to stand trial and it is doubtful whether she ever saw Spaulding again.

Spaulding was court-martialled and acquitted and went on to serve in Europe where he was promoted to captain. The only real casualty of the whole affair seems to have been the baroness' son, who was expelled from Annapolis.[26]

Chapter Eleven

*Mr von Papen, very naturally, never informed me of any instructions
he might have received from his superiors to arrange for questionable
enterprises of the character indicated. Without further evidence I do
not consider it to have been proved that such instructions were received
by him.* Count Johann von Bernstorff [1]

THE KAISER'S MEN IN AMERICA

Even before it was accepted—particularly after the Battle of the Marne
—that the war would not be 'over by Christmas', the more astute of
German diplomatic minds (and they certainly included Count von
Bernstorff, German ambassador to Washington) realized that the key
to victory would be to keep the United States out of the conflict. Once
America entered on the side of the Allies, Germany could never win.

From the time of the declaration of war in Europe, President
Woodrow Wilson maintained a policy of absolute neutrality. The
Kaiser's men in America, therefore, had a triple purpose. The first aim
was legitimate propaganda to influence America against joining the
war on the side of the Allies. The second was the illegitimate one of
fomenting strikes and sabotage to prevent munitions going to Europe
and Russia. And, as the war staggered on, the third was to lure Mexico,
and later Japan, into joining the German cause. In particular, if Mexico
could be persuaded to wage war on the United States this would keep
American troops out of Europe. The reverse was just as welcome: if
sufficient money were spent fomenting trouble in Mexico, the United
States might just be persuaded to attack it.

To promote these aims, the Germans used a mixed bag of spies:
immigrants loyal to Germany; German military officers; and adventurers or, less romantically, mercenaries, 'up for kicks'. They appear to
have had a degree of independence in the execution of their missions.

The principals of the German *klatch*, centred around New York's Broadway, were headed by the ambassador, the elegant, urbane, charming von Bernstorff, a man who held degrees from five universities including Princeton. With him were the military attaché Franz von Papen at 60 Broadway; the naval attaché Karl Boy-Ed—the half-Turkish protégé of Admiral von Tirpitz—in the German consulate facing Bowling Green; and at 45 Broadway in the Hamburg-American building, the commercial attaché, Heinrich Albert, six feet tall, slender, blond and bearing duelling scars. Albert was the paymaster of all undercover operations and was described by Wilson as 'the directing and most dangerous mind in all these unhappy intrigues'.[2] They used the German-American club at 112 Central Park South as a rendezvous; other meetings were held at the Manhattan Hotel at 42nd and Madison. Within months they were joined by a man sent from Berlin with a seemingly bottomless pocket, who was said to have had £7 million at his disposal—Franz von Rintelen. He would cause both the Americans and the Germans all sorts of problems.

From the start von Papen, accredited to both Washington and Mexico, had favoured the criminal line, suggesting to von Bernstorff that it would be possible to launch a series of attacks on Canada from the Great Lakes, so ensuring their American troops remained at home to defend their country rather than sailing for Europe.[3]

It was not a line of thought which appealed to von Bernstorff, and so von Papen turned his attention to sabotage. He planned to dynamite the Welland canal running between Lake Erie and Lake Ontario, through which shipping had to pass to avoid the Niagara Falls and which was the principal supply artery of grain from the northwest. Canadian troops were already training at Valcartier, Quebec; the idea was that they would now have to be kept at home.

Sabotage began, however, in the early hours of 1 January 1915 at the Roebling plant at Trenton, New Jersey, which, among other things, made anti-submarine netting. With 300 workers on the premises, saboteurs managed to disable the fire alarm system and start a number of small fires which quickly spread. Within a matter of hours, eight acres of factory buildings and a block of workers' homes were destroyed. The next month von Papen paid Werner Horn, a one-time coffee-plantation manager and naval reservist who had been sent to New York, $700 to blow up the Vanceboro bridge across the St Croix river in Maine. In the early hours of the morning Horn, who claimed he had been anxious not to cause any loss of life, bungled the job, causing only minor damage. His hands had frozen in the cold and after the explosion was heard, he was found by the manager of his hotel trying to thaw them in the bathroom. It did not take much intelligence to put two and two together.[4]

Others in von Papen's pay included Albert Kaldschmidt from Detroit (one of a number of American cities considered to be a hotbed of German spies and saboteurs), who carried out a series of explosions at the Peabody company in Walkersville, Ontario, the Windsor armouries and the Detroit screw works.

As for propaganda, the Germans made a series of terrible blunders from which the Allies were largely free. First, there was the burning of Louvain,[5] then the shooting of Edith Cavell and, perhaps the greatest political catastrophe of them all, the sinking of the liner *Lusitania*.

Back in England on 30 March 1915 Neville Chamberlain wrote to Vernon Kell that he had just received information from a reliable source that there was a scheme to destroy the liner:

> A very close German friend has confided to my informant that an effort will be made to blow up the *Lusitania* at Liverpool after arrival there across the ocean. So far as he knows the idea is for a passenger to take the explosive with him as personal luggage and to secrete it on the vessel shortly before arrival at Liverpool with a time fuse to give the passengers sufficient time to leave the ship before the explosion takes place. No attempt will be made to destroy any ship on sea carrying American citizens. When the attempt will be made or by whom is not within my knowledge but my informant thinks from what he knows of his German friend and his means of getting information, that the matter should be very carefully attended to by the Cunard Co.

Chamberlain's informant was partially wrong about the *Lusitania*, but the ship did not last much longer. On 22 April 1915 the German Embassy in Washington gave notice that it considered the liner an ammunitions ship and so a legitimate target, even though it was carrying women and children. It was torpedoed 15 kilometres off the Old Head of Kinsale on 7 May, sinking in 18 minutes with the loss of over 1,000 passengers and causing widespread condemnation of German policy.

Chamberlain had gone on to say that his informant had told him there would be no more attempts at procuring false passports but that:

... any work of espionage that can be carried out in England will be done by German-Americans who have qualified as American citizens and whose presence in England would not be likely to cause any suspicion if they went as tourists. Any person with a German name will be worth supervising. There is money in America for the work and persons will be found to take the risk of earning it.[6]

The passport ramp took many forms including sending suitably qualified derelicts from the Bowery in New York to obtain passports and then buying them from them for $10 apiece. They were then sold on for $30. For a time this operation was run from Bridge Street, Lower Manhattan by Hans von Wedell, a former New York journalist. When Wedell was recalled to Germany, his successor Carl Ruroede made the mistake of buying four passports from Albert Adams, a New York detective, and compounded it by explaining how the forgeries were done.[7] He received three years' imprisonment, but overall he fared better than Wedell: the *Bergensfjord* on which Wedell was sailing back to Europe was intercepted on the way to Germany, and he was taken off by a British patrol boat which then sank.[8]

Three weeks before the sinking of the *Lusitania* in 1915 the German High Command had sent Franz von Rintelen to America, travelling on a Swiss passport under his sister Emilie's married name of Gasche. His instructions were to restore the currently deposed Mexican General Victoriano Huerta to power—and so steer President Wilson into another political indiscretion, preferably one of even greater magnitude than that of Vera Cruz in April 1914.

Having seized power in an earlier coup, in February 1913 Huerta had organized the assassinations of the previous incumbent Francisco Madero and his deputy, in an operation known as *La Decena Trágica*. Wilson had refused to recognize Huerta, instead supporting his rival General Venustiano Carranza. After a minor diplomatic incident at Tampico, when sailors from the USS *Dolphin* went on shore to unload supplies and were arrested, on 21 April 1914 Wilson heard that the German steamer *Ypiranga* was bringing 200 machine guns and 15 million cartridges to be unloaded at Vera Cruz for Huerta. An American ship blocked the *Ypiranga*; American marines landed at the port and seized the Customs House in a battle which killed 19 Americans and 126 Mexicans. Although the Americans were obliged to make a humiliating apology to the Germans for blocking the *Ypiranga*, Huerta never recovered politically from Vera Cruz and, after defeats by Dorote Aranbuto (or Pancho Villa as he was better known), went to Spain shortly before the outbreak of the First World War.

The 38-year-old aristocratic von Rintelen spoke good English and had been in America with the Disconto Gesellschaft, Germany's second largest bank, for three years from 1906 before leaving for Mexico. As a result, he already had a wide and charmed range of business and social acquaintances. After he left New York he had married and, when war broke out, he rejoined the navy as a financial adviser to the Admiralty General Staff. Together with Robert Fay, who had fought in the Vosges and been awarded the Iron Cross, he returned to America on 3 April 1915.

Fay, who had lived in Manitoba just after the turn of the century, and his brother-in-law the mechanic Walter Scholz, had opened the Riverside garage in New Jersey and from there ran a factory making 'pencil' bombs used to cripple ships carrying supplies to the Allies. Over 40 ships were attacked and several sunk. In May 1916 the *Kirk Oswald* arrived safely in Marseilles where the bombs were discovered and traced back to Fay. The authorities had become suspicious when Fay tried to buy a large quantity of Trinitrotoluol from the French Chamber of Commerce. When his rooms were raided dynamite was found. He and Scholz were followed to Grantwood, New Jersey and, so one story goes, after a detective sneezed they had to be arrested prematurely. At the time they had been planning to travel to Chicago. Scholz commented, 'It looks like 20 years doesn't it?', but in fact it was only seven. Fay escaped from Atlanta Federal prison and made his way to Baltimore where he was told by the German detective Paul Koenig to go to San Francisco. Fearing he would be killed, instead he went to Mexico and then Spain. He was arrested in September 1918 and was returned to America to serve the remainder of his sentence.

Apart from the task of enticing Wilson into attacking Mexico, von Rintelen's other aims were to buy out DuPont's munitions works and, with a series of strikes and sabotage, to put a halt to production in other companies. After setting up the financial company Bridgeport Projectile with Heinrich Albert, he bought up gunpowder and then destroyed it. He also worked to organize the Labor National Peace Council which was intended to be used to cause strikes and go-slows on the waterfront and in factories. Through his business agent David

Lamar, von Rintelen invested over half a million dollars in the Council, much of it siphoned off by Lamar for his own use. He also worked with Fay on the improvement of the pencil bombs on the liner *Friedrich der Grosse* then interned at Hoboken.

In the midst of all this activity, one counter-espionage success came when Wolf von Igel, ironically dubbed the Arnold von Winkelried of Wall Street,[9] attached to the German embassy and masquerading as an advertising man, was arrested, tried and imprisoned. On 18 April 1916 when American Secret Service agents raided his offices he claimed to be on German territory saying, 'Shoot and a war will start'. They did not, and it did not, but boxes of incriminating documents were seized. In von Igel's safe was also a letter from the German Consul General in Shanghai giving an account of Secret Service activities in the Far East.

Von Rintelen was recalled on 6 July 1916, his usefulness apparently exhausted. It was also thought his activities were becoming too well-known, and his arrest was imminent. Certainly the Americans had been dogging both him and General Huerta, now returned from Spain, to the extent that their every meeting and telephone call had been logged. His recall came two days after the detention of Huerta in Newman, New Mexico. Huerta was charged with conspiracy to violate United States neutrality laws. For a time he was under house arrest but was later sent to jail in El Paso where he died of cirrhosis of the liver on 13 January 1916.

Travelling once again as Emile Gasche on a neutral Dutch–American liner, von Rintelen ran out of luck when in August 1916, following a tip-off, he was arrested after the vessel came into English waters and he was found in his cabin at Southampton with a well-known West End actress.[10] He knew enough of his sister's home life and his brother-in-law's business to provide convincing answers about his assumed identity and nearly survived the interrogation at Scotland Yard by Basil Thomson. He also convinced the Swiss minister. At the last minute 'Blinker' Hall, who had come to the interview, suggested that the English legation in Berne be asked whether it was at all possible for Emile Gasche to be in London.[11]

Von Rintelen's version of the story is slightly different. He claims that he was allowed to go to the Hotel Cecil in the Strand that evening, but when he heard the words Swiss Legation he realized the game was up, asked to speak to Hall and admitted to being a German officer. He was wined and dined by Hall before he was sent to Donnington Hall where he was to be interned for the next 21 months but from which he escaped. He was retrieved from Leicester a few hours later.[12] In 1917 he was sent back to America to be tried for conspiracy to foment labour agitation and received a year's imprisonment. When on 7 February 1918 he was sentenced for passport fraud and a conspiracy to plant bombs on British ships, the judge commented that he was sorry the death penalty was not available. In all he received a total of 50 months.[13]

Various theories have been advanced about von Rintelen's recall and arrest. One suggestion is that von Papen, jealous of his success, sent a coded message to Germany saying he was becoming a risk; he knew that the British had broken the code and would keep a watch on his rival. Another, which was confirmed by Lord Newton in 1933, is that 'Blinker' Hall himself sent the recall telegram. Yet another is that he was recalled over his 'social gallivanting' with Anne Leward, the niece of Abraham Lincoln's Secretary of State. On 2 July 1915 she wrote that von Rintelen was a secret but intimate emissary of the Kaiser. 'His utterances are distinctly offensive and his threats alarming'.[14]

Von Papen first met Horst von der Goltz at the German consulate on 22 August 1914 and sent him to Baltimore, under the name of Bridgeman Taylor, with a letter instructing the German consul there, Karl Luederitz, to supply him with whatever help he needed. He was to recruit men from the crew of a German ship then lying in the north German Lloyd docks. He had already recruited Charles Tucker, or Tuchhaendler, in New York, and von Papen supplied him with three more: A. A. Fritzen of Brooklyn, a discharged purser on a Russian liner; Frederick Busse, 'an importer'; and Constantine Covani, a New York private detective.

The Baltimore sailors reported for duty, but were sent back because von der Goltz believed he was being watched so aborted the mission. He was then sent to Captain Hans Tauscher of the Krupp factory offices at 320 Broadway to obtain 300 lbs of dynamite. This consignment was loaded on a barge near Black Tom Island and taken to 146th Street from where it was carried in suitcases to the German Club in Central Park South and later to von der Goltz's home.

Using his Bridgeman Taylor alias, he set off for Buffalo on 10

September and took rooms at 198 Delaware Avenue. Suddenly that mission was also aborted. He claimed this was because the Canadians had already left camp. He also maintained he was being watched by US Secret Service agents. Nevertheless he had kept two incriminating telegrams, so arrests followed.

The purser Fritzen, who had tried to cross the border into Mexico before being arrested in Los Angeles in March 1917, was sentenced to 18 months. The detective Covani was never found. Tucker and Busse gave evidence at the Tauscher trial. Tauscher tried to plea bargain for a non-custodial sentence, but this was refused. There was evidence that he had purchased 7,000 Springfield rifles, 3 million revolver cartridges and 2.5 million rifle cartridges and stored them at 200 West Houston Street on 21 June 1915. He claimed these were job lots purchased for speculation, but the prosecution maintained they were for use in India. He was acquitted but deported. By now, von der Goltz had fled.

Things began to go seriously wrong for the Germans in America when one afternoon in July 1915 their embassy official Heinrich Albert lost an important collection of documents when he fell asleep on the subway. He and the German poet and propagandist George Sylvester Viereck, editor of the pro-German magazine, *The Fatherland*,[15] left the German beehive at 45 Broadway and took the Sixth Avenue El. After Viereck got off at 23rd, Albert nodded off. He woke as the train pulled into 50th but forgot to take his briefcase when he got off the train. The pair had been followed by the American Secret Service agent, Frank Burke, who picked up the case and made off into the crowd. Albert ran back to the train, saw the case had gone and, as Burke stood by the subway wall, rushed out to the street. Burke took another exit and telephoned headquarters.

Albert put an advertisement in the *New York Telegram* offering $20 for the return of his briefcase and its priceless contents. He would see them soon enough, but not in the context he hoped.[16] There may not have been enough in Albert's papers to justify prosecutions, but the contents were leaked to the *New York World*. The first in a sensational series, which did much to influence uncommitted Americans in favour of joining the war, appeared on 15 August 1915.

Things went no better when in the same August the Austro-Hungarian Ambassador Konstantin Theodor Dumba (who had already been in trouble for assisting the recruitment of ex-pat Austrians into the army in violation of American neutrality) sent home a letter with a sympathetic American journalist, John James Archibald, who was sailing for Europe.

The letter indicated that Dumba recommended 'most warmly' von Bernstorff and von Papen's proposals in relation to causing trouble at Bethlehem Steel and in the mid-west. 'We could if not entirely prevent the production of war material at Bethlehem and in the middle west, at any rate strongly disorganise it and hold it up for months.'

Unfortunately, the letter was discovered when Archibald's luggage was searched when the vessel reached Falmouth. 'Blinker' Hall added it to the collection of a hundred or so other documents in which von Papen and Boy-Ed sent their sabotage reports and a letter in which von Papen described Americans as 'idiotic Yankees', and passed them to the pro-Allies American Ambassador Walter Page, who in turn forwarded them to President Wilson. As a result, the Secretary of State Robert Lansing asked for Dumba's recall. He left for Rotterdam on 5 October. Home in Austria he was ennobled for his efforts, an honour excoriated in the British press.[17] Wilson, never keen to upset the Germans unnecessarily, left von Papen and the others where they were.

In November 1915 Karl Boy-Ed was implicated in the trial of officials of the Hamburg-Amerika line, charged with falsification of clearance papers which had enabled the Germans to send out supply ships to fuel their destroyers. Boy-Ed's part in the operation, said to have cost $200 million, was fiercely denied by the German Embassy and, after the New York District Attorney accused Boy-Ed of 'riding roughshod over the laws of the United States treating them as if they were scraps of paper', they demanded an apology. It was not received, because on 1 December President Wilson demanded the Germans recall both Boy-Ed and von Papen.[18]

The Hamburg-Amerika line also provided a cover for Paul Koenig. His small detective agency, the Bureau of Investigation, handled inquiries for its subsidiary, the Atlas line. Koenig was active from the beginning of the war. In September 1914 he recruited an Irishman, Edmund Justice, to find out the number of troops being sent from Canada to Europe. When Justice was arrested on 23 December 1915 and asked if he was pro-German, he replied, 'No, I'm anti-British'. Koenig also recruited Frederick Schleindl to steal letters and telegrams which related to the business secrets of the Allies, from his employers, the National City Bank. Koenig's downfall came when he quarrelled over the payment of a day's wages owed to a distant cousin, George Fuchs. Koenig's telephone had been tapped and Fuchs was heard making abusive calls. Investigated by detectives, Fuchs told all.

At 2.12 on the morning of 30 July 1916 barges at Black Tom Island, which was linked by a long pier to Jersey City, exploded. The Brooklyn Bridge was rocked and the clock on the *Jersey Journal* stopped at that moment. One thousand tons of TNT and shrapnel destined for the Allied Forces in Europe blew up with the barges. Munitions plants were not the most stable of places and initially officials were charged with criminal and gross negligence. Then came the question of sabotage.

Anna Rushnack, the landlady of 23-year-old Michael Kristoff, was suspicious about his arriving home in a distressed state at 4 a.m. on the morning of 30 July and reported him to the police. Kristoff was interviewed and described as 'insane but harmless'.[19] Suspicion then fell on Kurt Jahnke and Lieutenant Lothar Wiztke. Both were known spies who were thought to have been sent by the German Consul, General von Bopp, to carry out the explosion.

On 1 February 1918 Wiztke, who gave his name as Pablo Waberski and who had escaped from internment in Valparaiso, was arrested in Nogales, New Mexico, and a cryptogram was found sewn in the upper left sleeve of his jacket. It was broken by Herbert Yardley who had been working with 'Blinker' Hall in London. Witzke confessed but later recanted. Both he and Jahnke had alibis that they were in San Francisco at the time of the explosion and the question was, assuming the alibis were genuine, whether they could have travelled to New York and back in the time available.[20] Nevertheless, on 17 August Witzke was convicted and sentenced to death, the only man in America to be sentenced for espionage.[21]

Fritz Duquesne was really 'the only man who could lay claim to being a master spy', thought Scotland Yard detective Herbert Fitch. Duquesne had fought in the Boer War and developed a pathological hatred of Lord Kitchener after his sister was murdered and his parents' farm destroyed in the general's scorched earth policy. In the First World War Duquesne, who operated mainly from South America, dynamited the SS *Salvador*, SS *Vauban* and HMS *Pembrokeshire*. He is also credited with planting a bomb on HMS *Hampshire* which sank on its way to Russia with the loss of Lord Kitchener and 642 others off the northwest coast of Orkney on 5 June 1916. Duquesne claimed to have escaped on a raft shortly before the explosion. For his efforts he received the Iron Cross.[22]

Dr Armgaard Karl Graves was still around causing mischief. On 8 October 1916 he turned up in Washington charged with trying to extort £600 from Prince Hatzfeldt, the First Secretary to the German Embassy, over three over-affectionate letters to the Countess von Bernstorff, allegedly written in code by a woman in Germany. The letters had, he said, come to the United States by three separate routes and involved three couriers. Graves had told Hatzfeldt the postage would come to £600. He confidently predicted the German Embassy would never go through with the prosecution and he was correct. The next day he told reporters that von Bernstorff had known the submarine U53 was in American waters, 24 hours before it surfaced in Newport, Rhode Island, so enabling him to make a killing on the stockmarket by seeling stocks short before the news became public.

A year later, on 16 August 1917, Graves was found at Union station, Kansas City, and charged with being in a zone closed to enemy aliens without permits. Said to be without funds and poorly dressed, he claimed to be able to show that the Hohenzollern lineage was illegitimate. This time he was detained until the war ended.

What, if anything, had the British been doing about the German activists in America? Quite a lot, was the answer but, as was the situation throughout the war, the players were niggling at each other. The dashing and indiscreet British naval attaché Captain Guy Gaunt, who reported to 'Blinker' Hall, was the man on the ground, publicly alleging that von Bernstorff and the others were violating America's neutrality. After the sinking of the *Lusitania*, a tap was put on the German Embassy telephones and now typists worked around the clock transcribing the calls.

Favourable propaganda by the British played a key role in inducing America to play its part on behalf of the Allies. Sir Gilbert Parker was director of British propaganda in the United States, leading a secret campaign to get American support. Few, if any, Americans approached by Sir Gilbert realized they were targets of a propaganda crusade run from London. By 1916 his list of potential supporters contained over a quarter of a million names.

The Cambridge boxing blue Sir William Wiseman, gassed at Ypres, was sent to New York, ostensibly to head the British Purchasing Commission but in reality to run Section V, the American branch of what would become MI6, replacing Gaunt.

On 1 February 1917 Germany announced that in future she would make use of unrestricted submarine warfare. Two days later von Bernstorff was recalled. He left New York for Copenhagen on the Danish steamer *Friedrich VIII*. The British had agreed a safe conduct for him only if it was agreed that the vessel would be searched at Halifax, Nova Scotia, before being allowed to proceed. The ship was held there while it was gone over, inch by inch, by customs officials for contraband. It was feared that the Germans might be taking home coded messages recorded on phonographs. It was also said that military orders were being passed on a disc of a duet from *Robert le Diable*. Although the customs officers remarked on the German predilection for cotton nightshirts, after nearly a fortnight nothing was found so the *Friedrich VIII* was allowed to sail away.[23]

After his expulsion von Bernstorff—as all good ambassadors should —issued a statement endeavouring to exculpate himself from the illegal acts, playing down those which he could not actually avoid and distancing himself from von Papen.

> Mr von Papen, very naturally, never informed me of any instructions he might have received from his superiors to arrange for questionable enterprises of the character indicated. Without further evidence I do not consider it to have been proved that such instructions were received by him. But in regard to these questions I can only speak for myself for I never concerned myself in purely military matters. Soon after Captain von Papen started home I energetically protested against the government's sending a successor, because I considered that with a situation such as existed in America, there was nothing for a military attaché to do and that the presence of such an officer at the embassy would merely feed enemy agitation.[24]

On 6 April 1917 President Wilson announced that America was at war with Germany.

Chapter Twelve

'If you do well, you'll get no thanks. If you get into trouble, you'll get no help' Sir John Wallinger to Somerset Maugham[1]

SWITZERLAND

Switzerland was a nest of both spies and deserters, which were sometimes the same thing. Much of the population was German-speaking and, as such, was pro-German, and the head of the police in Berne was taking 500 German marks a month from Prince von Bülow — but, despite this, the Swiss police generally acted impartially when arresting foreign agents on both sides. In October 1915 they arrested 120 alleged German spies. A visit from the Swiss police could lead to arrest or deportation; in *Miss King*, one of the Ashenden stories about a British agent in Switzerland, Somerset Maugham recounts how his protagonist dreaded their knock on the door.

If burglaries to steal official papers from embassies and consulates in Switzerland did not take place on a regular basis it was only because of the fear of upsetting the Swiss.[2] Nevertheless, the Italians had the Austro-Hungarian consulate in Zurich burgled on 25 February 1917 by Italian cracksmen released from prison for the purpose. Meyer, the Austrian consul, was lured away to a bogus dinner engagement; when he returned to the embassy and saw what had happened he shot himself. Eighteen Italians in Austria's pay were later arrested and shot.

The police weren't the only people detecting spies. Jacques Mougeot, a French agent wounded early in the war, established an information service at the Château de Bellegarde at Thonon-les-Bains, Lake Geneva, spotting German agents working in Switzerland,

and was very successful.[3] One particular centre of espionage was the Hôtel Royal in Lausanne, where a whole host of German sympathizers was camped out. The Prince de Hohenlohe, head of Nazi propaganda in Switzerland, was spending large sums of money trying to buy Paris newspapers for propaganda. On 26 February 1915 a French report showed that his wife, Princess Alexandrine de Hohenlohe, was in contact with the Comtesse A.L. Pecci in Rome who was part of a 'vast organisation of propaganda and pacifism through the Catholic Church and the Vatican being financed by Austria and Germany'.[4]

The Comtesse Rucclai of Florence was also spying, making visits to Holm of the German General Staff. Their aim was to arrange for defeatist propaganda to be circulated in France.

Maurice Wolff, *aka* Jacobson, had cameras in the windows of his Lausanne bureau opposite the French consulate. And Somson, director of both the Savoy and Cecile hôtels in Lausanne, had an English mistress, Alice Bond; both could be found at the Hôtel Rosat in Château d'Oex, where she questioned British officers and soldiers on recuperation or rest. She had let her flat in Lausanne to a Polish woman, Sfronski, who was in touch with the German vice-consul.[5]

Earlier in the war Somerset Maugham had been recruited for espionage work in Switzerland by Ernest Wallinger's elder brother, Sir John, to replace an agent who had had a nervous breakdown. They met through social connections: John Wallinger, who had been in the Indian police and later became head of the French and Swiss Intelligence service, was the lover of a friend of Maugham's mistress, Syrie Wellcome. Maugham's mission was to collect and forward reports from agents in Frankfurt, Trier, Koblenz and Mainz.

Kirke thought that Wallinger's service was ineffectual, producing only one useful report.[6] Nor did Maugham think any great deal of his employer, regarding him as:

> A very ordinary man on the fringe, I would have said of the upper
> middle class… I perceived he was excessively flattered to be the lover
> of a handsome woman, who in his simple-minded innocence of social
> conditions, he took for a great lady.[7]

He may have made a correct assessment. Wallinger was generally regarded as a poor judge of character. As head of the Swiss service, he was described by Walter Kirke as having 'cold feet' and being

psychiatric reports, he managed to escape after eight days and was reportedly still at large in the 1930s. Barroz also managed to escape and went to Switzerland. Guaspare had his sentence commuted half an hour before he was due to be shot. He decided he wished to marry Schadeck—but she had already left for Guyana. Corbeau received 20 years for spying for the Germans.[11]

At the other end of the social scale to the Café Amodru set was the 24-year-old Dora Charlton, who posed as an American. Said to be well-dressed, very beautiful, and known as the 'Lady of the Camellias' after the flowers she always wore, she obtained high-class information from Allied soldiers, and passed it on while travelling to Germany and Italy. She committed suicide when she was arrested in Turin in June 1919.[12]

It was not only the Guaspares of this world who fled to Switzerland. Monsignor Rudolph von Gerlach went there in the summer of 1917 shortly before he would have been arrested in Rome for his part in blowing up the Italian battleships *Benedetto Brin* and *Leonardo da Vinci*. He had also funnelled money into pro-German Italian newspapers in an attempt to destabilize the country. In his absence, he received 30 years. The Pope is said to have been unable to comprehend his guilt, saying he was such a 'jolly' man. Some habits die hard: prior to taking the cloth, von Gerlach had apparently been a cavalry officer.[13]

In war, as in peace, Switzerland was a financial centre where money could be paid out to spies and propagandists, and it was there that Marx de Mannheim, the German financier, met the unfortunate Emile Duval in Berne. The Germans wanted to acquire an interest in a leading Parisian newspaper so that, by introducing an editorial policy of defeatism and appeasement, condition the French public into accepting peace on terms more favourable to the Germans. The owners of a number of papers including *Le Bonnet Rouge* and *Le Journal* were approached. It was this that led to a number of Frenchmen including Duval facing a firing squad.

On 16 May 1917 Duval was found at Bellegarde with a cheque for 157,000 French francs which he could not explain. He was the go-between for de Mannheim as well as for the pimp and adventurer, Pasha Bolo, and Pierre Lenoir (one-time chauffeur for Georges Ladoux of the Deuxième Bureau) who was later to face the firing squad. Again the aim was to purchase a leading newspaper to use for propaganda purposes. When Duval was at the stake on 17 June 1918 and was offered a blindfold he is said to have replied 'It isn't worth it'. Pasha Bolo was shot on 17 April 1918 and Lenoir, in a complete state of breakdown and having to be carried to the stake and tied to a chair, on 24 October 1919.[14]

In 1918 there was information from France that there was a 'Bolo II' investigating the strength of the peace movement in England. It was decided by MI5 that a wine shop should be opened in London's West End on the off-chance of capturing this man. The shop did good business but unsurprisingly the man was never caught.[15]

The sentences for spying and treason continued after the war. In February 1919 two others, American-born Charles Hartman and Henri Guilbeaux (who, pre-war, had been an associate of the Bonnot motor-car gang of robbers in Paris), were sentenced to death by the French in their absence for having committed treasonable acts. They had run pro-German propaganda newspapers in Switzerland during the war. In April 1924, still *in absentia*, Guilbeaux announced that he was going to stand in the forthcoming French parliamentary elections.

IN AND OUT
OF RUSSIA

Just as the Germans wished to keep the Americans out of the war, so the British wished to keep Russia in it—fighting on the Eastern Front prevented a transfer of troops to the Western. But by 1917 Russia was in a very difficult position: its army had suffered humiliating defeats; the old social order was breaking down; there were food shortages and inflation; the power of the Tsar was waning; and the government was inefficient and corrupt.

Back in 1914, Cumming had established agents in Russia with Major Archibald Campbell as the station chief. Campbell's time there, however, was a story which was repeated throughout the war all over Europe. GHQ had its own men on the spot and they resented Campbell. Not that the heads at GHQ's mission liked each other any better. General Sir John Hanbury-Williams had been sent to Moscow because he ranked higher and was better socially connected than the incumbent Ulsterman Colonel Alfred Knox, reasons which caused resentment and bickering.

Campbell did not fare well. His attempts to improve signals intelligence failed when the Russians refused to co-operate and, just as GHQ had quarrelled with Cumming over the Belgian networks, so in 1915 Knox, supported by the austere ambassador Sir George Buchanan,[1] tried to have Campbell recalled. Indeed, they thought there was no need for a Cumming representative at all. Honours were even: Campbell was recalled, but replaced by Major C.M.J.Thornhill. Unfortunately, he became Knox's man, not Cumming's, and in turn he was replaced by Samuel Hoare, who later became Foreign Secretary.

Hoare lasted until March 1917, by which time he had reported on the likelihood that the Russian war effort was going to collapse because of the number of casualties and the resulting mistrust of the government. By the time Hoare left, the influential monk, Rasputin, a favourite of the German-born tsarina, had been assassinated on the night of 29 December 1916 by a group led by Prince Youssoupoff and possibly his friend and biographer, Oswald Rayner, who worked for British Intelligence. The story goes that when the first two bullets failed to kill Rasputin, Rayner fired the final and fatal shot. The killing, which did not displease British Intelligence, was just one more step on the road to the forthcoming revolution.[2]

Six weeks later the tsarist regime collapsed in the revolution of February 1917. It began on 8 March (in the Gregorian calendar) with demonstrations in bread queues in Petrograd, and quickly spread. There had already been a series of strikes but when the police failed to quell the rioters, Tsar Nicholas II disregarded Buchanan's advice to 'Break down the barrier that separates you from your people to regain their confidence',[3] and ordered the army to take control. Many of the lower ranks were disloyal and on 13 March the tsar abdicated.

The abdication was followed by a provisional government, led first by Prince Lvov and then by Alexander Kerensky. The last great Russian war effort ended in July 1917 and General Lavr Kornilov became commander-in-chief. It was then that Hanbury-Williams' successor, General Sir Charles Barter, seems to have given his blessing to an abortive coup by Kornilov, who was not co-operating with Kerensky. The coup failed dismally. Few of the army leaders joined the call to arms, although a British armoured car squadron led by Oliver Locker-Lampson did.[4] That month the Germans allowed Pytor Ilyich Lenin to travel back to Russia in a closed railway compartment from Zurich, where he had been since the outbreak of war.

Meanwhile, as was often the case, British intelligence systems were pulling in opposite directions. Sir Charles Barter continued to connive against Kerensky, with Cumming actively supporting him. William Wiseman, last heard of in connection with the Zimmermann telegram, was busy recruiting Somerset Maugham, last heard of spying in Switzerland, to go to Russia to try to persuade Kerensky to keep Russia in the war.

Whether it was the $150,000 at his disposal, supplied by the Foreign Office and American interests, or a desire to please his old friend, Maugham agreed. Maugham at least had an introduction to Kerensky through a former mistress, Sasha Kropotkin, daughter of the exiled Prince Pyotr Kropotkin. He would later write that he met Kerensky at Sasha's apartment, where the man harangued him for hours on end as if he were at a public meeting. Maugham's assessment—but what did he really know of these matters?—was that Wiseman should run a programme of covert action and propaganda which he estimated would cost $500,000 a year. There were also to be secret organizations 'unmasking...German plots and propaganda in Russia'. Wiseman took the proposition seriously, but on 31 October Maugham was given an urgent message by Kerensky to take to Prime Minister David Lloyd George asking for guns and weapons. He left Russia that night.

Maugham's meeting with Lloyd George was cordial enough, with the prime minister asking about his plays, but when it came to the content of the message the meeting ended abruptly. Lloyd George instructed Maugham to tell Kerensky it simply could not be done, and with that he left for a cabinet meeting. Kerensky lasted a few more days before, on 7 November, he was overthrown in the Bolshevik revolution and fled to France. Wiseman was apparently pleased enough to offer Maugham another job, this time in Romania, but the playwright had already contracted tuberculosis and spent the next months in a sanatorium in Scotland.[5]

All of this left Cumming's agents in disarray. The next up to bat in Moscow was Robert Bruce Lockhart, who had had an innings there before. Lockhart was generally regarded as a man of high ability, but lacking the required morals of the day. He had already had one entanglement in Malaya when he had run off with Amai, the ward of Dato Klana, the chief of Sungei Ujong. The relationship lasted a year before Lockhart became ill, apparently with malaria, and was sent home. Much more romantic was his claim that he had been poisoned.[6] In late August 1917 there had been another indiscretion in Moscow, and Lockhart had once again been sent home on sick leave.

However, once the revolution had started, Lockhart's star began to rise again. He began lobbying in London for contact to be established with the Bolsheviks, and his reward was a posting back to Russia to coincide with the recall of Buchanan and Knox. He was instructed to re-establish relationships with Trotsky and Lenin.

On 3 March 1918 the Russians signed a peace treaty with the Germans at Brest-Litovsk. Lockhart reported to London that the treaty might not last. He then contacted the anti-Bolsheviks led by Boris Savinkov, who had been responsible for a number of assassinations including that of the minister of the interior in 1904 and Grand Duke Serge the following year. Savinkov believed that if the Allies invaded he could have all the Bolshevik leaders assassinated the same night; Lockhart duly forwarded this message to London where it was not well received. Lockhart had, after all, earlier advised against a strike against the Bolsheviks, with or without the assistance of Japan, and had changed his mind. His advice was rejected out of hand.

What was Cumming doing all this time? Nothing much worthwhile was the answer. The head of station was now Lieutenant Ernest Boyce. A string of agents passed through the bureau, none capable of determining the political situation, according to Lockhart—as if he could.

Also in Russia at the time, sent by the War Office, was George Hill, known as 'Jolly George', who had been in both the Intelligence Corps and the Royal Flying Corps and who, according to his memoirs, up until the Brest treaty spent his time plotting how to keep the Bolsheviks in the war.[7] After the treaty he still found plenty to occupy him. He gave lectures to Trotsky and enjoyed nights at the theatre and rounds of supper parties. If a film of Hill's exploits had been made, then surely Errol Flynn would have had the leading role.

> I helped the Bolshevik military headquarters to organise an
> Intelligence Section for the purpose of identifying German units on
> the Russian front…Time and again I was able to warn London that
> a German division had left the Russian for the Western Front.
>   Secondly I organised a Bolshevik counter-espionage section to
> spy on the German Secret Service …We deciphered German codes.
> Opened their letters and read most of their correspondence without
> even being suspected.[8]

Someone in an apparently official position was needed who could report on what was really happening. Now, the second most famous spy of all time, *pace* his literary son James Bond, entered the scene. Sidney Reilly, a man whose career has spawned biographies, auto-biographies, novels, countless newspaper articles, television series and films was, it seems, first approached by Cumming at the beginning of March 1918.[9]

Reilly is credited with holding eleven passports and having a wife to go with each. But just how much that is written of his exploits is true? Just about the only thing that can be said of him with absolutely certainty is that he was born. Exactly where is by no means clear. Four of his biographers have Reilly born in or around Odessa; three have him born in Russian Poland. He himself often claimed he had been born in Ireland, either in Clonmel or in Dublin. His father was variously a clergyman or sea captain (both Irish) or a landowner or aristocrat (both Russian). Alternatively, he was the illegitimate son of a doctor (Viennese). His family was almost certainly Jewish.[10]

He also certainly married on a number of occasions—but did he kill his wife's first husband and some years later a woman who could have identified him? Andrew Cook suggests that in March 1898 he may have poisoned the ageing and ill Reverend Hugh Thomas at the grandly named London & Paris Hotel in Newhaven where the packet from France docked. Sometime later, Louisa Lewis, who was working at the hotel when Thomas died, disappeared from the fashionable Hotel Cecil, which stood next to the then far less impressive Savoy, at a time when Reilly was staying there. Cook offers the suggestion that Reilly may have killed her because she recognized him as 'the doctor' who certified Thomas' death from heart failure. But at that time, many young women disappeared after botched abortions. There is no evidence that Louisa was pregnant, nor is there any evidence that Reilly killed her. Like so much about his life, it is conjecture.

As to his espionage work, it is likely that Reilly met the Scotland Yard officer William Melville when Melville was engaged in tracking down the anarchists of the 1890s. There have been suggestions that in 1906 Melville, by then involved in Secret Service work, employed him in a matter relating to Britain's oil interests, but this is another disputed story. According to his ghosted autobiography, Reilly also obtained secrets from a crashed plane at the Berlin airshow in 1909, but research has shown there was no such crash at the time. He was definitely employed by MI6 during the First World War. His story that, dressed in an officer's uniform, he attended a meeting of the German High Command and reported back to Cumming is more than likely another invention.

What is interesting is that Cumming apparently did not meet Reilly for the first eight years of his tenure, although Melville, Cumming's subordinate and indeed confidant, had been using Reilly sporadically for the better part of 20 years. Alan Judd has Cumming recording in his diary for 15 March 1916:

> Major Scale introduced Mr Reilly who is willing to go to Russia for us.
> Very clever – very doubtful – had been everywhere and done
> everything… I must agree tho' it is a great gamble.

Reilly was to go with £500 in banknotes and a further £750 in diamonds to visit Cumming's agents throughout the country.[11]

Reilly had spent a good deal of time in America during the war, where he was reputed to have made a fortune. Some of his biographers have him working for German interests, claiming he was involved with Kurt Jahnke in the explosions at Black Tom and the DuPont power plant near Tacoma, Washington. For a variety of reasons the claims do not stand up.[12]

One of the few undisputed facts of Reilly's life is that in 1917 he went to Canada to join the Royal Flying Corps before he came to London to meet Cumming. With his languages and resourcefulness, what more suitable man to send to Russia?

In August 1917, when Reilly had been in Russia for some five months, he became involved in the 'Reilly Plot' or the 'Lockhart Plot' to assassinate Lenin and Trotsky. This plot seems to have been the brainchild of the double agent Colonel Eduard Berzin, who thought that the two assassinations would take so much starch out of the Bolsheviks that they would never recover from the blows. Reilly, it is said, was not happy with the idea, preferring that the leaders should suffer the humiliation of being publicly debagged in a Moscow street —but Ernest Boyce favoured Berzin's idea and put out a tentative offer of a contract.

It came to nothing because, on 30 August 1918, there were two unconnected shootings. In the first, Moisei Solomonovitch Uritsky, head of the Petrograd Cheka—the state security organization—was shot and killed by a military cadet, Leonid Kanegieser, possibly as a reprisal for the execution of his friends. In the second, Lenin himself was seriously wounded when he was shot in the chest and jaw getting into his car as he left a meeting at a Moscow factory. His attempted assassin was probably the Left Socialist revolutionary Dora, or Fanya, Kaplan, who had been released from Siberia 18 months earlier. She had been sent there for an assassination attempt on Novitsky, the head of the gendarmerie, in 1907 and was not released until 3 March 1917. It was an experience which left her partially blind and subject to fits. At one time the Left Socialists had been partners of the Bolsheviks but they had fallen out over the Treaty of Brest-Litovsk and they now considered Lenin a traitor. Kaplan confessed, and when it became clear she would not name her co-conspirators, if any, she was shot on 3 December 1918.[13] There was never any evidence that the attacks were linked but, safer than sorry, Felix Dzerzhinksy, head of the Cheka, swung into action, rounding up and executing some 500 former officials of the tsarist régime.

Who was the ruthless Felix Dzerzhinsky, much admired by Lenin, who would go on to cause so much trouble for British agents in Russia? Born in 1877 to a well-off family in Poland, Dzerzhinsky joined the Socialist Revolutionary Party in 1897 and began to work as a courier between the underground cells of the party in Russia and overseas groups. After a spell in a labour camp, in 1903 he joined Lenin's wing of the Social Democrats, the Bolsheviks.

In October 1917 he was one of the masterminds behind the Communist coup in which Kerensky was overthrown. It was now that Dzerzhinsky set up the Cheka, using former tsarist police officers to build the organization which became the KGB. At the end of December Dzerzhinsky had two dozen men, no money and little experience. By the next year he was said to have over 100,000 agents and had begun overseas operations. In 1918, with information from a Communist French agent, he arrested the chief American agent in Russia, the Greek-American Xenophon Kalmatiano.

Throughout 1918 Lockhart was toiling away trying to set up a counter-revolution, dealing with two Letts including Colonel Berzin who reported to him that there was serious trouble among Lettish troops. Lockhart obtained 1.2 million roubles which he handed over to Berzin. Unfortunately Berzin and his fellow Lett were Dzerzhinsky's men.[14]

The plan—before Lockhart was infiltrated and the money went astray—was that there should be an anti-Bolshevik coup to coincide with a British and French landing in north Russia. A company of marines led by Major General Frederick Poole had landed at Murmansk on 6 March and a second arrived on 1 August to coincide with the staging of a small-time coup which left Captain Georgi Chaplin in control of the area. By August, however, the agents sent over in advance of the coup had been captured.

Things now started to go very badly wrong for the French and British communities. On 29 August 1918 the offices of Colonel de Vertement, head of the French Secret Service in Moscow, were raided by the Cheka. The colonel got away over the rooftops, but explosives were found and a number of his agents were arrested.

Lockhart was arrested on 31 August, released within 24 hours and rearrested four days later. He was not the only one. Into prison went the head of station, Ernest Boyce. Reilly escaped, taking a seat in a first-class carriage on a train to Moscow. For a time some of his numerous mistresses, including Elizaveta Otten, whom he used as a courier, were imprisoned on his behalf. Hill claims Reilly wanted to surrender himself in exchange for Lockhart, but that Hill dissuaded him.

On 4 September the British Embassy was attacked and Captain Francis Cormie, the naval attaché, was killed, but not until, so it was reported, he had killed three of the insurgents. The newspapers reported that barbarous things had been done to his body and, worse, that an English chaplain had been refused permission to say prayers over him. His Cross of St George was ripped from him and worn by one of the invaders, and his body was said to have been hung in one of the windows of the embassy. Cormie was awarded a posthumous Order of the Bath. The attack was the start of a pogrom in which all the French and British between the ages of 18 and 40 in the area of Petrograd were rounded up and imprisoned.[15]

The reprisal by the British was the 'preventative' arrest of the Bolshevik ambassador Maksin Litvinov who went straight to Brixton prison to be held as a hostage against the release of Lockhart.[16]

Reilly stayed in hiding in the flat of another mistress in Moscow where he was visited by George Hill, who wanted him to get to the Ukraine through a series of safe houses. Reilly preferred to travel north to Finland. Hill gave him his own false papers in the name of

Bergmann (Hill with a German suffix) and saw him off on the sleeper back to Petrograd. Reilly, who had long black hair, had long coveted Hill's pair of hairbrushes. At the station Hill gave him one of them along with a bottle of wine and a package of food. When they met again in London Reilly gave Hill a pair of silver-backed brushes engraved with Hill's regimental crest.[17]

Once he had reached Petrograd, Reilly went into hiding until he could obtain different papers and a protection certificate which allowed him to leave for Kronstadt. From there he travelled to Revel (now Tallin) and thence to Helsingfors, Stockholm and London. The journey took him just over two months and he arrived back just in time for the Armistice — only to be accused of being a double agent by the Americans who were blaming him for the failure of the Lockhart plot.

Other people were now trickling back to England including Boyce, now released from prison, and an Italian woman who had hidden Hill for a time. With them were Lockhart and Hill, who was sent to work in Sofia — he had learned Bulgarian in four weeks at the beginning of the war.

There were claims that the shooting of Uritsky, the head of the Petrograd Cheka under Dzerzhinsky, was as part of an English conspiracy, but there were other more serious charges against Lockhart: for a start, that he had been caught, along with Reilly, dealing with Lettish *agents provocateurs*. In December 1918 both Reilly and Lockhart were outlawed and sentenced to death in Russia in their absence. Reilly remained in London until the December when he and Hill went back to Russia in disguise and under the cover of the British Trade Corporation to obtain information on the Black Sea coast and south Russia for possible use at the forthcoming Paris peace conference.[18]

The First World War may have ended but Russia had now replaced Germany as a prime place of interest for the intelligence services.

Chapter Fourteen

I have made no revisions whatever in regard to the cases of spies, and unless the S. of S. thinks otherwise, I have no intention of doing so. To extend clemency to men who have been responsible for the loss of thousands of British soldiers seems to me to be an extraordinary proposal, and I am rather surprised at Maj. Gen. Seeley as a soldier endorsing it. B. Child [1]

GONE TO GRAVEYARDS

An immediate problem at the end of the war was what to do with the spies, male and female, who were still in custody in England. One line of Home Office thought was that since all British spies imprisoned in Germany had been released in November 1918, German spies should also be sent home. This did not appeal to many: Germany had been defeated and had no option but to release the British agents.

Attitudes depended on the motivation of the spy in question. Here again Carl Hans Lody was cited as the epitome of what a patriotic gentleman spy should be. Those who had spied for their country were in a far better position than those who had done so for money. The latter, it was decided, should be kept in custody, although their life sentences were generally commuted to 10 years from the date of conviction.

But over the years, one by one most of the spies were sent home. On 17 July 1920 Eva de Bournonville's trial judge, Mr Justice Darling, wrote to the Home Office suggesting that as a 'merciful course' she should be released when she had served 10 years. She was repatriated in 1922.

In December 1920 the last woman convicted during the war, Louise Smith, was recommended for release, subject to her reapplying for German nationality and deportation.

Poor Lizzie Wertheim was never released. During her time in

Aylesbury her physical and mental condition had deteriorated. 'Chicago May' Sharpe, the notorious American criminal who met her there, thought that the cause of Wertheim's collapse was a combination of a broken heart and the treatment she received in the prison. In January 1918 she was suffering from the delusion that no one could leave England without her authority, and she also suspected that she was being poisoned. She was sent to Broadmoor. By June 1920 she had been confined to bed for some months and died on 29 July of pulmonary tuberculosis.[2]

On 20 August 1920 Percy Thellusson, a prison visitor at Parkhurst on the Isle of Wight, wrote to Major J.E.B Seeley about one particular spy there: 'Now that the war is over it seems hard on the taxpayers to pay for the keep of this man'. The man to whom he referred was Friedrich Greite; perhaps Thellusson could have chosen a more sympathetic prisoner.

Since his imprisonment in 1916 Greite had regularly petitioned for his release. Notes on his file describe him as 'Very skilful and utterly untrustworthy' (1916), 'Absolutely untrustworthy and not good enough for this country' (1918) and 'Quite of the slimy, spy type: not trustworthy' (1921).[3]

Seeley forwarded Thellusson's letter to the War Office and received a thoroughly dusty response stating that Greite would 'in all probability' have been sentenced to death if the Antwerp spy bureau records — his name appeared on the list of German spies as A7 — had been available at the time of his trial. He would certainly stay where he was. In 1923 Greite was sent to Maidstone; his file notes read: 'Greatly improved: will make a good German!' The next year he was released and deported on 14 December.

Of another spy, the Belgian diamond-cutter Leon Francis van der Groten, it was written:

> There is no doubt that this man ought to have been shot and but for
> the intervention of the Belgian Government at the time he would have
> been… A traitor to the Allied cause, who deserves no consideration
> whatsoever.[4]

The cinema owner Leopold Vieyra, who later spuriously claimed responsibility for sinking the *Hampshire*, was released in 1923.

Special opprobrium was reserved for the traitor Kenneth Rysbach who, on 14 July 1924, was the last spy to be released in England. Rysbach was in and out of the courts over the years, mainly being acquitted of fraud. Two years later he tried to go to Australia to take up a theatrical engagement, but permission was denied. His Requirement to Report was remitted in 1930. He celebrated by prosecuting his employer for criminal libel.

There was never any sympathy for Rysbach. He claimed that being on licence was a 'social imputation and business impediment'. A note on his Home Office file reads 'Great social imputation might be expected to arise from the fact that he was convicted of espionage in war time. Rysbach has no known merits'. In 1927 he was acquitted of a jewel swindle at the Old Bailey and on 25 February 1937 he was again acquitted, this time at Bristol Assizes, of obtaining money by false pretences. After that he seems to have disappeared.[5]

Trebitsch Lincoln's certificate of naturalization, granted on 5 May 1909, was revoked. Later, he dabbled in mystic religions and became the Abbot Chao-king. He died in Shanghai in 1943, possibly poisoned by the Nazis.

On 2 March 1926 his son Ignatius, known as John, who had joined the British army, was hanged at Shepton Mallet for the murder of Edward Richards, who had surprised him and another soldier when they were burgling his house on the previous Christmas Eve.

The last First World War spy to be released in Europe was Paoli Schwartz, the son of a dismissed French police superintendent. German Agent 39 Strasbourg, Schwartz was not convicted until 1921, when he was sentenced to hard labour on Devil's Island. Over the years the German newspapers campaigned for his release, which came in 1932 when he returned to Germany in something approaching triumph.[6]

Major Cecil Cameron, the man credited with establishing the railway-watching networks in Belgium, and who had been convicted over a pre-war fraudulent claim for a pearl necklace, committed suicide at Hillsborough Barracks, Sheffield, on 18 August 1924. At the time he was commanding the 46th Battery Royal Artillery. Although his wife denied it, hinting that the cause of his death was that he was continually being transferred from one battery to another, letters he left behind indicated that he was in financial difficulties.[7]

After the war, the naval journalist Hector Bywater, who had spied in Germany for Cumming, wanted a year's leave with pay. This was turned down and, in pique, he refused an OBE. He returned to Fleet Street, wrote a number of books, translated others from the German, and became convinced there would be a war between America and Japan. He died, allegedly from alcoholic poisoning, on 16 August 1940, but there have been suggestions that he was murdered by a Japanese agent. Less than three weeks before, Bywater's principal contact in Tokyo had apparently leaped, or been thrown, from the third-floor windows of the police headquarters.

The underrated and often maligned Richard Tinsley, controller of the Secret Service in Holland, expanded his Uranium Steamship Company after the war and also continued in espionage. At the time of the Versailles Peace Treaty Conference in August 1919 it was alleged by the German legation that he was now working in Germany, employing Arthur Caenpenne and Frederic Promper, Belgians who had been arrested on 12 July 1919 amid allegations that they had corrupted 42 German soldiers. Promper was in possession of a parcel of skeleton keys; it was suggested that Caenpenne was obtaining quantities of morphia, opium and cocaine to render victims talkative and/or to rob them. Caenpenne pleaded guilty. Tinsley, awarded a CBE in 1919, was the Rotterdam consul for Nicaragua from 1917 to 1928. He died in 1941. For a time his Rotterdam police officer friend, François van Sant, lived in London.

Tinsley's colleague Ernest Maxse became the consul-general in Rotterdam, but when it was suggested he might take the same office in Paris, questions were asked in Parliament about the desirability of employing a man of German origin. He died in March 1943.[8]

Both the South African Henry Landau and his underling Major Hugh Dalton terminated their careers in something approaching disgrace. For a time both remained in the Secret Service with SIS, but Landau soon headed off to smuggle diamonds out of Russia, and later published *The Secrets of the White Lady*, about the Belgian train-watchers, in America, which annoyed the authorities and was banned in Britain.

When the agent TR/16, working for the British and believed to be Danish, was arrested and shot at the beginning of the Second World War, for a time Landau was blamed for leaking his identity. In fact the arrest had nothing to do with Landau and was simply a terrible mischance. TR/16 was not a Dane but a German, Herman Krueger, who had served a sentence for insulting the Kaiser by hitting one of his relatives. It was reported that Krueger was executed with an axe, but he may have committed suicide.[9] That Landau never knew the Dane's real identity shows how tightly Tinsley ran his ship.

Dalton survived his denunciation by Sigismund Payne Best, which alleged that he was helping in Tinsley's blackmail scheme of Dutch businessmen, and later became station chief in the Netherlands. But in September 1936 he fell like Lucifer when, accused of embezzling nearly £3,000 from SIS funds at The Hague, he shot himself.

Sigismund Payne Best continued his Secret Service career. In September 1921 he married a Dutch girl, Marie van Rees. He was described in *The Times* as a noted amateur musician. In November 1939 he was kidnapped by German intelligence at a café at Venlo on the Dutch–German border. He had been recruited into the new Z organization founded by Cumming's one-time deputy Colonel Dansey, and was in the area to meet what the authorities thought were dissident Germans plotting to overthrow Hitler. It was in fact an SS-organized trap. Best was held in a concentration camp throughout the war and was liberated by the Americans in 1945. He died in 1978.[10]

Over the last half century Richard Meinertzhagen, from the Egypt bureau, has been exposed as a fraud, thief and possible murderer. Much of his accumulation of ornithology was found to have been stolen from other people's collections including that of the Natural History Museum. His work seems to have been plagiarized and the death of his first wife in a shooting accident was possibly a murder to stop her exposing him as a fake. He almost certainly beat a servant to death in India and arranged that the cause of death was certified as due to the plague.[11]

Somerset Maugham divorced his wife Sylvie in 1928 and remained with Gerald Haxton until his lover's death in 1944. The highest-paid English writer in the 1930s and a great traveller, he had bought the Villa Mauresque near Nice where he lived until his death at the age of 91 on 16 December 1965. During the Second World War he spoke publicly in America urging support for Britain. In later life he quarrelled with his daughter Liza and adopted one of Haxton's successors, Alan Searle, as his son. William Wiseman, who had sent Maugham to Russia, died in New York on 17 June 1962.

In the 1920s Compton Mackenzie was offered the position of second in command to Mansfield Cumming, which he declined. According to John Coleby in his memoir, *A Marine or Anything,* Cumming's staff sent a round-robin saying they would resign if Mackenzie was appointed.[12] He ended up in court, when in 1932 he was prosecuted under the Official Secrets Act over *Greek Memories,* his account of his experiences as an agent in Athens in 1916. At the end of a trial in which the judge became increasingly exasperated with the prosecution, he was merely fined £100 and was not challenged when the memoirs were reprinted in 1939. He had already had a spat with Somerset Maugham, whose Ashenden stories came out just prior to Compton Mackenzie's novel, *Extremes Meet.* Later he wrote the bestseller *Whisky Galore.* He died on 30 November 1972 aged 89.

Mackenzie's assistant, Edward Knoblock, received no honours for his service in England, but was awarded the Chevalier of the Order of the Redeemer by the Greeks. After the war he wrote the screenplay for the Douglas Fairbanks' vehicle, *The Three Musketeers.* He died aged 70 in July 1945.

On 24 November 1922 in the aftermath of the Troubles which followed the First World War, the author of the *Riddle of the Sands,* the Irish patriot Erskine Childers, was shot by the Army of the Free State for possessing two pistols. He was another who shook hands with each of his firing squad, saying 'Take a step or two forward, lads. It'll be easier'. Half a century later his son Erskine Hamilton Childers became the fourth President of Ireland.

William Tufnell Le Queux continued to write mainly detective fiction. In 1923 he published his often specious autobiography, *Things I Know about Kings, Celebrities and Crooks*, in which he claimed he had seen a manuscript written in French by Rasputin, stating that Jack the Ripper was a Russian doctor named Alexander Pedachenko who had committed the murders to confuse and ridicule Scotland Yard. He died in the Belgium seaside resort of Knocke-le-Zoute on 13 October 1927.

Wilhelm Wassmuss, the 'German Lawrence' who lost his codebook, was finally imprisoned by the British. He was released in 1920 and made his way back to Berlin. Once there he struggled to persuade the German Foreign Office to honour his pledges to the tribesmen and pay the money he had promised to them. The German government refused, but Wassmuss could not forget his pledges. He returned to Bushehr in 1924 and, purchasing cheap farmland, promised to repay the tribesmen from the profits he hoped to make from farming. The farm failed and Wassmuss returned to Berlin in April 1931. He died virtually forgotten and in poverty seven months later.

Of the French, as well as writing his highly fictionalized memoirs and those of Marthe Richard, Georges Ladoux survived his trial for treason and later became an inspector of casinos. After he died in 1933 his widow claimed that he had been poisoned by Fräulein Doktor. Shortly before his death Ladoux had received a letter from a French journalist in Berlin proposing a meeting with the Fräulein and sending two photographs of her, one old and one new. Mme Ladoux claimed the photographs had been infected with a *bacile photogene*, but the police found no traces of poison.[13]

Marthe Richard, described as a 'charmless mythomane', prospered greatly after Ladoux wrote her memoirs, in which he changed her name from Richer. She also wrote her own fictional memoirs, and a film was made of her story in which she was played by the great Edwige Feuillière, with Eric von Stroheim as von Khron. In 1926 she married an Englishman, Thomas Crompton. She spent the Second World War in Vichy, where she was thought to be too close to certain German officers for the good of France. Other reports, however, have her organizing an escape route for Allied soldiers. Afterwards, quite improperly since she now had British nationality, she was elected to the French Parliament, leading a successful campaign to close the country's brothels. Towards the end of her life she claimed she regretted her campaign because the tax from brothels would pay for schools. She died aged 93 in 1982, and was buried under the name Crompton in the Père Lachaise cemetery in Paris.[14]

During his time on Devil's Island Charles Ullmo, convicted in 1908 for attempting to sell French naval secrets, converted from Judaism to Catholicism. He was finally pardoned in 1934 and returned from Cayenne. He found he did not like life in metropolitan France and, after selling his story to a magazine, went back to Cayenne where he spent the remainder of his life helping ex-prisoners. He died in September 1957.

Of the German spymasters, Gustav Steinhauer wrote his more or less truthful memoirs, *I was the Kaiser's Master Spy*, with S.T. Felstead. In 2009 it was suggested that Ian Fleming might have based the plot of

Goldfinger on a hitherto unrevealed attempt by Steinhauer to blow up the Bank of England's gold reserves. Given the threadbare quality and quantity of Steinhauer's agents at the time it seems highly improbable, but it makes a good story.

His successor, Walter Nicolai, was replaced by Colonel Gempp in 1921. Described by Ellis Zacharias of the US Naval Intelligence as a 'ruthless and unscrupulous spy-master, devoted to Secret Service work with the unconditional devotion of an ascetic monk', Nicolai was never promoted above lieutenant-colonel. Gempp was replaced by Captain Patzig of the German navy when Hitler came to power in 1933. At the end of the Second World War Nicolai was arrested by the Russian Secret Service and taken for questioning in Moscow, where he died on 4 May 1947.[15]

Mata Hari's prepared grave was left empty and when her body was not claimed by relatives it was given to the Museum of Anatomy in Paris for dissection. Her head went missing in July 2000.[16]

After the war, the dubious Maria de Styzinska Brett-Perring continued to spy for any country or organization that would pay her. By the end of the 1930s, it was thought that she had worked at one time or another for the German, French, Italian, Japanese and Polish intelligence services as well the Canadian—to whom she reported on pro-Soviet movements—and for Russia itself. In 1939 she was associating with a pro-Nazi group in England. But she and the authorities were not quite finished. In 1942 she received three months at Bow Street for evading censorship regulations, using American and Chinese diplomatic bags, and was then detained under section 18B of the wartime Defence Regulations, during which she spent her time in Holloway prison denouncing other prisoners as Nazi sympathizers. By 1944 it was decided that, whatever she may have been, she was now harmless and, given £1 by the s. 18B Detainees Aid Fund, she was discharged on 14 September. In 1948 she wrote to Sir Oswald Mosley asking him for a job. After that she finally disappeared from view.[17]

Some of the Germans in America remained there after the war. One of them was Dr Armgaard Karl Graves. The details of his post-war career are obscure, but it seems he did not prosper. In 1928 he was acquitted of burning a woman alive, and he seems to have been imprisoned in 1934. He is thought to have died in America.[18]

Contrary to British intentions, Captain Horst von der Goltz, a.k.a.

Bridgeman Taylor, did not return to England. After he gave evidence in the Tauscher trial, Goltz was granted asylum in America and, drifting to the west coast, in 1918 appeared, typecast as the German spy, in Raoul Walsh's *Prussian Cur*. The film was not well received. What happened to him after that is more obscure. He possibly married Estelle Gray Cooper in 1923 and also her daughter Margaret in 1929. He is said to have died in East Orange, New Jersey, in 1969. At some time he had kept a pet shop on Broadway, Manhattan.

Much to the indignation of the American press, von der Goltz's master, Captain Franz von Rintelen, was pardoned on 19 November 1920. He returned to England, becoming a friend of 'Blinker' Hall and, along with the novelist A.E.W. Mason, who had worked for Hall in the Mediterranean and later in Mexico, dined at Hall's home shortly before Christmas 1925.

In 1932 von Rintelen wrote his self-serving and almost wholly specious version of events with an introduction by Mason and prefaced by a letter from Hall. No doubt helped by this friendship, von Rintelen survived questions in the House of Lords intended to lead to his deportation. He volunteered his services for the Royal Navy in the Second World War, but the offer was declined and he spent the duration in an internment camp. His offer to travel to Nuremberg to defend 10 of the Nazi war criminals was also declined. He died in London on 30 May 1949.[19] (Mason died in 1943 aged 83. His best-known work after the war was *The House of the Arrow*.)

Of the German Embassy staff, on his recall in 1917 Johann von Bernstorff was appointed ambassador to Turkey. He was, however, in great disfavour with both the Kaiser and the General Staff. After the war he declined an appointment to head the Foreign Office and resumed private life. He died in 1939.

Karl Boy-Ed became director of the German Navy's press bureau. He married an American girl, Virginia Mackay Smith from Washington, and they settled in Hamburg. In 1926 he was refused a visa to travel to America. He died in September 1930 at the age of 58 following a horse-riding accident.

Dr Heinrich Albert, who had gone to sleep on the subway in July 1915, returned to Germany where, after the war, he became Treasury and Reconstruction Minister. In 1923, after an unsuccessful attempt to form a government, he resumed his practice as a lawyer in Berlin.

He died on 1 November 1960 aged 86.

The man who had left him asleep at 23rd Street, George Viereck, resumed his career as a poet and editor. In 1942, described by *Time* as 'Bespectacled, thick-lipped' and now a Nazi propagandist, he was interned under the Foreign Agents Registration Act, after which he wrote *Men into Beasts* which was sold on the promise of an account of homosexual rape in prison. It is regarded as one of the first examples of gay pulp literature, just as his 1907 novel *The House of the Vampire* was an early contribution to gay vampire literature. He died on 18 March 1962.[20]

Hans Tauscher, acquitted of involvement in the Welland canal case, returned to New York in 1934 where, amazingly, he was permitted to revive his gun-dealing business, which flourished during the Second World War. His wife, the opera singer Joanna Gadski, died in 1932 in a car accident in Berlin.[21]

In 1919 Fritz Duquesne, 'The Man who Killed Kitchener', was arrested in New York wearing the uniform of a captain in the Australian Light Horse. He was due be extradited on charges of murdering British seamen but, feigning paralysis, he was sent to Bellevue hospital from which he escaped. He made his way to Philadelphia and then flew to Mexico. Although he was thought to have returned to America and to have worked for the anti-British Joseph Kennedy, he did not reappear on the authorities' radar until 1932, when he was betrayed by a woman friend and arrested, again in New York. An application for his extradition to Britain was refused on the grounds that the limitation statutes had expired. America might have done better to expel him: in the Second World War Duquesne was the leader of a 300-strong German spy group trapped by the double agent William Sebold. An illegal immigrant into America, Sebold had returned to Germany where he was approached by the Nazis who threatened to expose him if he did not work for them. Immediately on his return to America he contacted the FBI. He ultimately infiltrated Duquesne's network, becoming its radio operator. Duquesne was sentenced to 18 years, which he served in Leavensworth. He was released in 1954 and died in poverty on 24 May 1956.[22]

Lothar Witzke, involved in the Black Tom explosion, was pardoned on 22 November 1923 after he rescued a number of fellow prisoners in a fire. Deported to Germany, he was awarded the Iron Cross. Kurt

Jahnke spied for the Germans in the Second World War, mainly in Pomerania. He and his wife are said to have been arrested by the Russians in 1945, tortured and executed. Another account is that he escaped to Switzerland. Michael Kristoff later joined the American army and seems to have died in 1928. At least that was when a body with his papers was found in Potters Field, but the dead man's dental records apparently did not match those of Kristoff. The claim for damages against the German government arising out of the explosion ran until 1930, when an award of $50 million was made.

Of those who had been in and around Russia at the time of the Revolution, Sidney Reilly was unable to resist causing more trouble or the opportunity to refinance his failing business or set up new enterprises. In 1925 he returned to Russia, in theory to meet leaders of the seemingly anti-Bolshevik Monarchist Union of Central Russia, which was in fact controlled by the OGPU, the state police organization that had replaced the Cheka. Reilly crossed from Finland into Russia where, after a meeting in which he proposed financing the Monarchist Union by looting the country's museums and selling the artefacts to the West, he was arrested and told of his existing death sentence. It is difficult to see how he cannot have known of it: it had been in all the newspapers. An appeal to Felix Dzerzhinsky in which Reilly promised to betray British and American intelligence officers and Russian emigrés failed. He was shot in early November. However, like the 7th Lord Lucan and Elvis Presley, Reilly has lived on after his death. It was variously reported that he was working for the OGPU, or again that he was working against it.[23] An application by Reilly's last wife Pepita that she should work for British intelligence in the Second World War was rejected.

George Hill remained in intelligence work and went on to publish his memoirs *Go Spy the Land*.

In 1932 Robert Lockhart published his highly successful memoirs, which in 1943 were filmed as *British Agent* with Leslie Howard in the title role. In the Second World War he became the Director General of the Political Warfare Exchange which controlled propaganda. He was knighted in 1943. A friend of the black magician Aleister Crowley, he died in 1970 aged 83.

As for the chiefs of MI5 and MI6, Colonel James Edmonds, whose efforts led to the creation of the modern Secret Service, served in the First World War and broke down during the retreat from Mons. For the remainder of the war he served at GHQ. In 1919 he was appointed director of historical research and, four years later, produced the first volume of *The History of the Great War*. The final volume appeared nearly 30 years later in 1949. He died in 1956.

After the war Mansfield Cumming continued to operate a much-reduced bureau. He died on 23 June 1923 at his home in Melbury Road, west London, shortly before he was due to retire. Cumming claimed he was going to publish his memoirs, 'The Indiscretions of a Secret Service Chief'. It was to be bound in red with the title and his name embossed in gold, and every one of the 400 pages would be blank.

'Blinker' Hall went into politics, becoming the Conservative MP for West Derby in 1919. In the Second World War he was an active member of the Home Guard until his death in 1943.

William Melville retired in 1917 in poor health, and died following kidney failure on 1 February the following year. His son James became a barrister, appearing in the celebrated case over the prosecution of Radclyffe Hall's *The Well of Loneliness* for obscenity. He died while serving as solicitor-general in Ramsay McDonald's government.

After the war, Cumming's Sir Vernon Kell fought a long battle to maintain control of his department, which was under attack from the empire-building anti-semitic Basil Thomson, and which over the years became badly run down. By the end of the war, Thomson's Special Branch had increased from fewer than two dozen employees in 1914 to over 700, and he had his sights on an appointment as commissioner of the Metropolitan Police. His downfall was, however, swift. In 1919 he was appointed Director of Intelligence at the Home Office, but resigned in 1921 after a quarrel with Lloyd George—the circumstances of which were never made clear. Worse was to follow.

On 12 December 1925 he was charged with committing an act violating public decency with a prostitute, Thelma De Lava, who was seen masturbating him in Hyde Park. Thomson claimed that while dining at his club he had decided to go to Hyde Park to hear a Communist orator and possibly question him. By the time he arrived, sometime after 10 p.m., the speakers had left and he was solicited by a woman. He was writing a book about prostitution in London and, although he initially rejected her advances, he realized here was the opportunity to get a first-hand account of life in the park. He gave her two or three shillings to sit and talk and if he was seen fiddling in his waistcoat it was because he was putting silver away. His defence was not helped by the fact that De Lava had earlier pleaded guilty. Thomson called an impressive number of character witnesses including 'Blinker' Hall, but the stipendiary magistrate was against him, saying that had he really been researching a book he would have told the constable this straight away. There was also a suggestion that Thomson had tried to bribe the officer and had prevaricated when asked his name, giving it as Home Thomson and pronouncing it Hume. He was fined £5 and 5 guineas costs. When he appealed to Inner London Sessions on 5 February 1926 the chairman, Sir Robert Wallace, said that the majority of the Justices (13 in all) were of the opinion that the appeal should be dismissed and he thought it better to say nothing more.

Thomson's supporters claimed that he had been set up by enemies in the Metropolitan Police. But, at a time when he was angling for an appointment as commissioner, his behaviour was foolishness in the extreme. He went to live in Paris where he kept up a correspondence with the shady Maundy Gregory, convicted in a cash for honours scandal and suspected of at least two murders, at a time when Gregory was thought possibly to be spying for a revived Germany. Thomson wrote a number of detective novels before his death in March 1939 at the age of 78.[24]

In the immediate aftermath of the war, MI5 concentrated its attention on the new enemy, Communism, with its stated intent of the overthrow of the bourgeoisie. In 1929 its name was changed to the Defence Security Service, and in 1931, to the Security Service. That year it assumed formal responsibility for security threats, with the exception of Irish terrorism and anarchists. By the middle of the 1930s the next target was Fascism and its links with Hitler.

Kell never got on well with Churchill, who sacked him in 1940. He was replaced by a veteran police officer, Sir David Petrie, who reformed the department thoroughly. While serving as a special constable Kell caught a cold which developed into pleurisy and pneumonia. He died on 27 March 1943.

The German Secret Service, on the other hand, had reorganized quickly, and by April 1919 its agents were circulating freely on the streets of Paris. By October 1920 Germany was spending £400,000 a year on foreign intelligence.

This side of the Channel the Intelligence Corps soldiered on, shamefully neglected, until 1929, when it was dissolved, not to be re-formed until the first days of the Second World War.

NOTES ON THE TEXT

Introduction

1 Ex-Intelligence Officer [Lionel James], *The German Spy System from Within*, 1914.

2 Herbert Fitch, *Traitors Within: The Adventures of Detective Inspector Herbert T. Fitch*, p. 99.

3 *The Times*, 10 December 1898.

4 Jean-Denis Bredin, *The Affair: The Case of Alfred Dreyfus*. Frederick Brown, *Zola*, ch. XXVII.

5 Arrested in 1898, Colonel Henry cut his throat after drinking most of a bottle of rum in his cell at Fort Mont-Valérian. Esterhazy shaved his moustache, crossed into Belgium and then came to England, where he continued to write anti-semitic articles for French papers until his death Harpenden in 1923. The charges against Picquart were dropped and he became war minister under Clemenceau. He died in 1914 after a fall from his horse. Dreyfus was reinstated and fought with great distinction at Verdun and Chemin des Dames. He died on 12 July 1935. His son Pierre was awarded the Croix-de-Guerre. Two of his nephews were killed in the First World War. Dreyfus' grave in Paris was desecrated in 1988.

6 Both quoted in Michael Smith, *The Spying Game*, p. 398.

7 Marthe McKenna, *I was a Spy!*, p. 39.

8 *Yorkshire Telegraph and Star*, 25 April 1916.

9 John Jones, *The German Spy in America*, p. 27.

10 *Daily Mirror*, 17 March 1911.

11 Letters between Repington, Hardinge, Sanderson and Claeys in The National Archives HD 3/133; Gustav Steinhauer, *Steinhauer: The Kaiser's Master Spy*, p. 11.

12 Vernon Kell lecture, 1934. Imperial War Museum.

13 S. T. Felstead, *German Spies at Bay*, p. 164.

14 Holger H. Herwig, 'Imperial Germany' in Ernest May (ed.), *Knowing One's Enemies: Intelligence Assessment before the Two Wars*, p. 65; David Kahn, *Hitler's Spies*, p. 58; Cees Wiebes, *Intelligence and the War in Bosnia, 1992–1995*; Pohlmann, 'Talking about Schluga'. Another aristocratic spy in France for Germany in the late 1890s was Sidney O'Danne, probably Prussian, born in 1838, who sometimes passed himself off as the Earl of Irishannon and sometimes as von Schwerin. Over the years he was expelled from France on a number of occasions. In January 1900 the Sûreté Interieur was particularly keen to have one of their agents interview O'Danne before he was deported for the fifth time. *Archives du Préfet de Police*, BA 916; *Le Petit Journal*, 3 February 1900.

15 The National Archives KV 6/47.

16 Lady Constance Kell, 'A Secret Well Kept: An Account of the Work of Sir Vernon Kell', unpublished manuscript in the Imperial War Museum.

17 HL Debate, 3 May 1933, vol. 1 87- cc 695–705.

18 After the war Norton-Griffiths sat as a Member of Parliament and later worked as an engineer in Egypt, but after a project collapsed in 1929 he committed suicide on 27 September 1930. Unfortunately Woodhall does not give any more details of Ginhoven's talents. Ginhoven was dismissed from the Metropolitan Police in April 1929 for leaking Special Branch information. He may at one time have been a prisoner of war but he certainly gave evidence in one or two spy trials. E. T. Woodhall, *Spies of the Great War*, p. 18; The National Archives KV 2/1398.

19 Paul Lanoir, *The German Spy System in France*, p. 219.

20 *Confessions*, 28 January 1937.
21 Venita Datta, 'Opium, Gambling and the Demi-Mondaine: The Ullmo Spy Case of 1907'; Ex-Intelligence Officer, *The German Spy System from Within*.
22 Richard Grenier, 'Colonel Redl: The Man Behind the Screen Myth', *New York Times*, 13 October 1985. John Osborne's 1965 play *A Patriot for Me* is based on the Redl case and the 1985 István Szabó film, itself based on the play, starred Klaus Maria Brandauer as *Colonel Redl*.
23 *The Times*, 21, 22 July 1914.
24 Edward Knoblock, *Round the Room*, p. 208.
25 John Kish and David Turns, *International Law and Espionage*.
26 The National Archives KV 1/8.
27 Robert Boucard, *The Secret Services of Europe*, p. 28. Boucard was a French major who worked with British Intelligence at Folkestone in the First World War.
28 De Brézé Darnley-Stuart-Stephens, 'Wolves in Sheeps' Clothing' in *English Review* pp. 241–2, March 1916.
29 William Kalush and Larry Sloman, *The Secret Life of Houdini*, ch. 6.
30 John Maclaren, *Bibliography and Guide to British Intelligence Conducted during the Great War and the Wars of Intervention in Russia 1914–1920*.
31 Louis Rivière, *Un Centre de Guerre Secrète*.

PART ONE

1 Spy Panic

1 The National Archives CAB 16/8.
2 Darrell Bates, *The Fashoda Incident of 1898*.
3 *Daily Telegraph*, 28 October 1908.
4 Quoted in the *Guardian*, 'First World War: Day One, The Road to War,' partwork series in *The Guardian*, 2008.
5 *The Times*, 28 December 1891, 4 February 1892.
6 *The Times*, 25 May, 8 June 1904; *Le Petit Journal*, 5 June 1904.
7 William Tufnell Le Queux was a curious man. Born in July 1864, the son of a French draper and an English mother, he studied art in Paris before embarking on a walking tour of Europe. In the 1880s he edited magazines in London and in 1891 became the parliamentary correspondent of *The Globe* before becoming a full-time writer, which began his successful association with the newspaper magnate Lord Northcliffe. A wireless and flying buff, for a time he was also the honorary consul for San Marino.
8 First published in *Blackwood's Magazine* in May 1871, it was reprinted as a sixpenny pamphlet and sold over 80,000 copies. It was translated into French, German, Dutch and Italian.
9 For a full account of these novels and an assessment of their influence on pre-First World War thinking, see Niall Ferguson, *The Pity of War*.
10 The National Archives HD 3/130. Colonel Francis Davies to Sir Thomas Sanderson, 31 January 1905.
11 Bernard Porter, 'M: MI5's First Spymaster', *The English Historical Review* 120 (2005).
12 The National Archives KV 1/5.
13 The National Archives KV 1/8.
14 The National Archives KV 6/47.
15 The National Archives HD 3/133.
16 The National Archives HD 3/130, KV 6/47, Colonel Francis Davies to Sir Thomas Sanderson, 31 January 1905.
17 *Police Review*, 19 March 1906.
18 The National Archives KV 4/183.
19 The National Archives MEPO 3/243.
20 William Le Queux, *German Spies in England: An Exposure*, p. 55.
21 The National Archives KV 1/7.
22 *Notes on invasion supplied to Mr Balfour*, The National Archives CAB 3/2/42C;

John Gooch, *The Prospect of War: Studies in British Defence Policy 1847–1942.*

23 The National Archives CAB 3/2/42A.

24 Slade papers III, National Maritime Museum MRF 39/3.

25 The National Archives HO 3/139, Hardinge to British Ambassador in Constantinople, 12 January 1909.

26 The National Archives FO 371/80, file 40513, pp. 191–2.

27 *The Times,* 10, 15 August 1905.

28 The National Archives KV 1/2.

29 The National Archives KV 6/47.

30 De Brézé Darnley-Stuart-Stephens, 'Wolves in Sheep's Clothing' in *English Review,* March 1916.

31 The National Archives 106/47B, p. 8. Remarks on Col. Repington's figures by MO2.

32 James Edmonds, *Memoirs,* p. 9.

33 When, somewhat surprisingly, the play was produced in Berlin at Easter that year, the German papers were quick to ridicule the idea that England would be invaded by Germany. The *Lokalanzieger* wrote 'We suppose Du Maurier wishes to warn Englishmen against the danger of invasion by Servia [*sic*] or Montenegro or some other great power'. Quoted in *New York Times,* 4 April 1909.

34 Jane, another who was obsessed with the spy fear, had kidnapped a German in Portsmouth and taken him to what is now Whipsnade Zoo, where he had released him. This jape had resulted in a shoal of letters telling of suspicious Germans making enquiries about railway bridges, gas and water supplies and maps.

35 Spy panic was not confined to Britain. In March 1909 *Navy,* the journal of the Navy League, reported that in Schleswig-Holstein and along the Friesland coast extraordinary powers had been given to 'petty office-holders'. Half a dozen 'harmless folk wearing an English look have been seized, run in and searched on the flimsiest evidence,

but so far as is known nobody has been detained'.

36 A.J.A. Morris *Scaremongers,* p. 160.

37 James Edmonds, *Memoirs,* ch. xx. p. 9.

2 Kell and Counter-Espionage

1 Lady Kell, 'A Secret Well Kept'. The quote continues, 'I was sure he would succeed, so he decided to accept the suggestion of the Committee of Imperial Defence that he should start a scheme of Special Defence to counter Espionage.' Unpublished biography of Sir Vernon Kell, Imperial War Museum.

2 The National Archives KV 1/3, KV 1/46.

3 The National Archives KV 1/5.

4 Valentine Williams, *The World of Action,* p. 335.

5 *The Autocar,* 6 June 1903.

6 Paul Dukes, *Red Dusk and the Morrow,* p. 11.

7 Edward Knoblock, *Round the Room.*

8 For an account of Cumming's early struggles in the office see Alan Judd, *The Quest for C,* ch. 4.

9 The National Archives CAB 16/8. In the file Brodtmann is spelled Brockmann.

10 BA-MA RM. 5/3712. Bundesarchiv-Militärarchiv, German Military Archives, Freiburg.

11 The National Archives KV 1/7.

12 The National Archives FO 1093/28.

13 Letter Ewart to Churchill, 28 April 1910. The National Archives HO 317/44.

14 The National Archives KV 1/39.

15 *The Times,* 5 November 1911.

16 The National Archives KV 1/39. Tobler was described as aged about 50, 5'6" or 5' 7" in height with dark hair and beard.

17 Peterssen's commercial spy agency in Brussels was not the only one in existence. There was said to be two more in that city alone. In Geneva Captain Paul Larguier ran the International Spy Agency until he was deported from Switzerland following a scandal in November 1913 when he was accused

of espionage to the detriment of
Switzerland, Italy and Germany. He
and a number of others of what the
newspapers described as the 'Larguier-
Rosselet gang' had been peddling
information regarding German airships
supplied by an officer in the Landwehr.
The Times, 17 November 1913,
4 February 1914.
18 The National Archives KV 1/39.
19 A.K.Graves, *Secrets of the German War
Office*, pp. 12–13.
20 James Edmonds, *Memoirs*, ch. xx.
21 Lady Kell, 'A Secret Well Kept', p.143,
Imperial War Museum.
22 The National Archives KV 1/41,
KV 4/112; *The Times*, 3 June 1914.
23 The National Archives KV 1/41.
24 The National Archives KV 1/41.
25 The National Archives KV 1/41 para 921.
26 The National Archives CRIM 1/151/2.
27 Gustav Steinhauer, *The Kaiser's Master
Spy*, pp. 48–50.

3 British Spies under Cumming

1 George Hill, *Go Spy the Land*, p. 6.
2 Alan Judd, *The Quest for C*, pp. 209–210.
3 Alan Judd, *ibid.*, pp. 118–121. The chapter *Formation and Frustration* has a most
entertaining account of Cumming's
struggles for independence and even to
purchase a typewriter.
4 Alan Judd, *ibid.*, p. 158.
5 Alan Judd, *ibid.*, p.210.
6 At the time of his death in 1934, which
was possibly murder, Clarkson was
under investigation over a series of
fraudulent arson claims. His forged will
resulted in the London solicitor Edwin
O'Connor and the clerk William Cooper
Hobbs both serving lengthy sentences.
James Morton, *Gangland: The Lawyers*.
7 Alan Judd, *The Quest for C*, pp.213–15.
8 *The Times*, 10, 23 March 1916.
9 RG Box K-2-B File 9788 Agent Z
Report, 24 August 1901. United States
National Archives.

10 The National Archives ADM 12/1481.
11 Royal Marine Museum, AECG
11/11/2 and Arch T-3 Trench papers.
12 *The Times*, 2, 23 December 1910.
13 On 1 July 1911 the German gunboat
Panther arrived at Agadir at a time
when Morocco was rebelling against
the French. Its appearance was intended
to intimidate the French and resulted
in the Treaty of Fez which, in return for
Germany's acceptance of the French
position, ceded to Germany certain
territory in what is now the Republic of
Congo. It also unintentionally resulted
in a stronger French alliance with
Britain.
14 For an account of this fiasco see
Nicholas Hiley, 'The Failure of British
Espionage against Germany, 1907–
1914', *The Historical Journal*, 26, 4
(1983) pp. 867–9.
15 *Hamburger Nachrichten*, 12 February
1912. There is a copy of the letter in
The National Archives' FO 371/1373;
Hector C. Bywater, *Strange Intelligence*.
16 Hector Bywater, *ibid.*, p. 176.
17 Alan Judd, *The Quest for C*, pp. 230–31.
18 Quoted in Alan Judd, *ibid.*, pp. 224–5.
19 *The Times*, 2 January 1912.
20 Brussels had long been an international
exchange for naval and military secrets
of every country. In December 1898
Victor Decrion, once of a French artillery regiment, was said to be carrying
on such an agency for the sale of confidential military documents. He had
two other former soldiers, Bonnasse and
Le Rendu, helping him and they had
obtained the specifications of a new rifle
from a Brigadier Groult.
21 C. Lux, *L'Evasion du Capitaine Lux*;
Pascal Krop, *Les Secrets de l'Espionnage
Français*.
22 *The Times*, 2 January, 22 February, 9 July
1912. Stewart later wrote 'Germany and
Ourselves' for the *National Review*, June
1914 and 'An Active Service Pocket
Book'. He was killed in September 1914

rallying troops who were under attack. 'I was with him at the time and must tell you I am certain it was the death near Braisne he would have chosen', wrote a companion to his parents. His regiment awarded an annual essay prize in his name. Some time later three men were arrested at a hotel in the Place Vendôme in Paris. One gave the same rank and number as Stewart. Shortly after, he and the others admitted they were Germans. Harry J. Greenwall, *The Underworld of Paris,* p. 153.

23 Much against the advice of Cumming, Stewart's widow was finally paid the £10,000. Alan Judd, *The Quest for C,* pp. 241–2.

24 *The Advertiser,* (South Australia), 10 April 1911. Maimon was an interesting man. Born in Syria he had spied on behalf of Abdul Hamid, the ex-Sultan of Turkey and was also suspected of disclosing details of Russian-German proposals arranged at Potsdam.

25 William James, *A Great Seaman, The Life of Admiral of the Fleet Sir Henry F. Oliver,* pp. 123–4; *The Times,* 21, 23 September 1911.

26 *The Times,* 6 August 1912.

27 Robert Baden-Powell, *My Adventures as a Spy,* pp. 52 et seq.

28 'Britain's Greatest Spy Captured' in *Daily Mirror,* March 1911.

29 Henry Landau, *All's Fair,* p. 44.

30 Nicholas P. Hiley, 'Failure of British Espionage against Germany 1907–1914' in *Historical Journal,* vol. XXVI, 1983; The National Archives FO 608/128/12.

31 William H Honan, *Bywater.*

32 Robin Bruce Lockhart, *Ace of Spies,* p. 54.

33 Alan Judd, *The Quest for C,* p. 384.

34 Christopher Andrew, *Secret Service,* pp. 129–30; The National Archives FO 383/22.

35 *The Times,* 3 July 1912, 31 January, 1 February 1913.

36 *The Times,* 29 August 1912.

37 Hector Bywater, *Strange Intelligence,* p. 180; *The Times,* 26 June 1914. A month earlier the French airship constructor Clément Bayard caused similar consternation but his was seen as a rather more serious attempt at espionage. He and friends were found rather too close to a Zeppelin hangar at Cologne. Worse, they had taken photographs of the Fuhlsbüttel aerodrome after which they had been followed by the Hamburg police. Arrests followed but explanations and apologies were eventually accepted. *The Times,* 27 May, 3 June 1914.

PART TWO

1 Too young to receive the death penalty, Princip was sentenced on 28 October 1914 to 20 years' hard labour, and Cabrinovic 16 years'. Other leaders of the conspiracy to kill the Archduke were hanged on 3 February 1915. Princip and Cabrinovic died in prison. They had both contracted tuberculosis in prison and Princip, who had had an arm amputated, had died at Theresienstadt on 28 April 1918. Cabrinovic died in 1916. In the Second World War, the prison became a Nazi concentration camp. *The Times,* 29 October 1914.

2 For a proponent of the latter theory see Fritz Fischer, *War of Illusions: German Policies from 1911 to 1914.*

3 Gary Sheffield, 'First World War: Day One, The Road to War', partwork series in *The Guardian,* 2008.

4 *The Times,* 1 September 1914.

5 *The Times,* 2 September 1914.

6 The National Archives CAB 45/206. Diary of Sir Horace Smith-Dorrien.

7 *The Times,* 1 September 1914.

8 *The Times,* 12 August 1914.

9 *The Times,* 7 September 1914.

10 *Matin,* 23 August 1914.

11 Harry Greenwall, *The Underworld of Paris*, p. 160 *et seq.*

4 The Intelligence Corps

1 Quoted by Colonel F.G. Robson, *History of the Intelligence Corps 1914–1984,* unpublished manuscript, Intelligence Corps Archives.
2 Kirke manuscript, Imperial War Museum.
3 Torrie was killed at Grandcourt on 18 November 1916.
4 Walter Kirke, *The Origin of the Intelligence Corps*, p. 1. Intelligence Corps Archives.
5 Woolrych Papers, ICA; A.F. Judge, *The 'Intelligence Corps' 1914–1928*, p. 154.
6 Blennerhasset became a brilliant interrogator and received the Croix de Guerre. D.S.Hawker, 'An Outline of the Early History of the Intelligence Corps'. For a highly entertaining account of some of the other recruits and the early days of the Corps, see Christopher Andrew, *Secret Service*, pp. 195–200.
7 Intelligence Corps Archives
8 A.F. Judge, *The 'Intelligence Corps' 1914–1928*, p. 140.
9 Walter Kirke, *The Origin of the Intelligence Corps*, p. 1.
10 The story was repeated as fact in 'MI5: A Century in the Shadows', on BBC Radio 4 on 27 July 2009. A. Judd, *The Quest for C*, p. 283–5.
11 Kirke, *The Origin of the Intelligence Corps*, p. 38.
12 Sigismund Payne Best, *The Origins of the Intelligence Corps*, BEF 1914, p. 2. Unpublished account in Imperial War Museum.
13 A.F. Judge, *The 'Intelligence Corps' 1914–1928*, p. 16.
14 S.T. Felstead, *German Spies at Bay*, ch. VII.
15 Colonel F.G.Robson, *History of the Intelligence Corps 1914–19*, vol. I, unpublished MS in IC archives; L.S.

Amery, *My Political Life*, vol. II, ch. 2.
16 Sigismund Payne Best, *The Origins of the Intelligence Corps, BEF 1914.*
17 Lieutenant Colonel R.J. Drake, Drake Papers, para 75, Intelligence Corps Archives, Chicksands.
18 Walter Kirke, Diary, 4 October 1915, Intelligence Corps Archives.
19 Letter Ernest Wallinger to R. J. Drake, 2 April 1918, Intelligence Corps Archives.
20 One Intelligence officer, M.G. Pearson, reported that he had been successful in crossing a parrot with a pigeon so that the bird could deliver its message verbally. He was taken literally and was fortunate not to be prosecuted under the Official Secrets Act.
21 H.C. O'Neill, *Royal Fusiliers in the Great War*, quoted by A.F. Judge, *The 'Intelligence Corps' 1914 to 1919*, p. 34.
22 A.F. Judge, *The 'Intelligence Corps' 1914 to 1919*, p. 58.
23 In 1920 Toplis killed a taxi driver and, after a chase across England and Scotland in which he killed a police officer, he was shot dead.
24 Drake Papers, para 89.
25 Lieutenant Colonel R.J. Drake, *ibid.*, para 54.
26 Kirkpatrick, *The War 1914–18*, p. 69.
27 Kirkpatrick, *ibid.*, pp. 69–71.
28 Kirkpatrick, *ibid.*, p. 76.
29 General Sir Ian Hamilton, *Gallipoli Diary*, quoted by A.F. Judge, *The 'Intelligence Corps' 1914 to 1919.*
30 For an account of espionage in Greece generally, see Compton Mackenzie's *Greek Memories*, Edward Knoblock's *Round the Room* and John Coleby 'A Marine or Anything', *Royal Marine Spies.*
31 *The Times*, 2 January 1916; The National Archives WO 32/4898.
32 Other archaeologists working in intelligence included T.E. Lawrence, who was never officially attached to the Intelligence Corps, and Gertrude Bell.

33 Hillel Hankin, *A Strange Death; The Sun* (New York), 1 June 2005.
34 N.M.E.Bray, *A Paladin of Arabia*.
35 N.M.E.Bray, *ibid*.; A. F. Judge, *The 'Intelligence Corps' 1914–1928*, p. 17. Leachman was murdered by Sheik Dhari near Fallijah on 12 August 1920.

5 In Holland and Belgium

1 James Dunn, *Paperchase*, p. 42.
2 Baron Guido Errante, 'The German Intelligence Service during the World War', *United States Infantry Journal*, Nov–Dec 1933.
3 For a discussion on the subject, see Tammy M. Proctor, *Female Intelligence*, citing Leon Schirmann, who believes the Fräulein existed, *Mata-Hari:Autopsie d'une machination*, and Pascal Krop, who does not, *Les Secrets de l'espionnage Français de 1870 à nos Jours*.
4 Magnus Hirschfeld, *The Sexual History of the Great War*, ch. 14.
5 Magnus Hirschfeld, *ibid*.
6 Magnus Hirschfeld, *ibid*.
7 E. T. Woodhall, *Spies of the Great War*, p. 12.
8 *The Times*, 9, 18 December 1919; *Le Soir* 28 September 1934; *Paris-Midi* 19, 24 November 1933.
9 Vernon Kell lecture, p. 28. Imperial War Museum PP/MCR/120.
10 David Khan, *Hitler's Spies*, pp. 35–6.
11 James Dunn, *Paperchase*, p. 42.
12 *Ibid.*, p. 42.
13 *Ibid.*, p. 42.
14 The National Archives WO 106/6189; Lieutenant M.R.K. Burge, *History of the British Secret Service in Holland 1914–1917*.
15 Kirkpatrick papers p. 58.
16 *The Times*, 31 May, 1, 5 June 1911. In *Armour against Fate* Michael Occleshaw proffers an interesting but probably ultimately unsustainable theory that Cameron's trial and sentence was a cover to enable him to vanish from his regiment and into the Secret Service without further inquiries. It is difficult to accept this. It is not as if reports of the trial showed anything but deep complicity unless the evidence was wholly rigged. Nor were efforts to obtain a pardon for Cameron kept secret. As for his suggestion that he was released a year early, prisoners were entitled to remission for good behaviour and an officer, if not a gentleman, whose father had been awarded the VC, would certainly be in line for maximum remission.
17 Ivone Kirkpatrick, *The War 1914–1918*, p. 59. Imperial War Museum.
18 Drake papers, p. 2.
19 Henry Landau, *All's Fair*, pp. 131–2.
20 Ivone Kirkpatrick, *The Inner Circle*, pp. 146–7.
21 The National Archives FO 371/2163.
22 The National Archives KV 6/47. The file itself is a collection of a number of disparate papers on espionage culled for historical reasons when other files were destroyed.
23 S.H.C. Woolrych, *Recollections of World War I*, p. 32, Intelligence Corps Archives.
24 S.H.C. Woolrych, *ibid.*, pp 34–35.
25 S.H.C. Woolrych, *ibid*.
26 Christopher Andrew, *Secret Service*, pp. 238–9; P. Decock, *La Dame Blanche*, pp. 65–72; Tammy Proctor, *Female Intelligence*.
27 Ivone Kirkpatrick, *The War 1914–1918*, p. 127.
28 Ivone Kirkpatrick, *The War 1914–1918*, p. 18; Hubert P. Van Tuyall, *The Netherlands and World War I: Espionage, Diplomacy and Survival*, p. 162.
29 Walter Kirke was more impressed with Marié than some, giving him the name of the moustache-twirling Jean Bart in a post-war novel. Mervyn Lamb [Kirke] Diary, Part 1, p. 444; Ben MacIntyre, 'Solved: The Riddle of Executed First World War Soldier Robert Digby'.
30 Ivone Kirkpatrick, *The War 1914–1918*, p. 19–20.

31 Ivone Kirkpatrick, *The War 1914–1918*, appendix, p. 4.

32 Walter Kirke, papers at Intelligence Corps Archives.

33 He was not alone. When Deputy-Brigadier Henry Wilson said he saw no reason for an officer to know any language but his own and he knew of no commander who did, it was pointed out to him that the line went back to Julius Caesar who preferred to speak in Greek. Sir James Edmonds, *How Different Then: Reminiscences and Comments of a Nonagenarian 1861–1951*, unpublished manuscript, Kings College London; Kirke Diary, 29 November 1915; Payne Best transcripts at IWM; Henry Landau, *Spreading the Spy Net*, pp. 31–3.

34 Kirke Diary, 30 November 1915. In addition to his other duties Tinsley was heavily involved in propaganda and formed close links with the socialist journalist Carl Minster who fomented insurrection in Germany and supported the left-wing newspaper *Der Kampf*.

35 Henry Landau, *All's Fair*, p. 37.

36 Ivone Kirkpatrick, *The Inner Circle*, pp. 16–17.

37 In fact Fryatt had received two gold watches. In the same month he had escaped from another submarine. He had also used the *Brussels* to help evacuate Allied troops. His funeral service took place at St Paul's Cathedral. A Pathé newsclip can be seen on the web. A similar incident occurred in the Ionian Sea when an Austrian submarine fired on a Greek vessel containing bags and officers. Capt Stanley Wilson flung a bag of diplomatic papers overboard which was retrieved by the submarine captain. Major Stanley, 'R' Head of Intelligence in Athens was not pleased as a complete list of Constantinople agents was in the bag. An American lady stood over another bag which was not searched. Yet another bag was captured in Russia in not dissimilar circumstances and its contents published in the neutral press. Compton MacKenzie, *My Life and Times*, p. 41; *First Athenian Memories*, p. 339.

When Bertie Sullivan, the nephew of Sir Arthur Sullivan, was used as a courier by the Naval Intelligence Department carrying secret documents to the Continent his dispatch case was loaded with lead. On one occasion he was torpedoed and clung to a raft until he was rescued. Later he was offered the chance of a recuperatory holiday and, an hour out of Newcastle, was torpedoed again. Once more he survived, this time in a small boat. Hugh Hoy, *40 OB*, pp. 43–4; Ivone Kirkpatrick, *The War 1914–1918*.

38 Ivone Kirkpatrick, *The War 1914–1918*, pp. 65–6.

39 C.F. Oppenheimer, *Stranger Within*, p. 266 *et seq*.

40 Peterson, described by Henry Landau as Tinsley's general factotum, was, in fact, Dmitch de Peterson, also known as Jong and Stern, and was the son of the Russian consul general.

41 F. Kluiters, *R.B. Tinsley, a Biographical Note*.

42 The National Archives WO 106/6189: Lt M.R.K. Burge, *History of the British Secret Service in Holland 1914–1917*.

43 Henry Landau, *All's Fair*, p. 46.

44 Ivone Kirkpatrick, *The War 1914–1918*, pp. 150–51.

45 *Ibid*.

46 *Ibid*.

47 The National Archives WO 106/6189. Lt. M.R.K. Burge, *History of the British Secret Service in Holland 1914–1917*. Intelligence Corps Archives.

48 Henry Landau, *All's Fair*, pp. 139–40.

49 For an account of Mme Rischard and her network, see Janet Morgan, *The Secrets of Rue St. Roch*.

50 Lieutenant Colonel R.J. Drake, *History of Intelligence (B) British Expeditionary*

Force, France from January 1917 to April 1919, para. 48. Intelligence Corps Archives.

51 The Bosworth papers, Intelligence Corps Archives.

6 Spies in the Tower

1 The National Archives WO 71/1236.
2 John Frazer, *Sixty Years in Uniform*, pp. 220–21.
3 The National Archives WO 71/1236.
4 Hugh Hoy, *40 O.B. or How the War was Won*, p. 66.
5 The Irish patriot and one-time British consul, Casement went to Berlin to try to raise an Irish brigade from among Irish prisoners of war captured after the Battle of Mons. He only recruited about 60; they were sent to a camp near Berlin and given green uniforms with gold harps on the collars. Casement was arrested when he returned to Ireland, convicted of treason and hanged on 3 August 1916. Sir Basil Thomson, *Queer People*, p. 132.
6 Michael Smith, *The Spying Game*, p. 398.
7 Basil Thomson, *Queer People*, p. 99.
8 The National Archives WO 71/1236;
9 The National Archives WO 71/1236; The National Archives WO 94/103 Frederick Lloyd to Field Marshal Sir Evelyn Wood, 9 June 1915. British army deserters were usually executed at Wandsworth.
10 The National Archives WO 71/1236.
11 The National Archives WO 141/2/2; C. Olsson in *Picture Post*, 26 November 1938, pp. 61–71.
12 The National Archives KV 1/44; The National Archives WO 141/1/3; Sir Vernon Kell papers PP/MCR/120, Imperial War Museum; S.T. Felstead, *German Spies at Bay*, pp. 33–40.
13 The National Archives WO 141/1/7; WO 71/1312; Basil Thomson, *Queer People*, pp. 136–7.

14 The National Archives WO 71/1237; Basil Thomson, *ibid.*; S.T. Felstead, *German Spies at Bay*.
15 The National Archives WO 141/61; Basil Thomson, *ibid.*, p. 145; S.T. Felstead, *ibid.*, pp. 130–31.
16 The National Archives WO 71/1313; S.T. Felstead, *German Spies at Bay*, pp. 142–3.
17 The National Archives WO 71/1313.
18 The National Archives DPP 1/41. A greengrocer and illegal bookmaker, Pierrepoint was a member of a long-serving family of hangmen. First appointed in 1906 he later became hangman for the Irish Free State.
19 The National Archives WO 141/3/1.
20 *Ibid.*
21 The National Archives WO 141/3/1; S.T. Felstead, *German Spies at Bay*, pp. 118–19. Most writers take the view that the pair were in love or at least that Wertheim was in love with Breeckow but S.T. Felstead in his biography of Sir Richard Muir, who prosecuted them, suggests that Wertheim was a fading *demi-mondaine* in need of money and that Breeckow had been recruited very much against his will.
22 The National Archives WO 71/1238; S.T. Felstead, *ibid.*, p. 151; Basil Thomson, *Queer People*, pp. 156–7.
23 The National Archives WO 141/83; S.T. Felstead, *ibid.*
24 In his excellent account of the German spies shot in the Tower, Leonard Sellers provides an interesting footnote to the Zender story. In September 1975 a cartridge, said to have been found on the beach below the Tower promenade, was advertised for sale in *Exchange and Mart*. It was engraved *H. Zender, The Tower of London, 22nd January 1916*. Its provenance must therefore be seriously in question. The National Archives WO 141/2/4; S.T. Felstead, *ibid.*; Leonard Sellers, *Shot in the Tower*, pp. 172–3.

7 Survivors

1 To his arresting officer. The National Archives DPP 1/42.

2 S.T. Felstead, *German Spies at Bay*.

3 Valentine Williams, *The World of Action*, p. 331; Henri Beland, *My Three Years in a German Prison*, pp. 138 *et seq*.

4 *New York Times*, 22 October 1915.

5 J.B. Sterndale Bennett, 'I Guarded Spies in The Tower' in *The Great War: I Was There*, pt. 22.

6 *New York Times*, 8 October 1915.

7 The National Archives ADM 178/99.

8 The National Archives KV 1/43.

9 The National Archives FO 228/2945.

10 The National Archives WO 32/4898; H.T. Fitch, *Traitors Within*, pp. 166–7.

11 The National Archives PCOM 8/257.

12 The National Archives FO 373/1059, KV 2/4; Herbert Yardley, *The American Black Chamber*, pp. 69 *et seq*; *Saturday Evening Post*, 4 April 1931.

13 The National Archives KV 1/43, G branch report for 1916; WO 32/4898.

14 Basil Thomson, *Queer People*, pp. 161–4.

15 The National Archives DPP 1/48; Basil Thomson, *Queer People*.

16 Horst von der Goltz, *My Adventures as a German Secret Service Agent*.

17 The National Archives HO 144/21710; H. Brust, *I Guarded Kings;* Horst von der Goltz, *My Adventures as a German Secret Service Agent*.

18 The National Archives DPP 1/42.

19 The National Archives DPP 1/42.

20 *The Times*, 13 June 1918.

21 The previous man to be stripped of his honours had been Sir Roger Casement. The next was Lord Kagan, following his conviction and imprisonment in 1981 for theft and false accounting. It is curious that the Jonas case is omitted in the biographies of most of the barristers at his trial but is referred to briefly in Edward Marjoribanks, *The Life of Sir Edward Marshall Hall*.

22 Basil Thomson, *Queer People*.

23 The National Archives WO 32/4898.

24 The National Archives KV 2/1094.

25 Ronald Seth. *The Spy Who Wasn't Caught;* David Khan, *Hitler's Spies*, p. 32.

26 Valentine Williams, *The World in Action*, p. 334.

27 *Ibid*.

8 Room 40 and the Zimmermann Telegram

1 To Senator Henry Cabot Lodge, selections from the correspondence of Roosevelt and Lodge, Scribner's, New York, 1925.

2 Barbara Tuchman, *The Zimmermann Telegram*, pp. 10–11.

3 After Tannenberg the blame was placed on the Russian Minister of War who had a Jewish wife and a week before had sent a letter to a friend in Austria saying because of bad weather 'long walks are out of the question'. This was deemed to be in code. He was perhaps fortunate to receive a sentence of life imprisonment, but there again, perhaps not. W. Bruce Lincoln, *Passage through Armageddon: The Russians in War & Revolution 1914–1918*, p. 64; Robert B. Asprey, *The German High Command at War: Hindenburg and Ludendorff Conduct World War I*, p. 93.

4 A. G. Denniston, undated and untitled manuscript on Room 40, MSS DENN 1/3 Churchill College Archives Centre, Cambridge; Sir Henry Oliver, 'Notes about Room 40 and Sir Alfred Ewing in the 1914–1918 War'; Oliver MSS OLV/8, National Maritime Museum.

5 A. G. Denniston, undated and untitled MS on Room 40, MSS DENN 1/3; Churchill College Archives Centre, Cambridge.

6 Hall, the son of William Henry Hall the first DNI, had captained the battle cruiser *Queen Mary* until ill-health had forced him to retire from active service in the first months of the war. The author Compton Mackenzie thought

that he and Mansfield Cumming were caricatures of each other and both looked like Punch. In 1909, when commanding a cadet training ship, Hall had run a successful but unauthorized 'raid' on Kiel, taking photographs. Compton Mackenzie, *Life and Times, Octave Five*, p. 113.

7 Christopher Andrew, *Secret Service*, p. 147; W.F. Clarke, Narrative of Captain Hope and '40 OB & GC to CS 1914 to 1945', ch. 3, Churchill College Archives, Cambridge MSS CLKE 3.

8 Patrick Beesly, *Room 40*, pp. 3–4. On another occasion early in the war no intelligence officer was on the flagship of the Australian squadron sent to destroy a German wireless station at Rabaul in Papua New Guinea. The fleet could not find Rabaul and returned to base. Sir George Aston, *Secret Service*.

9 The SKM is now in The National Archives ADM 137/4156 where it shows no sign of sea-staining; W. S. Churchill, *World Crisis*, vol. 1, p. 462; Patrick Beesly, *Room 40*, pp. 4–6.

10 Szek's father appears to have believed his son survived the war and attempted to obtain compensation for his son's efforts. Alan Judd does not believe that Szek was killed thinking that Cumming [*sic*] was incapable of such an action. Alan Judd, *The Quest for C*, ch. 15. See also Robert Bouchard, *Revelations from the Secret Service*.

11 Christopher Sykes, *Wassmuss 'The German Lawrence'*.

12 For a full but succinct account of the Battle of Jutland, see Christopher Andrew, *Secret Service*, pp. 162–167. In 1923 Winston Churchill prosecuted Lord Alfred Douglas, the one time lover of Oscar Wilde, for criminal libel over allegations of a Jewish conspiracy linking him, the Battle of Jutland and the death of Lord Kitchener. Douglas received six months.

13 Barbara Tuchman, *The Zimmermann Telegram*, p. 107 *et seq.*

14 Charles Seymour, *The Intimate Papers of Colonel House*, quoted in Barbara Tuchman, *The Zimmermann Telegram*.

15 *New York Times*, 25 October 1915; Charles F. Horne, (ed.) *Source Records of the Great War*, vol. III.

16 Woodrow Wilson, 18 December 1916. Barbara Tuchman, *The Zimmerman Telegram*, p. 128

17 Various sources, quoted in Barbara Tuchman, *The Zimmermann Telegram*, p. 152.

18 *Ibid.*, p. 151.

19 *New York Times*, 1 March 1917.

20 There was more bad news for Zimmermann. On 14 April he was told that Mexico had decided to remain neutral. That summer he was involved in preliminary negotiations with Papal Nuncio Eugenio Pacelli, later Pius XII, which were designed to lead to peace talks. The basic terms were to have been no annexation of territories, no border changes with Russia, Poland to remain independent, all occupied territories to be evacuated and Alsace-Lorraine returned to France. The *quid pro quo* was that all German colonies would be returned to Germany. The talks came to nothing after Zimmermann resigned on 6 August 1917.

9 Women Spies for the Allies

1 Ferdinand Tuohy, *The Secret Corps: A Tale of 'Intelligence' on All Fronts*, pp. 17–18.

2 *Norddeutsche Allgemeine Zeitung*, 20 November 1915.

3 Ferdinand Tuohy, *The Secret Corps : A Tale of 'Intelligence' on All Fronts;* see also Mervyn Lamb, *On Hazardous Service*.

4 The National Archives FO 383/15.

5 On 25 August 1914 as a reprisal for the shooting of the German military commander by the son of the town's

burgomaster and a quickly suppressed uprising in which 50 German soldiers were killed, the town of Louvain, including its precious library, was razed and its 42,000 inhabitants forced to flee. On 7 May 1915 the *Lusitania*, known as the 'Greyhound of the Sea', carrying both passengers and munitions, was torpedoed without warning off the Irish coast with a loss of over 1,000 lives. 114 Americans died. America had made a point of not shooting Elizabeth van Lew, Rose Greenhow and Belle Boyd during the Civil War and the Cavell incident was an early contribution to the eventual entry of the United States into the war.

6   Charles F. Horne, *Source Records of the Great War*, vol. III.

7   *The Times*, 27 November 1915.

8   After the war Petit became a national heroine. There are statues of her in Brussels and Tournai. In 1920 a play was produced about her life and a film was made in 1928.

9   *The Argus* (Melbourne), 7 October 1915.

10 *Gazette de Liège*, 24 June 1919.

11 Bishop of London, Trafalgar Day Sermon, 1915.

12 Marie-Anne Claire Hughes, 'War, Gender and National Mourning: The Significance of the Death and Commemoration of Edith Cavell in Britain', *European Review of History*, November 2005.

13 Walter Kirke, Diary 2, 5, 6 November 1915; Tammy M. Proctor, *Female Intelligence*, pp. 116 *et seq*; Marthe McKenna, *I was a Spy!*

14 Archives de État à Liège, Parquet Genéral, Affair Thielens, boite 3, dossier no 7018; Tammy Proctor, *Female Intelligence*, ch. 5.

15 Paul Durand, *Agents Secrets, L'Affaire Fauquenot-Birckel*.

16 In France, prostitutes were given cards by the authorities, which they were meant to show to get work in brothels.

17 Dossier Marthe Richard in Bibliothèque

Marguerite Duras, Paris; Marthe Richer, *I Spied for France*; Natacha Henry, *Marthe Richard L'Aventurière des Maisons Closes*; 'La Farce des Services Secrets', *Crapouillot*, no. 15.

18 *New York Times*, 1 April 1917; 'Les Femmes 'Croix de Guerre', in an undated and unidentified French newspaper, 940. 3 GUE in Bibliothèque Marguerite Duras.

19 Mathilde Lebrun, *Mes Treize Missions; Canberra Times*, 10, 17 February 1927.

20 Archives Générales du Royaume, *La Belgique Occupée, 1914–1918*, Service Éducatif, Dossiers, Première Série , no. 20 Brussels, 1998, p. 63.

21 Ferdinand Tuohy, 'Women as Secret Service Agents', *The Statesman*, 17 January 1926.

10 Fräuleins for the Kaiser

1   To Basil Thomson. The National Archives MEPO 3/2444.

2   Sam Waagener, *The Murder of Mata Hari*, pp. 10–11.

3   The National Archives MEPO 3/2444.

4   Nederlande Gezantschap in Groot-Brittanie (en Ierland) 1813–1932 (849) Alegmeen Rijsarchief (NGG-B AR).

5   Service Historique de l'Armée de Terre, Vincennes, cited in Julie Wheelwright, *The Fatal Lover*; The National Archives MEPO 3/244.

6   The National Archives MEPO 3/2444.

7   The Second Battle of l'Aisne took place in April 1917 when the French, led by Robert Nivelle, attacked German machine-gun strongholds in an all-out offensive designed to be the attack which ended the war. After two days it was clear that it would not succeed and over the next month other attacks only gained seven kilometres. Nivelle, who had been advised the tactic would not be successful, was replaced. One consequence was that men in 49 infantry divisions mutinied and deserted

complaining about the way the war was being conducted. 554 were sentenced to death although the number actually shot is estimated at between 30 and 50. The Stanley Kubrick anti-war film *Paths of Glory* is based on the aftermath of the Chemin de Dames attack. Guy Pedoncini, *Les Mutiniérs de 1917*.

8   For a full account of the investigation into her alleged spying, see Julie Wheelwright, *The Fatal Lover*, ch. 4.

9   Archives de France F/7/15978/2.

10 'Is Mata Hari Still Alive?', *Daily Mail*, 3 September 1929.

11 Emile Massard *Female Spies in Paris*, ch. 9.

12 Magnus Hirschfeld, *The Sexual History of the Great War*.

13 Emile Massard, *Les Espionnes à Paris*, ch. 5.

14 Emile Massard, *Les Espionnes à Paris*, ch. 9.

15 Roger Faligot and Rémi Kauffer, *Histoire Mondiale du Renseignement Tome I 1870–1939*; Magnus Hirschfeld, *The Sexual History of the Great War*; Emile Massard, *ibid*.

16 J.M. Spaight, *Air Power and War Rights*, p. 288; F. Baumann, *Der Fall Edith Cavell* p. 117; K. Baschwitz, *Der Massenwahn, seine Wirkung und seine Beherrschung*, p. 196. Part of the problem lies in the translation of documents. For example Josie-Maria dei Posi is often given as Marie José di Basi, a female spy, but in fact the name is Dei Posi and the spy was an Argentinian male. Similarly the actress Suzy Depsy is often listed as having been 'condemned' but she was only 'condemned' to a short period in prison. James Morgan Read, *Atrocity Propaganda 1914–1919*, p. 215.

17 Archives Nationales BB/24/2116; *New York Times*, 22 October 1915.

18 Archives Nationales BB/24/2121.

19 E.T. Woodhall gives slightly different names. *ibid.*, p. 113.

20 Robert Boucard, *The Secret Services of Europe*; Winfred Lüdecke, *Behind the Scenes of Espionage*, p. 232. Lüdecke also has the story of Olga Bruder employed by the International Secret Service Bureau in Brussels to find out the plans of a Russian fortress on the eastern frontier of Germany. It was claimed she had committed suicide but in reality she was poisoned after she had formed a 'very intimate friendship' with the local chief of the Russian espionage, p. 231. There is also the story of a French agent who fell in love with a German officer with whom she was to 'make up'. She passed on details of the French espionage system as a result of which 66 agents were arrested, p. 234. It is almost impossible to determine the truth of these tales.

21 E.T. Woodhall, *Spies of the Great War*, p. 113.

22 Magnus Hirschfeld, *The Sexual History of the Great War*, ch. 14.

23 *The Times*, 10 June 1916.

24 Robinson's appeal against his conviction was allowed when the court held that it could not be sustained on the evidence of one witness together with circumstantial evidence even though it was 'well-nigh' conclusive. *US v Robinson*, District Court S D, New York, 26 May 1919.

25 *New York Times*, 13 August 1920.

26 'Has Uncle Sam Caught One of the Kaiser's "Vampire Spies"?, *San Francisco Chronicle*, 27 January 1918. Despite its lurid title it is a reasonably balanced account of the case and the Baroness's exploits.

11 The Kaiser's Men in America

1   Charles F. Horne (ed.), *Source Records of the Great War*, vol. III.

2   Wilson to Lansing, 5 December 1915, U.S. Lansing Papers, i 90.

3   In Europe consideration was given to introducing the Colorado beetle to German potato crops. There had been

earlier outbreaks in France in 1914 and on the Lower Elbe. Although the advantages were considerable—the beetle would ruin the crop and so enhance a blockade and troops would have had to be pulled back from the front line to deal with the emergency—the scheme was never implemented. Anon, 'Colorado Beetle in France', *Journal of the Ministry of Agriculture*, vol. 29, 1923.

4 George Baker, 'The Artless German who dynamited the Vanceboro Bridge', *More Real Spies*.

5 From 25 August 1914, a reprisal for the shooting of some German soldiers, the town of Louvain, including churches and the library, was effectively destroyed. The mayor and university rector were shot and some 300 male inhabitants were sent to Germany.

6 The National Archives KV 1/46.

7 Ernest Wittenberg, 'The Thrifty Spy on the Sixth Avenue El', *American Heritage Magazine*, December 1965, vol. 17, issue 1.

8 Ernest Wittenberg, *ibid*.

9 Basil Thomson, *Queer People*, p. 194. *New York Times*, 23 September 1917. In 1386 during a battle with the Habsburg army the rather more heroic Swiss patriot Winkelried is said to have cried out, 'I will open a passage into the line; protect, dear countrymen and confederates, my wife and children'. He then threw himself at the Habsburg pikemen bringing down a number of soldiers and so clearing a path.

10 Hugh Hoy, *OB 40*, p. 63.

11 Another version of this story is that Lord Abinger, who was present and who spoke fluent German, told von Rintelen to salute and he stood to attention and did so. Hugh Hoy, *OB 40*, p. 64. In fact this version sounds very much like the story of the questioning of Captain Hans Boehme, but perhaps this is the way Germans behaved in real life as well as in fiction.

12 Franz von Rintelen, *Dark Invader*.

13 *The Times*, 7 February 1918.

14 Box 209, Records of the Office of Counsellor, RG 59, NA; Franz von Rintelen *Dark Invader*, p. xxi; HL Debate, 3 May 1933, vol. 1 87- cc 695–705; *New York Times*, 4 October 1939, 3 January 1940.

15 Money was readily available for propaganda. George Viereck, said to have been the illegitimate son of Kaiser Wilhelm I and the actress Edwina Viereck, received a salary of $1,750, paid through a series of women intermediaries.

16 Officials were just as careless with documents then as now. In 1918 in Paris a Colonel Devignies left important documents in a taxi where, fortunately, they were found by the young film star Odette Rousseau, 'Florelle', who handed them in. There is another story that Prince Udo of Stolberg taking documents to Ghent left them in an officers' brothel in Cintra. They were not returned until two days later. Magnus Hirschfeld, *The Sexual History of the Great War*, ch. 14.

17 In 1932 Dumba published *Memoirs of a Diplomat* setting out his version of the affair. He died in 1947 aged 93.

18 *New York Times*, 28 November 1915.

19 Norman Thwaites, *Velvet and Vinegar*, p. 137.

20 Chad Millman, *The Detonators : The Secret Plot to Destroy America and an Epic Hunt for Justice*.

21 However the American Defense Society claimed that since the declaration of war 14 enemy spies, including two from Detroit, had been put to death. 'In the opinion of the Defense Society this information should be made public as a warning to the enemies of the United States now in this country'. The Society declined to say from where it had obtained its information. *New York Times*, 25 January 1918.

22 The National Archives KV 2/1953.

23 'L'Espionage Chante' in *L'Excelsior*, 3 June 1919; Barbara Tuchman, *The Zimmermann Telegram*, pp. 191–4.

24 Charles F. Horne (ed.), *Source Records of the Great War*, vol. III.

12 Switzerland

1 Anthony Masters, *Literary Agents*, p. 44.

2 The Commissaire of the Surété Nationale, Charpenter, revealed that during the war he had organized a burglary at Frankfurt with the talented burglar Cyrille Vercruysee, a man said to be able to clear a two metre wall in one leap, who was then in prison at Poissy. The terms of a successful operation were his immediate release. Vercruysee stole the required papers, but also a watch and some jewellery 'to keep his hand in'. Henri Danjou, *France-Soir*, 12 May 1950.

3 Robert Boucard, *The Secret Services of Europe*, pp. 53 *et seq.*

4 Archives Nationales de France F/7/14607.

5 Archives Nationales F/7/14607.

6 A.F. Judge, *The 'Intelligence Corps'*, p. 34.

7 In fact Wallinger had more experience with the upper classes than Maugham credited him. He just had not benefited from it. He had married Lady Michaella Tuchner in August 1911 in Paris. His wife left him the next day and took up with a Romanian banker. *The Times*, 25 June 1929.

8 Kirke Diary, 19 July 1916.

9 Anthony Masters, *Literary Agents*, p. 44. Maugham's close friend Gerald Kelly, the painter and later president of the Royal Academy, became an intelligence agent in Spain. Maugham portrayed him in two Ashenden stories, *The Hairless Mexican* and *The Dark Woman*. In *The Hairless Mexican* the wrong man is killed but, according to Kelly, after

considerable expenditure of time and money, he followed the suspect agent to Seville railway station where he boarded a train for Madrid, got out onto the tracks and was lost by him. Maugham also portrayed him as the painter Lionel Hillier in *Cakes and Ale*.

10 In 1916 the Hotel d'Angleterre on the Kongens Nytorf in Copenhagen was German headquarters for espionage, as was the Hotel Astoria in Brussels.

11 Emile Massard, *Les Espionnes à Paris*.

12 *New York Times*, 12 June 1919.

13 *New York Times*, 11 January 1917.

14 'L'Affaire Bolo', *Les Procès de Trahison*, no. 1, 2 March 1918; Bernard Zimmer, 'Les Mystères de la Guerre', *Le Crapouillot*, Le Numero Special (n.d. *c*.1931).

15 Hugh Hoy, *OB 40*, p. 104.

13 In and out of Russia

1 In Somerset Maugham's Ashenden stories, *Mr Harrington's Washing* and *His Excellency*, Buchanan becomes Sir Herbert Witherspoon.

2 Karyn Miller, 'British Spy fired the shot that finished off Rasputin', in *Daily Telegraph*, 19 September 2004.

3 Sir George Buchanan, *My Mission to Russia and Other Diplomatic Memories*, 12 January 1917, vol. II.

4 After the coup Kornilov was arrested but escaped from prison on 19 November 1917 and, going to the Don region, fought a savage war with the Bolsheviks. He was killed when a shell hit his cottage on 13 April 1918. For a succinct account of the period and the intriguing, see Christopher Andrew, *Secret Service*, ch. 6.

5 At the beginning of the Second World War Kerensky went to America. He married Nell Tritton, an Australian journalist, and they lived in Brisbane for a time. After her death he returned to New York. When he died in 1970 the

Russian Orthodox Church refused to bury him and his body was flown to London. He is buried at Putney Vale cemetery.

6 R. H. Bruce Lockhart, *Memoirs of a British Agent*. Lockhart played football for a season for Morozov, a factory team owned by a Lancastrian, which won the Moscow League in 1912.

7 George Hill, *Go Spy the Land*.

8 George Hill, *ibid*.

9 Alan Judd, *The Quest for C*, p. 429.

10 In *Ace of Spies*, his exhaustively researched biography of Sidney Reilly, Andrew Cook examines the various stories of Reilly's parentage, life and death, discarding many of them. But even he is reduced very often to 'could have'.

11 Alan Judd, *The Quest for C*, p. 429. Christopher Andrew suggests Cumming may have met and used Reilly before the war. *Secret Service*, p. 317.

12 Richard B. Spence, 'Sidney Reilly in America 1914–1917', *Intelligence and National Security*, vol. 10, no. 1, January 1995.

13 Because of her blindness there have been suggestions that Kaplan was not the assassin and the name of her friend Lidia Konopleva has been put forward. Certainly there were said to have been two women involved.

14 An alternative view suggested by George Hill, who was not willing to accept the Letts were double agents, is that the plot was betrayed by the French. George Hill, *Go Spy the Land*, p. 238.

15 *The Times*, 5 September 1918.

16 Such arrests were not uncommon. In 1916 the German commercial attaché in Athens Alfred Hoffman was arrested for spying despite German claims that he was merely a retired officer. It was believed he would continue operations from Switzerland and so he was specifically excluded from a safe conduct. As a reprisal two middle-aged men in

northern France John Platt and Harry Falkener were arrested effectively as hostages for Hoffmann. In turn the British arranged for four middle-aged Germans to be held 'and retained'. The National Archives FO 383/22.

17 George Hill, *Go Spy the Land*, p. 246.

18 For accounts of the period and the lives of the protagonists see Christopher Andrews, *Secret Service*; Andrew Cook, *Reilly, Ace of Spies*; R. H. Bruce Lockhart, *Ace of Spies*; Alan Judd, *The Quest for C;* George Hill, *Go Spy the Land;* Gordon Brook-Shepherd, *Iron Maze*.

14 Gone to Graveyards

1 The National Archives WO 32/4898. Note dated 3 September 1920 on War Office file asking for remission for Friedrich Greite.

2 Broadmoor Hospital File 879; The National Archives WO 141/3/1; May Sharpe, *Chicago May, Her Story*.

3 The National Archives PCOM 8/324.

4 The National Archives WO 32/4898.

5 The National Archives HO 144/20603.

6 Archives Nationales de France no. 233 2009/1.

7 *Sheffield Daily Independent*, 20–22 August 1924.

8 *The Times*, 3 June 1919.

9 *The Times*, 10 October 1939.

10 Christopher Andrew, *Secret Service*; C. A. MacDonald, 'The Venlo Affair' in *European Studies Review, 8* (1978), pp. 443–64; D. Cameron Watt in *Dictionary of National Biography*.

11 Brian Garfield, *The Meinertzhagen Mystery*.

12 Donald Bittner, *Royal Marine Spies of World War One Era*.

13 Georges Ladoux, *Mes Souvenirs*.

14 'Marthe Richard, Escroc et Prostituée' in *Paris Villages*, no. 9 1985; Mary Blume, 'A post war heroine who fooled France' in *New York Times*,

3 August 2006; Dossier Marthe
Richard in Bibliothèque Marguerite
Duras, Paris.

15 Henry Hohne, *The General was a Spy*.

16 Adam Sage, 'Mystery of how Mata
Hari lost her head', *The Times*, 13 July
2000.

17 The National Archives KV 2/1097.

18 *New York Times*, 12 March 1925, 21
February 1928, 5 December 1935,
15 April 1937.

19 *New York Times*, 25, 27, 28 1920, 30
May 1949.

20 *Time*, 16 March 1942.

21 There is a recording of her and Enrico
Caruso singing from *Aida* on YouTube.

22 The film *The House on 92nd Street* is
partly based on the World War Two
story. Thomas Joseph Tunny and Maul
Merrick Hollister, *Throttled: The Detection of the German and Anarchist Bomb
Plotters*; Clement Wood, *The Man who
killed Kitchener: The Life of Fritz Joubert
Duquesne*.

23 Andrew Cook, *Ace of Spies*.

24 The National Archives MEPO 10/10;
News of the World, 10 January 1926.
Quite what was Gregory's relationship
with Thomson is open to question.
Possibly he had sent Thomson information during the war and Thomson
tried to prevent him being called up.
He certainly appealed far more to Basil
Thomson than to Kell and Major John
Carter, who could not abide him,
regarding him, quite correctly, as an
absolute rogue. In 1916 Thomson wrote
to MI5 saying that Gregory was asking
for money to cover the outgoings he
had incurred supplying information.
Would Kell contribute £50 from his
funds? No, he wouldn't. So far as MI5
was concerned some of Gregory's
information was 'laughable' and, as for
the rest, it was mostly a case of 'What's
true is not new'. MI5 did not want to
pay because they had no control over
Gregory. If it was 'to help BT out of a
hole that's another affair but if it is so,
let's have it stated frankly'.

In April 1917 Gregory then wanted
to be put on the 'not to be called up' list.
The extension was to be for not longer
than a month. Thomson clearly was
batting for him again 'He has from time
to time furnished useful information to
this department' (Scotland Yard). But
Captain S. Russell Cooke said that any
application should be treated with suspicion. 'I can give you full information
about him if necessary'. Gregory
wanted out of service. The 'boastful'
Gregory was rejected by Cooke on
behalf of Major Carter on 1 May 1917.
'He is not a 'Sahib'. Cooke thought he
should be enlisted and put on gate duty
as soon as possible. The National
Archives KV 2/340.

SELECT BIBLIOGRAPHY

AGRICOLA [A.Bauermeister] (trans. H. Bywater), *Spies Break Through* (Constable, London, 1934).

ALLARD, P., *Les Enigmes de la Guerre* (Editions des Portiques, Paris, 1933).

ANDREW, C.M., *Secret Service: The Making of the British Intelligence Community* (Heinemann, London, 1985).

— (intro) *The Secret Service 1908–1945* (The National Archives, London, 1999).

— *The Defence of the Realm: The Authorized Biography of MI5* (Allen Lane, London, 2009).

ANTIER, C., Walle, M. and Lahair, O., *Les Femmes Espionnes dans la Grande Guerre* (Librairie Le Écho, Rouen, 2008).

ASPREY, R.B., *The German High Command at War: Hindenburg and Ludendorff Conduct World War I* (Morrow, New York, 1991).

ASTON, G., *Secret Service* (Faber & Faber, London, 1930).

BADEN-POWELL, R., *My Adventures as a Spy* (Pearson, London, 1915).

BARTON, G., *The World's Greatest Military Spies* (Page, Boston, 1917).

BASCHWITZ, K., *Der Massenwahn, seine Wirkung und seine Beherrschung*, (C.H. Becksche, Munich, 1923).

BATES, D., *The Fashoda Incident of 1898* (Oxford University Press, Oxford, 1984).

BAUMANN, F., *Der Fall Edith Cavell* (Otto Schlegel, Berlin, 1933).

BAXTER, R., *Guilty Women,* (Quality Press, London, 1943).

BEESLY, P., *Room 40, British Naval Intelligence 1914–1918* (Oxford University Press, Oxford, 1984).

BELAND, H., *My Three Years in a German Prison* (William Briggs, Toronto, 1919).

BENNETT, R.M., *Espionage: an A–Z of Spies and Secrets* (Virgin, London, 2002).

BERNDORFF, H.R. (trans. Bernard Miall), *Espionage* (Nash & Grayson, London, 1930).

BEST, S.P., *The Origins of the Intelligence Corps* (unpublished manuscript, Imperial War Museum).

BITTNER, T.D., *Royal Marine Spies of World War One Era* (Royal Marine Historical Society, 1993).

BIZARD, L., *Souvenirs d'un médecin de Saint-Lazare,* (Michel Albin, Paris, 1925).

BOGHARDT, T., *Spies of the Kaiser* (Palgrave Macmillan, Basingstoke, 2004).

BOUCARD, Robert, *The Secret Services of Europe* (Stanley Paul, London, 1940).

BOUCHARDON, P., *Souvenirs,* (Albin Michel, Paris, 1954).

BREDIN, J.-D., *The Affair: The Case of Alfred Dreyfus* (George Braziller, New York, 1986).

BROWN, F., *Zola* (Macmillan, London, 1996).

BRUST, H., *I Guarded Kings* (Stanley Paul, London, 1926).

BUCHANAN, G., *My Mission to Russia and Other Diplomatic Memories* (Cassell, London, 1923).

BULLOCH, J., *MI5* (London, 1963).

BURGE, M.R.K., *History of the British Secret Service 1914–1917* (unpublished manuscript, Intelligence Corps Archives, Chicksands).

BYWATER, H.C. and Ferraby, H.C., *Strange Intelligence* (Constable, London, 1931).

CAMPBELL, S., *Secrets of Crewe House* (Hodder & Stoughton, London, 1920).

CLARK, R.W., *Great Moments of Espionage* (Phoenix House, London, 1963).

COOK A., *Ace of Spies* (Tempus, Stroud, 2002).

— 'M'., *Britain's First Spymaster* (Tempus, Stroud, 2004).

CORDELL, R., *Somerset Maugham : A Biographical and Critical Study* (Heinemann, London, 1961).

CURTIS. A., *The Pattern of Maugham* (Hamish Hamilton, London, 1974).

DARROW, M., *French Women and the First World War: War Stories from the Home Front,* (Berg, Oxford, 2000).

DEACON, R., *Spyclopaedia* (Futura, London, 1987).

DOBSON, C., *The Dictionary of Espionage* (Harrap, London, 1984).

DRAKE, R.J., *History of Intelligence (B) British Expeditionary Force, France from January 1917 to April 1919* (unpublished manuscript, Intelligence Corps Archives).

DUKES, P., *Red Dusk and the Morrow* (Williams and Norgate, London, 1922).

DUNN, J., *Paperchase* (Selwyn Blount, London, 1938).

DURAND, P., *Agents Secrets, l'Affaire Fauquenot* (Birckel, Payot, Paris, 1937).

E 7, *I am a Spy; The Danger Zone* (Lovat Dickson, London, 1938).

—*Women Spies I have known* (Hurst and Blackett, London, n.d.).

—*Spies I knew* (Jarrolds, London, 1933).

Sir James, EDMONDS, 'How Different Then: Reminiscences and Comments of a Nonagenarian 1861–1951', unpublished manuscript in Liddell Hart Collection, Kings College, London.

EVERITT, N., *British Secret Service during the Great War* (Hutchinson, London, 1920).

Ex-Intelligence Officer [Lionel James], *The German Spy System from Within* (Hodder & Stoughton, London, 1914).

FALIGOT, R. and Kauffer, R., *Histoire Mondiale de Renseignement, Tome I 1870–1939* (Laffont, Paris, 1993).

FELSTEAD, S.T., *German Spies at Bay: Being an Actual Record of the German Espionage in Great Britain during the years 1914–1918 compiled from official sources* (Hutchinson, London, 1920).

FERGUSON, N., *The Pity of War* (Allen Lane, London, 1998).

FISCHER, F. (trans. M. Jackson), *War of Illusions: German Polices from 1911 to 1914* (Chatto & Windus, London, 1975).

FITCH, H.T., *Traitors Within: The Adventures of Detective Inspector Herbert T. Fitch* (Hurst and Blackett, London, 1933).

FRANKLIN, C., *The Great Spies* (Hart Publishing, New York, 1967).

FRAZER, J. *Sixty Years in Uniform* (Stanley Paul, London, 1939).

FRIEDMAN, W. and Mendelsohn, C.J., *The Zimmermann Telegram of January 16 1917,* (Aegean Park Press, Laguna Hills, Ca.).

GARFIELD, B., *The Meinertzhagen Mystery* (Potomac Press, Washington DC., 2007).

GIVIERGE, M., *Au Service du Chiffre 18 ans de souvenirs 1907–1925,* vol. III (NAF, Amiens, 1930).

GOOCH, J., *The Prospect of War: studies in British defence policy 1847–1942* (Taylor & Francis, London, 1981).

GRANT, H., *Spies and Secret Service: The Story of Espionage, its Main Systems and Chief Exponents* (Frederick A. Stokes, New York, 1915).

GRAVES, A.K., *The Secrets of the German War Office* (T. Werner Laurie, London, 1914).

GREENWALL, H.J., *The Underworld of Paris* (Stanley Paul, London, 1921).

GROSS, F., *I Knew Those Spies* (Hurst & Blackett, London, 1940).

HALSALLE, H. de and Sheridan Jones, C., *The German Woman and Her Master* (T. Werner Laurie, London, 1916).

HANKIN, H., *A Strange Death: A Story Discovered in Palestine* (PublicAffairs [sic]), New York, 2005).

HASWELL, C.J.D., *British Military Intelligence,* (Weidenfeld & Nicholson, London, 1973).

—*Spies and Spymasters* (Thames and Hudson, London, 1973).

HENNESSEY, T. and Claire Thomas, C., *Spooks* (Amberley, Stroud, 2009).

HENRY, H., *Marthe Richard l'Aventurière des Maison Closes* (Punctum, Paris, 2006).

HERWIG, H.H., 'Imperial Germany', Ernest May (ed), *Knowing one's Enemies, Intelligence Assessment before the Two Wars* (Princeton University Press , Princeton, NJ, 1984).

HEYMANS, Charles S., *La Vraie Mata Hari: Courtisane et Espionne,* Étoile (Paris, 1936).

HILL, G.A., *Go Spy the Land* (Cassell, London, 1932).

HINSLEY, F. H. and Simkins, C.A.G., *British Intelligence in the Second World War* (HMSO, London, 1990).

HIRSCHFELD, M., *The Sexual History of the Great War* (Panurge Press, New York, 1934).

HOFFMANN, M., *The War of Lost Opportunities* (Battery Press, Nashville, Tenn., 1999).

HOHNE, H. and Zollig, H., *The General was a Spy* (Conrad McCann & Geoghan, New York, 1972).

HONAN, W.H., *Bywater* (Macdonald, London, 1990).

HORNE, A., *The Price of Glory* (St Martin's Press, London, 1963).

HORNE, C.F., *Source Records of the Great War, Volume III* (National Alumni, USA, 1923).

HOY, H.C., *40 OB or How the War was Won* (Hutchinson, London, 1932).

JAMES, W.J., *The Eyes of the Navy: A Biographical Study of Admiral Sir Reginald Hall* (Methuen, London, 1955).

— *A Great Seaman, The Life of Admiral of the Fleet Sir Henry F. Oliver* (H.F. and G. Witherby, London, 1956).

JEFFREYS-JONES, R., *American Espionage* (The Free Press, New York, 1977).

JONES, J. P., *The German Spy in America: The Secret Plotting of German Spies in the United States and the Inside Story of the Sinking of the Lusitania* (Hutchinson, London, 1917).

JUDD, A., *The Quest for C: Sir Mansfield Cumming and the Founding of the Secret Service* (HarperCollins, London, 1999).

JUDGE, A.F., *The 'Intelligence Corps' 1914–1928*, unpublished MS in Intelligence Corps Archives, Chicksands, 2009.

KAHN, D., *Hitler's Spies*, Hodder & Stoughton, London, 1978.

— *The Reader of Gentlemen's Mail: Herbert Yardley and the Birth of American Codebreaking* (Yale University Press, Cambridge, Mass., 2006).

KALUSH, W., and Sloman L., *The Secret Life of Houdini* (Atria Books, New York, 2006).

KETTLE, M., *Sidney Reilly* (Corgi, London, 1983).

KIRKE, W., *The Origin of the Intelligence Corps* (unpublished manuscript, Intelligence Corps Archives).

KIRKPATRICK, I., *Inner Circle* (Macmillan, London, 1959).

KIRKPATRICK, I., *The War 1914–1928* (unpublished manuscript, Imperial War Museum, London).

KISH, J. and Turns, T., *International Law and Espionage* (1995).

KNOBLOCK, E., *Round the Room* (Chapman & Hall, London, 1939).

KROP, P., *Les Secrets de l'espionnage Français de 1870 à nos Jours* (Éditions Jean-Claude Lattès, Paris, 1993).

LADOUX, G., *Les chasseurs d'espions: Comment j'ai fait arrêter Mata Hari* (Librairie des Champs-Elysees, Paris, 1932).

— *Marthe Richard, the Skylark: The Foremost Woman Spy of France* (Cassell, London, 1932).

— *Mes Souvenirs* (Les Editions de France, Paris, 1937).

LANDAU, H., *All's Fair*, (G.P. Putnam's Sons, New York, 1934).

— *Secrets of the White Lady*, (G.P. Putnam's Sons, New York, 1935).

LANOIR, P., *The German Spy System in France* (Mills & Boon, London, 1910).

LEBRUN, Mathilde, *Mes Treize Missions*, (Fayard, Paris, 1926).

LE QUEUX, W., *German Spies in England: An Exposure* (Stanley Paul, London, 1915).

LE QUEUX, W., *Spies of the Kaiser* (London, Frank Cass, 1996).

LINCOLN, W.B., *Passage through Armageddon: The Russians in War & Revolution 1914–1918* (Simon & Schuster, New York, 1986).

LOCKHART, R.H. Bruce, *Memoirs of a British Agent* (Putnam, London, 1932).

LOCKHART, R.B., *Ace of Spies* (Hodder & Stoughton, London, 1967).

LUCIETO, C., *On Special Missions* (Robert M. McBride & Co, New York, 1927).

LÜDECKE, W., *Behind the Scenes of Espionage: Tales of the Secret Service* (Harrap, London, 1929).

LUX, C. *L'Evasion du Capitaine Lux* (Oeuvres Rares, Paris, 1932).

MACINTYRE, B., *A Foreign Field: A True Story of Love and Betrayal in the Great War* (HarperCollins, London, 2002).

MACKENZIE, C., *Greek Memories* (Chatto & Windus, London, 1938).

MAHONEY, H.H., *Women in Espionage* (ABC-Clio, Oxford, 1993).

MASSARD, E., *Les Espionnes a Paris: La Vérité sur Mata-Hari* (Albin Michel, Paris. 1922).

MASTERS, A., *Literary Agents: The Novelist as Spy* (Blackwell, Oxford, 1987).

MAUNOURY, H., *Police de Guerre* (Editions de la Nouvelle Revue Critique, Paris, 1937).

McKENNA, M., *I was a Spy!*, (Jarrolds, London, 1932).

MEINERTZHAGEN, R., *Army Diary 1899–1926* (Oliver & Boyd, Edinburgh, 1960).

MEJAN, A., *Bobo The Super Spy* (Odhams, London, 1918).

MILLMAN, C., *The Detonators: The Secret Plot to Destroy America and an Epic Hunt for Justice* (Little, Brown, New York, 2006).

MORAIN, A., *The Underworld of Paris: Secrets of the Sûreté* (Jarrolds, London, 1930).

MORGAN, J., *The Secrets of Rue St Roche* (Penguin, London, 2004).

MORRIS, A.J.A., *Scaremongers* (Routledge & Kegan Paul, London, 1984).

MORTANE, J., *Special Missions of the Air* (Aeroplane & General Publishing, London, 1919).

—*La Guerre des Ailes* (Baudinière, Paris, 1934).

MORTON, J., *Gangland: The Lawyers* (Virgin, London 2004).

MOYLAN, J., *Scotland Yard and the Metropolitan Police* (Putnam, London, 1929).

MURPHY, B., *The Business of Spying* (Milton House, London, 1973).

NEWMAN, B., *Secrets of German Espionage* (Right Book Club, London, 1940).

—*Spies in Britain* (Robert Hale, London, 1964).

NICOLAI, W., *The German Secret Service* (Stanley Paul & Co, London, 1924).

NIKITINE, B.V., *The Fatal Years* (William Hodge, London, 1938).

OCCLESHAW M., *Armour against Fate: British Military Intelligence in the First World War* (Columbus, London, 1989).

OFFENSTADT, N., *Les fusillés de la Grande Guerre* (Éditions Odile Jacob, Paris, 1999).

OPPENHEIMER, C.F., *Stranger Within* (Faber & Faber, London, 1960).

OSTROVSKY, E., *Eye of the Dawn; The Rise and Fall of Mata Hari* (Dorset Press, New York, 1978).

PALÉOLOGUE, M., *Un Grand Tourant de la Politique Mondiale 1904–1905* (Plon, Paris, 1934).

PAQUET, C., *Dans l'attente de la ruée : Verdun janvier-fevrier 1916* (Berger-Levrault, Paris, 1928).

PEDONCINI, G., *Les Mutiniérs de 1917* (Publications de la Sorbonne, Presse Universitaires de France, Paris, 1983).

PORCH, D., *The French Secret Services* (Macmillan, London, 1998).

PORTER, B., *The Origins of the Vigilant State* (Weidenfeld & Nicholson, London, 1987).

PROCTOR, T., *Female Intelligence: Women and Espionage in the First World War* (New York University Press, New York, 2003).

Public Record Office (ed.), *M.I.5: The First Ten Years 1909–1919* (PRO, Kew, 1997).

READ, J.M., *Atrocity Propaganda 1914–1919* (Yale University Press, New Haven, CT, 1941).

REDIER, A., *La Guerre des Femmes* (Editions de la Vrai, Paris, 1924).

—*The Story of Louise de Bettignies* (Hutchinson, London, 1926).

REILLY, S., *The Adventures of Sidney Reilly* (Elkin, Matthews and Marriott, London, 1930).

RICHELSON, J.T., *A Century of Spies: Intelligence in the 20th Century* (Oxford University Press, New York, 1995).

RICHER, M., *I Spied for France* (John Long, London, 1935).

—*Espions de guerre et de paix* (Les Editions de France, Paris, 1938).

ROBSON, F.G., History of the Intelligence Corps 1914–1984 (unpublished manuscript, Intelligence Corps Archives).

ROWAN, R., *The Story of Secret Service* (London, John Miles, London, 1938).

SANDERS, M.C. and Taylor, P.M., *British propaganda during the First World War 1914–1918* (Macmillan, London, 1982).

SCHIRMANN, L., *Mata-Hari: Autopsie d'une machination* (Editions Italiques, Paris, 2001).

SELLERS, L., *Shot in the Tower* (Pen & Sword, London, 1997).

SETH, R., *The Spy Who Wasn't Caught* (Hale & Iremonger, London, 1966).

—*Some of My Favourite Spies* (Chilton, Philadelphia, 1968).

—*Encyclopedia of Espionage* (New English Library, London, 1974).

SHIPMAN, P., *Femme Fatale* (Weidenfeld & Nicolson, London, 2007).

SILBER, J., *Invisible Weapons* (Hutchinson, London, 1932).

SMITH, M., *The Spying Game: the secret history of British espionage* (Politico's Publishing, London, 2003).

SNOWDEN, N., *Memoirs of a Spy* (Beacon Library, London, 1938).

SPAIGHT, J.M., *Air Power and War Rights* (Longmans Green, London, 1924).

STEINHAUER, G. with Felstead, S., *Steinhauer: The Kaiser's Master Spy* (John Lane, London, 1930).

SUMNER, I., *Despise it not* (Highgate of Beverley, Beverley, 2004).

SYKES, S., *Wassmuss 'The German Lawrence'* (Longmans Green & Co, New York, 1936).

TEAGUE-JONES, R., *The Spy who Disappeared* (Gollancz, London, 1980).

THOMPSON, W.H., *Guard from the Yard* (Jarrolds, London, 1938).

THOMSON, Sir B., *My Experiences at Scotland Yard* (Doubleday, Page & Co, New York, 1925).

—*Queer People* (Hodder & Stoughton, London, 1922).

—*The Scene Changes* (Collins, London, 1939).

THULIEZ, L., *Condemned to Death* (Methuen, London, 1934).

THWAITES, N. G., *Velvet and Vinegar* (Grayson & Grayson, London, 1932).

TUCHMAN, B., *The Zimmermann Telegraph* (Constable, London, 1959).

TUNNY, T.J. and Hollister, P.M., *Throttled: The Detection of the German and Anarchist Bomb Plotters,* (Small, Maynard, Boston, 1919).

TUOHY, F., *The Secret Corps : A Tale of 'Intelligence' on All Fronts* (Murray, London, 1920).

—*This is Spying: Truth and Fiction about Secret Service* (The World's Work, London, 1938).

VAN TUYALL, H P., *The Netherlands and World War I: Espionage, Diplomacy and Survival* (Brill, Boston, 2001).

VAN YPERSELE, L. *De la guerre de l'ombre aux ombres de la guerre* (Labor, Bruxelles, 2004).

VIOLAN, J., *Dans L'air et dans la boue* (Librairie des Champs Élysées, Paris, 1933).

VOLKMAN, E., *The History of Espionage* (Carlton, London, 2007).

VON DER GOLTZ, H., *My Adventures as a German Secret Service Agent* (Cassell & Co, London, 1918).

VON RINTELEN, F.K., *The Dark Invader* (Lovat Dickson, London, 1933).

VOSKA, E. and Irwin, W., *Spy and Counter-spy,* (Doubleday, New York, 1940).

WAAGENAAR, S., *The Murder of Mata Hari* (Arthur Barker, London, 1964).

WHEELWRIGHT, J., *The Fatal Lover : Mata Hari and the Myth of Women in Espionage* (Collins & Brown, London, 1992).

WIEBES, C., *Intelligence and the War in Bosnia 1992–1995* (LIT Verlag, Berlin, 2003).

WIGHTON, C., *The World's Greatest Spies* (Odhams Press, London, 1962).

WILLIAMS, V., *The World of Action* (Hamish Hamilton, London, 1938).

WITCOVER, J., *Sabotage at Black Tom* (Algonquin Books of Chapel Hill, Chapel Hill, 1989).

WOOD, C., *The Man who killed Kitchener: The Life of Fritz Joubert Duquesne* (W. Faro, New York, 1932).

WOODHALL, E.T., *Spies of the Great War* (Millifont Press, London, n.d.).

—*Detective and Secret Service Days* (Jarrolds, London, 1934).

WOOLRYCH, S.H.C., *Recollections of World War I* (unpublished manuscript, Intelligence Corps Archives).

YARDLEY, H.O., *The American Black Chamber* (Faber, London, 1931).

—*The Blonde Countess* (Faber, London, 1934).

YOUNGHUSBAND, *The Tower of London From Within* (Herbert Jenkins, London, 1920).

ZUCKERMAN, L., *The Rape of Belgium* (New York University Press, New York, 2004).

Articles etc.

ANON, 'Colorado Beetle in France', *Journal of the Ministry of Agriculture,* vol. 29, 1923.

Chantal ANTIER, 'Espionnage et espionnes de la Grande Guerre', *Revue historique des armées,* 247 / 2007.

George BAKER, 'The Artless German who dynamited the Vanceboro Bridge', *More Real Spies,* Nova, New York, 1966.

De Brézé DARNLEY-STUART-STEPHENS, 'Wolves in Sheeps' Clothing' in *English Review,* March 1916.

Venita DATTA, 'Opium, Gambling and the Demi-Mondaine: The Ullmo Spy Case of 1907', Lecture at 31st Annual Conference of Western Society for French History, California, 2003.

P. DECOCK, *La Dame Blanche,* unpublished dissertation, Université Libre de Bruxelles, 1981.

Sir James EDMONDS, 'How the Army lost its commander in chief', *Army Quarterly,* July 1938.

Baron Guido ERRANTE, 'The German Intelligence Service During the World War I', *United States Infantry Journal,* Nov–Dec 1933.

John FERRIS, 'Before Room 40: The British Empire and Signals Intelligence 1898–1914' in *Journal of Strategic Studies XII,* No 4, December 1989.

David FRENCH, 'Spy Fever in Great Britain 1900–15', *Historical Journal* 21 (1978).

Grant W. GRAMS 'Karl Respa and German Espionage in Canada during World War One', *Journal of Military and Strategic Studies,* Fall 2005, vol. 8, issue 1.

'Has Uncle Sam caught one of the Kaiser's "Vampire Spies"', *San Francisco Sunday Chronicle,* 27 January 1918.

Richard GRENIER, 'Colonel Redl: The man behind the screen myth', *New York Times,* 13 October 1985.

D.S. HAWKER, 'An Outline of the Early History of the Intelligence Corps', *Rose & Laurel,* no. 27, December 1965.

Nicholas HILEY, 'Counter-espionage and security in Great Britain during the First World War', *English Historical Review*, April 1986.

—'The Failure of British Espionage against Germany, 1907–1914', *The Historical Journal*, 26, 4 (1983), pp. 867–89.

—'The Failure of British Counter Espionage against Germany, 1907–1914', *The Historical Journal*, 28, 4 (1985), pp. 835–62.

Anne-Marie Claire HUGHES, 'War, Gender and National Mourning: The Significance of the Death and Commemoration of Edith Cavell in Britain', *European Review of History*, vol. 12, no. 3, November 2005.

—'Is Mata Hari Still Alive?', *Daily Mail*, 3 September 1929.

Lady Constance KELL, 'A Secret Well Kept: an account of the work of Sir Vernon Kell', unpublished manuscript in the Imperial War Museum.

F. KLUITERS, 'R.B. Tinsley, a Biographical Note', Den Haag, 2003 (unpublished).

'La Farce des Services Secrets', *Crapouillot*, no. 15.

Mervyn LAMB [Kirke], 'On Hazardous Service', *Blackwood's Magazine*, part I vol. CCVIII (1920); part II vol. CCIX (1921); part III vol. CCX (1921).

—'Les Femmes et L'Espionnage' in *Crapouillot*, no. 15, Paris 1951.

C.A. MACDONALD, 'The Venlo Affair' in *European Studies Review*, 8 (1978).

Ben MACINTYRE, 'Solved: The Riddle of Executed First World War Soldier

Robert Digby', *The Times*, 29 April 2009.

Karyn MILLER, 'British spy fired the shot that finished off Rasputin', *Daily Telegraph*, 19 September 2004.

M.E. OCCLESHAW, 'British Military Intelligence in the First World War', University of Keele Ph.D. thesis, 1984. Intelligence Corps Archives.

C. OLSSON in *Picture Post*, 26 November 1938.

Markus PÖHLMANN, 'Talking about Schluga', cited in Cees Wiebes, *Intelligence and the War in Bosnia, 1992–1995*.

Bernard PORTER, 'M: MI5's First Spymaster', *The English Historical Review* 120 (2005).

Gary SHEFFIELD, 'First World War, Day One The Road to War', partwork series in *The Guardian*, 2008.

Catherine SPECK, 'Edith Cavell: Martyr or Patriot' in *Australian and New Zealand Journal of Art* 2, no. 1, 2001.

Richard B. SPENCE, 'Sidney Reilly in America 1914–1917', *Intelligence and National Security*, vol. 10., no. 1 January 1995.

J.B. STERNDALE BENNETT, 'I Guarded Spies in The Tower', *The Great War: I was There, Pt 22*.

Ferdinand TOUHY, 'Women as Secret Service Agents', *The Statesman*, 17 January 1926.

Ernest WITTENBERG, 'The Thrifty Spy on the Sixth Avenue El', *American Heritage Magazine*, December 1965, vol. 17, issue 1.

R.A.B. YOUNG, 'Even Wars have Ears', *The Territorial*, February, 1938.

Picture credits   1 The National Archives KV 4/183; 2 Courtesy of the Council of the National Army Museum, London; 4, 5, 12, 13, 18 Getty Images; 6 NMeM Daily Herald Archive; 7 The National Archives ADM 223/783; 8 The National Archives HW 3/179; 9, 10 The National Archives KV 2/822; 11 Print Collector/HIP/TopFoto TopFoto.co.uk; 14 Popperfoto/Getty Images; 15 The National Archives WO 94/102; 16 The National Archives CRIM 1/683; 17 The National Archives KV 2/2; 19 The National Archives KV 2/1953; 20 Roger-Viollet/TopFoto TopFoto.co.uk; 21 The National Archives KV 1/74